New Basis for Business

PRE-INTERMEDIATE

David Christie

Cornelsen

New Basis for Business – Pre-Intermediate wurde verfasst von David Christie, Banbury, unter Mitarbeit von David Smith (*Self study*).

Berater/innen	Bob Muscutt, Solingen David Smith, Berlin Birgit Solf-Kellersohn, Monheim
Verlagsredaktion	Janan Barksdale
Redaktionelle Mitarbeit	Christine House, Fritz Preuss (Wortliste), Ingrid-Maria Sauer, Sylee Gore, Sigrid Janssen
Design / Herstellung	Oxford Designers & Illustrators
Bildredaktion	Uta Hübner

Außerdem sind zu diesem Lehrwerk erhältlich:

Key to Self Study	ISBN-13: 978-3-464-01987-2/ISBN-10: 3-464-01987-0
Audio-CD	ISBN-13: 978-3-464-01890-3/ISBN-10: 3-464-01890-3
Pocket Workbook	ISBN-13: 978-3-464-01893-4/ISBN-10: 3-464-01893-8
Handreichungen für den Unterricht	ISBN-13: 978-3-464-01891-0/ISBN-10: 3-464-01891-1

www.cornelsen.de

1. Auflage, 3. Druck 2006

Alle Drucke dieser Auflage können, weil untereinander unverändert, im Unterricht nebeneinander verwendet werden.

Druck: CS-Druck CornelsenStürtz, Berlin

ISBN-13: 978-3-464-01889-7
ISBN-10: 3-464-01889-X

Inhalt gedruckt auf säurefreiem Papier, umweltschonend hergestellt aus chlorfrei gebleichten Faserstoffen.

Preface

New Basis for Business – Pre-Intermediate ist der erste Band der neuen zweibändigen Ausgabe des bewährten Englisch-Grundkurses *Basis for Business*.

Ziel dieses Bandes ist es, Ihnen eine solide Grundlage für Ihr Geschäftsenglisch mit auf den Weg zu geben. Der Band führt Sie anhand alltäglicher Geschäftssituationen, in denen sich deutsche Muttersprachler befinden können, Schritt für Schritt an wesentliche Gegebenheiten der englischen Sprache heran. Dabei üben Sie typische Aufgaben des Arbeitslebens: Herantreten an Firmen, geschäftlicher Umgang per Telefon, E-Mail oder Brief, Kauf und Verkauf von Produkten oder Dienstleistungen, Beschreibung von Firmenkonzeptionen ... und vieles mehr. Nach Abschluss des Kurses werden Sie Sicherheit im Umgang sowohl mit Muttersprachlern als auch mit Personen, die Englisch als Verkehrssprache verwenden, gewonnen haben und mühelos über sich und Ihr Firmenprofil sprechen können. Für all diejenigen unter Ihnen, die mit den Einstufungen des CEF (*Common European Framework*) vertraut sind, bedeutet dies, dass Sie nach der Bearbeitung dieses Bandes Niveau B1 erreicht haben.

New Basis for Business – Pre-Intermediate ist außerordentlich „benutzerfreundlich“. Der Kurs ist in zehn Units unterteilt, die jeweils aus drei Teilen bestehen, welche ungefähr Unterrichtsmaterial von drei Doppelstunden ausmachen, je nachdem in welchem Rahmen Sie lernen. Der erste Teil jeder Unit (*A*) führt wichtige Grammatikstrukturen ein; der zweite Teil (*B*) hilft Ihnen, Ihre allgemeinen Sprachfertigkeiten weiter auszubauen; und der dritte Teil (*Business file*) führt Sie in authentische und typische Geschäftsaktivitäten ein, z. B. Telefonieren, Kundengespräche oder die Organisation einer Dienstreise. Im Anschluss an jede Unit finden Sie auf den *Self-study*-Seiten eine deutsche Zusammenfassung der behandelten Grammatik sowie eine Auswahl an Übungen, mit deren Hilfe Sie zu Hause das im Unterricht Gelernte festigen – oder etwas Versäumtes – nachholen können.

Am Ende des Buches finden Sie einen ausführlichen Abschnitt zum Thema Geschäftskorrespondenz mit Übungen zur Gestaltung von Briefen, E-Mails und Faxen, Materialien zur Partnerarbeit, Hörverstehenstexte, Wörterverzeichnisse und einiges mehr.

Wir hoffen, dass Ihnen die Arbeit mit **New Basis for Business – Pre-Intermediate** Spaß macht und wünschen Ihnen viel Erfolg beim Lernen!

Autor und Redaktion

UNIT 1

WHAT WE DO

In this unit you ...

talk about yourself, your job and your company:
I come from Austria.
I work for an Austrian company.
We sell/make/produce ...
meet people and practise the alphabet:
How do you do?/My name's ...
How do you spell that?

Business file
Here's my card

A Meet Lisa Schalk

WARM UP **Say 'hello' to a partner in your class.**

Hello. I'm ...
Pleased to meet you. My name's ...

A1 1/02 **Listen.**

"Hello. My name's Lisa Schalk and I come from Austria. I work for a company called Austrian Portal. We're an international business agency. We help foreign companies with start-ups in Austria and find Austrian business partners for them for joint ventures. I work in my company's office in Linz – and I live in Linz too. What do I do exactly? I'm a consultant. I specialize in contacts with firms in the EU. Do I like my job? Well, I meet a lot of interesting people. I speak English every day. And I travel around Europe a lot. So, yes, it's interesting."

A2 **Complete the English phrases.**

1 I come .... Austria. *Ich komme aus Österreich.*
2 I work .... a company .... *Ich arbeite bei einem Unternehmen namens ...*
3 .... consultant. *Ich bin Beraterin.*
4 What .... exactly? *Was bin ich genau von Beruf?*
5 I .... *Ich treffe eine Menge interessanter Leute.*

A3 Answer the questions about Lisa.

1 Where does she live and work?
2 What company does she work for?
3 What does she do?
4 What does her company do?
5 Where does she travel?
6 What language(s) does she speak every day?
7 Who does she meet in her job?
8 What do you think? Does she like her job?

A4 Listen and complete the table.

1/03

Where do these people come from/live/work?
What do they and their companies do?

The simple present FOCUS

I **work** for a company called Austrian Portal. Lisa **works** for ...

Fragen

What company **do** you **work** for?
What company **does** Lisa **work** for?

Remember

What do you do (exactly)? = What's your job?
What does your company do? = What's your company's business activity?

What do you do? – I'm a consultant.
What does your company do? – We're an international business agency.

Andrea Graf

Eckhard Kellermann

Lee Mazry

Helle GmbH

BlueSky Software

Amsel AG

who?	*Andrea Graf*		
where?			
what?			

A5

Look at the expressions in the box and complete the sentences below. Then compare your answers with a partner's.

What we do

We're a service company/a manufacturing company/a retailer/a bank/ an IT company/an insurance company ...

We make/manufacture/produce/sell/develop/provide (a service)/ transport ...

I work for Amsel in Germany. We're a .... (1) company. We .... (2) high quality kitchen knives. We .... (3) them in our factory in Solingen.

Andrea

My company, Helle GmbH, is a logistics company. We .... (4) goods worldwide. We're a service company – we .... (5) a service to customers.

Eckhard

My company, BlueSky, is a big .... (6) company. We .... (7) and .... (8) business software. You maybe have one of our software packages on your computer.

Lee

A6

Can you find and correct the ten mistakes in the notes below?

Lisa comes from Austria. She's a consultant. She lives in Vienna.
Andrea doesn't come from Austria. She comes from Germany. She's a consultant, too, with Amsel, a company in Hamburg. It manufactures cars.
Eckhard works for Helle, a big American logistics company. He's a sales manager. He lives and works in Solingen.
Lee doesn't come from Austria or Germany. He's British. He's the boss of BlueSky, a large insurance company. He works in the company's head office in London.

The simple present: negatives FOCUS

I **don't** live in Linz.
Lee **doesn't** work for an Austrian company.
He **isn't** a sales manager.

A7

Work with a partner.

1. Where do you come from/live/work? What company do you work for and what do you and your company do? Write a profile of yourself (approximately 50 words).
2. Now interview your partner. *(Where ... ? What ... ?)*
3. Then introduce your partner to the class. *(This is ... He/She ...)*

B Nice to meet you

WARM UP **Say 'hello again' to a partner.**

Nice to see you again. How are you?
I'm fine, thanks. Good to see you, too. How are you?

B1 1/04 **Listen. Is this Lisa's first face-to-face meeting with the two men? How do you know?**

Johan Eriksson and Per Lindstrom work for a mobile phone company in Sweden. It's one of Lisa's clients. Today the two men are in Linz. Lisa is at the airport to meet them.

Lisa Mr Eriksson? How do you do? I'm Lisa Schalk from Austrian Portal.
Mr Eriksson Oh, how do you do, Ms Schalk? We spoke on the phone. It's nice to meet you at last. Can I introduce our Project Manager, Per Lindstrom?
Mr Lindstrom How do you do, Ms Schalk?
Lisa Pleased to meet you, Mr Lindstrom. Welcome to Austria. So, how was your flight?
Mr Eriksson Ah, it was fine thanks ... [phone rings] Oh, sorry, could you excuse me? It's an important call.
Lisa No problem. So, Mr Lindstrom, is this your first time in Linz? ...

B2 **Find the English phrases.**

1 Wir haben telefoniert.
2 Freut mich, Sie endlich kennen zu lernen.
3 Darf ich Ihnen ... vorstellen?
4 Willkommen in Österreich.
5 Wie war Ihr Flug?
6 Würden Sie mich entschuldigen?

B3 1/05

Listen and learn the alphabet rhyme.

A B C D E F G, H I J K L M N O P, L M N O P Q R S T, U V W, X Y Z

B4

Ask a partner.

How do you spell your name?
And your company's name?

FOCUS

ee	double E (US: E-E)
nn	double N (US: N-N)
ß	double S/the German double S symbol
München	M-U-umlaut-N-C-H-E-N
A c	CAPITAL A, small c

B5

Can you spell these European countries (1–8)? Write the names, then spell the names to a partner.

B6

Now unscramble these country names and find them on the map (A–F).

ECEREG

DILREAN

HET ZHECC LICREPUB

TZIERSLAWND

LINNFAD

YEKTUR

B7 1/06

Listen. Which conversation (a–e) do you hear?

Conversation 1 ...b...... Conversation 3 .... Conversation 5 ....
Conversation 2 .... Conversation 4 ....

- **Listen again and practise saying each phrase.**

1 Pleased to meet you.
2 Please, call me Larry.
3 Come and join us.
4 Sorry. I didn't catch your name.
5 Great to see you again! How are you?
6 I'm fine, thanks. And you?

B8

In your class ...

1. Invent a name and a company for yourself and write a name badge.
2. You are at a conference. Introduce yourself, then other people that you meet.

Meeting people

FOCUS

How do you do?*
Pleased/Nice to meet you.
Great to see you again!
How are you?
Can I introduce ... ?
Can I introduce myself?
I'm/My name's ...
Sorry. I didn't catch your name.
Please come and join us.

* ***Vorsicht!*** *Die Antwort auf* How do you do *ist* How do you do (*oder* 'Pleased/Nice to meet you'), *NICHT:* ~~I'm fine, thanks~~.

Here's my card

In this business file you ...

- practise saying addresses, telephone numbers and email addresses.
- listen for information and write a memo.

1 **Try this quick test with a partner.**

TEST YOURSELF

Say (or write down in words) the telephone numbers and email and web addresses, and answer the questions about the British and American postal addresses. Then check your answers on page 140.

1 Telephone numbers

A My firm is based in Brighton in England. My work number is 01207 (the code for Brighton), then 455719.

B I live in Boston, Massachusetts and my home number is area code 617 635-4550.

2 Email addresses and URLs (web addresses)

A My email address is j-jones@aol.com.

B And my email address is t_thomas-321@hotmail.com.

C For more information visit our website, www.holidayparks.biz/htm.

3 Addresses

A One important thing is *wrong* in this British business address. What's the mistake?

B What's this part of the address called in the UK?

the post office
the post number
the post code

C What's this part of the address called in the US?

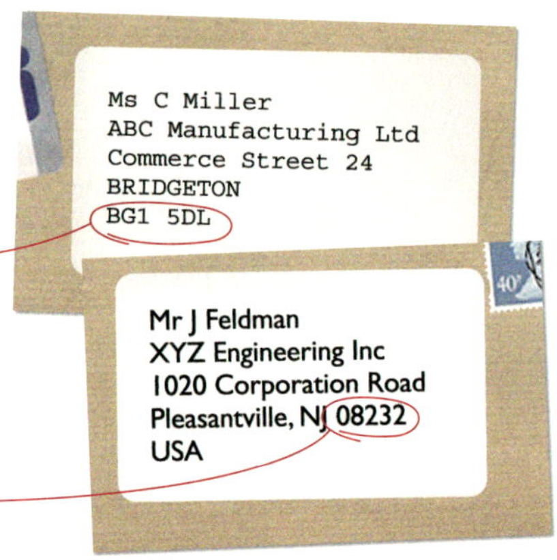

2 **Work with a partner and exchange information.**

Harry

Nina

Chantal

You work for a chain of department stores in your country. You meet Harry, Nina and Chantal at an international trade fair and collect their business cards. First look at Harry's details in the address book.

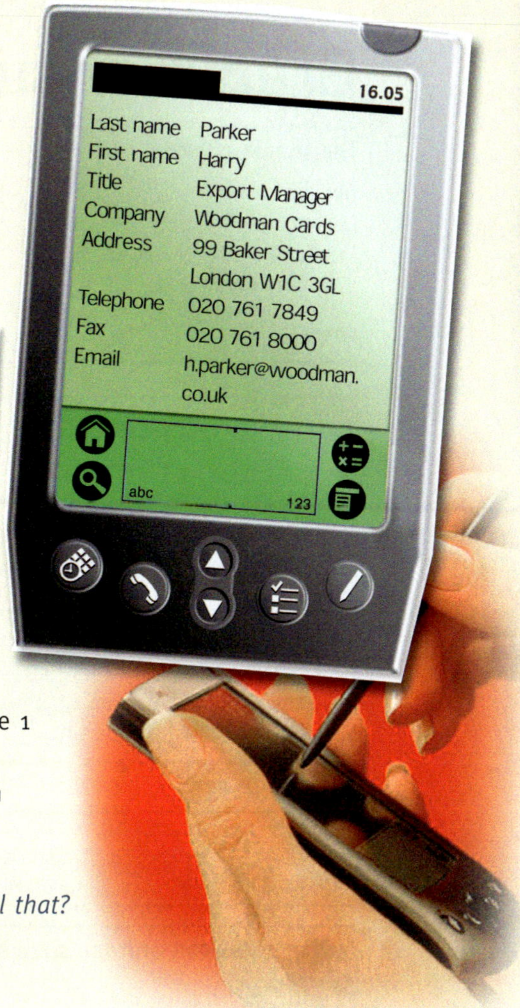

Now work with a partner.

PARTNER A Look at Nina's business card in File 1 on page 126.

PARTNER B Look at Chantal's business card in File 6 on page 128.

Ask each other questions and make notes:

What's Nina's last name? How do you spell that?
What's her (job) title? ... ?

3 1/07 **Listen, make notes and write a memo.**

After the trade fair, your boss is interested in the three companies. Listen to Harry, Nina and Chantal and make notes. Then write a memo to your boss (in German or English) with the main points and contact details for each of them.

Grammar summary

The simple present

USE

I **come** from Germany.
I **work** for a German company.
It **manufactures** cars.

FORM

	to come	to go	to fax
I	come	go	fax
he she it	come**s**	go**es**	fax**es**
we you they	come	go	fax

Where **do** you **live**?
What company **does** she **work** for?
I **don't work** for an Austrian company.
Lisa **doesn't come** from the UK.

Die einfache Gegenwart

VERWENDUNG

Mit dem *simple present* beschreibt man gleich bleibende Zustände und Fakten, beispielsweise Angaben zur Person, Arbeit oder Firma.

FORM

Das *simple present* wird mit der Grundform des Verbs, also dem Infinitiv *(z. B. to come)* ohne *to* gebildet.

In der dritten Person *(he/she/it)* wird meist -s angehängt. Bei einigen Verben, die auf *-o* enden wie *to go* und *to do,* und bei allen, die auf *-s, -ss, -sh, -ch* oder *-x* enden (wo die *-s*-Endung schwer auszusprechen wäre), wird -es angehängt.

Mit der Ausnahme von *to be* werden Fragen und Verneinungen im *simple present* mit *do/does* und *don't/doesn't* gebildet.

The verb *to be*

I	**am**	am not ('m not)
he/she/it	**is**	is not (isn't)
we/you/they	**are**	are not (aren't)

Das Verb *to be*

Das Verb *to be* ist unregelmäßig. Es werden oft die Kurzformen verwendet: *I'm, he's, she's, it's, we're, you're, they're, my name's* etc.

Asking questions with the simple present

Do you **live** in Linz? Yes, I **do**./No, I **don't**.
Are you a consultant? Yes, I **am**./No, I'**m not**.
Does Lisa **live** in Linz? Yes, she **does**./No, she **doesn't**.
Is she a consultant? Yes, she **is**./No, she **isn't**.

Where do you come from?
Who does she work for?
What do you do?
When do they start work?
How do you spell that?

Fragen stellen im *simple present*

JA-/NEIN-FRAGEN

Oft werden Ja-/Nein-Fragen mit einer Kurzantwort beantwortet.

FRAGEN MIT FRAGEWÖRTEN

Fragen werden auch mit Fragewörtern wie *where* (wo), *who* (wer **!**), *what* (was/welche/r/s), *when* (wann) und *how* (wie) gebildet. In Verbindung mit *to be* wird *is* nach Fragewörtern oft zu *-'s*: *Where's Jim today? What's your name?*

can and *could*

I he/she/it we/you/they	**can** **can't**	**speak** English

Can you speak English?
Can I introduce my colleague?
Could you spell that, please?
Could I ask a question?

can und *could*

Can bleibt in allen Personen unverändert. Die verneinte Form ist *can't.* Nach *can* und *can't* wird oft der Infinitiv eines zweiten Verbs ohne *to* verwendet.

Could ist eine Form von *can* und bleibt ebenfalls in allen Personen unverändert. *Could* wird oft als höfliche Form verwendet, beispielsweise um etwas zu bitten.

Grammar

1 Fill in the correct forms of the verb *to be*.

I *am*[1]
it ....[2]
she ....[3]
they ....[4]
we ....[5]
you ....[6]
he ....[7]

■ Now complete the gaps with the short form, where possible.

8 David *isn't* (not) a sales manager. He .... an account manager.
9 We .... a service company. We .... (not) a manufacturing company.
10 Bob and Sally .... in London now. They .... (not) in Oxford.
11 My number .... 456-6500. It .... (not) 456-6000.
12 .... you from Linz? No, I .... from Vienna.

2 Choose the correct alternative in each sentence.

1 What *do/does* your company do?
2 What company *do/does* you work for?
3 Which languages *do/does* she speak?
4 She *speak/speaks* English.
5 We *produce/produces* software.
6 I *don't/doesn't* live in Germany.
7 He *don't/doesn't* work here.

3 Match the questions to the answers.

1 Where do you come from?	a It makes cars.
2 What do you do?	b At 8.30 am.
3 Who do you work for?	c To France and Spain.
4 What does your company do?	d Italy.
5 Where do you travel in your job?	e I'm a sales manager.
6 When do you start work?	f Fiat.

4 Rearrange the words to make questions. There is one word you don't need in each sentence.

1 live ~~who~~ you do where? *Where do you live?*
2 company do for work which works you?
3 you company your does what do?
4 you does do your job like?
5 speak does languages which he do?
6 does her spell who name how she?

Words and phrases

5 Complete the sentences using the correct form of the verbs from the box.

manufacture live provide work transport be come

1 He .... a consultant.
2 She .... from the USA.
3 Susanne .... and .... in Frankfurt.
4 They .... computers.
5 We .... logistic services.
6 We .... goods all over the world.

6 There are 11 phrases hidden in this word square. Can you find them? They are either horizontal, going from left to right (→), or vertical, going from top to bottom (↓). The first one has been done as an example ('How are you?').

I	meet	to	how	are	you	he
you	great	yourself	do	you	nice	Mike
nice	to	meet	you	Claire	introduce	is
to	see	who	do	you	work	for
pleased	you	nice	come	and	join	us
to	again	I	didn't	catch	your	name
how	colleague	pleased	where	call	she	your
I'm	fine	thanks	me	for	I	work
you	do	who	can	I	introduce	myself
this	fine	please	call	me	Martin	me

7 Match person B's replies to what person A says.

PERSON A
1 How are you?
2 How do you do?
3 Nice to meet you.
4 Please call me Claire.
5 Sorry. I didn't catch your name.
6 Great to see you again.

PERSON B
a How do you do?
b And I'm Serge.
c Good to see you, too.
d I'm fine, thanks.
e Nice to meet you, too.
f It's Graham Klein.

8 Can you identify these European countries?

1 CAN REF *FRANCE*
2 REAL DIN
3 GRAY MEN
4 A ROT PLUG
5 WARD LIST ZEN
6 TENTH HEARS LEND
7 CCCP ZITHER EEL HUB

9 **Complete the table with the correct possessive adjectives.**

I	*my*
you	
he	
she	
it	
we	
they	

Translating

10 **Translate into English.**

1 Er kommt aus England, lebt aber in Deutschland.

2 Er arbeitet nicht für eine amerikanische Firma.

3 Sie arbeitet bei einer britischen Firma namens Brackstone.

4 Sie ist Verkaufsleiterin.

5 Er ist Österreicher und wohnt in Linz.

6 Was macht seine Firma?

7 Es freut mich, Sie kennen zu lernen. – Ebenfalls.

8 Wie geht es Ihnen? – Danke, gut.

TYPICAL MISTAKES

1 I come from Germany.
NOT I'm *coming* from Germany.
(Für Dinge, die immer gelten, wird das simple present *verwendet.)*

2 I work for a German company.
NOT I work *by* a German company.

3 Giles doesn't come from Germany. He comes from the UK.
NOT Giles *don't come* from Germany. He *come* from the UK.

4 I don't work for Siemens.
NOT I *work not* for Siemens.

5 What does your company do?
NOT What *does* your company?

6 How are you? – Fine, thanks.
NOT *Thanks, fine.*

7 I'm a project manager.
NOT I'm project manager.

8 She's German.
NOT She's *german*. *(Nationalitäten werden groß geschrieben.)*

CULTURE SPOT

Meeting people

Using first names

In British and American business circles, it is common to use first names.
Try to use first names as soon as possible when you meet someone. For example, if someone uses your family name ('Nice to meet you, Mr Schmidt'), you should say 'Oh, please call me (your first name)'. The other person will normally say 'And I'm (first name)'.

Mrs, Ms or Miss?

Do you know the difference between Mrs, Ms and Miss?

- *Miss* is used for unmarried women. It is not common today, and many women don't like it.
- *Mrs* is only used for married woman. Only use it if you know that a woman is married, *and* that she wants to be called 'Mrs'.
- *Ms* [mz] is used for married and unmarried women (like *Frau* in German). It is the best title to use in business.

UNIT 2
PROJECTS

In this unit you ...

talk about company and personal projects:

We're developing a new product at the moment.

I'm learning English.

describe where you work:

I work in Cologne. This is my office.

Cologne is on the Rhine in western Germany.

Business file

Could I speak to ... ?

A What we're doing at the moment

WARM UP **What clothes do you normally wear for work? Women: do you usually wear a skirt or trousers? Men: do you often wear a tie? Use your dictionary and make a list.**

A1 **Look at the picture and talk about Lisa's assistant, Felix Obermayr.**
He's the man in the blue shirt. Look at the list of things that Felix often does in the office at Austrian Portal. What's Felix doing (and not doing) *at the moment*?

He's helping Lisa.
He isn't making a phone call at the moment.

He helps Lisa.
He makes phone calls.
He writes emails.
He arranges meetings.
He attends meetings with Lisa.
He books flights and hotels for her business trips.
He drinks coffee.
He wears a tie.
He wears a suit.

A2

Look at the picture again.

1 First write the *-ing* forms of the verbs below.

to sit	....
to talk	....
to make (a phone call)	....
to listen	....
to wear	....
to use	....

2 Use the verbs to describe the picture. Do you remember the man in the white shirt? What are he, Felix and Lisa doing?

They're sitting in Lisa's office.
They're ...

> **The simple present** FOCUS
> Felix **comes** from Austria. He **works** for Austrian Portal. *(Tatsachen und Gegebenheiten mit langer Gültigkeitsdauer)*
> He often **arranges** meetings for Lisa. *(regelmäßige Handlungen)*
>
> **The present continuous**
> What**'s** Felix **doing** at the moment/right now?
> –He**'s helping** Lisa. He **isn't making** a phone call. *(eine im Moment des Sprechens vor sich gehende Handlung)*

A3

1/08

Now listen to Felix.

"As you can see, Lisa and I are in a meeting today. What are we doing? Well, the man with us is Per Lindstrom. Per is from Sweden and he's the project manager of a company called Nordik. It manufactures mobile phones and at the moment it's expanding into the Austrian market. That's where we come in. We're helping. Right now, we're talking about two possible sites for a sales office – one in Linz and the other in Vienna – and discussing the pros and cons."

A4

What's the English for ... ?

1 *(Die Firma) produziert Mobiltelefone*
2 *sie expandiert auf dem österreichischen Markt.*
3 *wir sprechen über zwei mögliche Standorte*
4 *wir diskutieren das Für und Wider.*

> **Talking about projects** FOCUS
> *Man verwendet das present continuous oft, um über laufende Projekte zu sprechen.*
> What**'s** your company **doing** at the moment?
> – We**'re expanding** into a new market.
> – We**'re opening** a new office.

A5

Work in a small group (3–4 people).

1 Look at the words in the box below. Check that you know their meanings.

2 Look at the example sentences. Can you see a pattern for the word order?

3 Now tell your group something that you always/normally/often/... do.

always normally usually often frequently sometimes occasionally never	I often **go** to work by bike. He usually **wears** a suit to the office. **I'm** never very friendly on Monday mornings! Pauline **is** always punctual for meetings.

A6

The simple present or the present continuous? Choose the correct forms.

1 Per Lindstrom *works/~~is working~~* for a Swedish company called Nordik.
2 He *comes/is coming* from Sweden.
3 At the moment he *visits*/he's *visiting* Linz.
4 He's in a meeting with Lisa. They *talk*/They'*re talking* about sites for a new office.
5 Per often *travels/is travelling* in his job.
6 Felix is Lisa's assistant. He frequently *attends/is attending* meetings with her. In fact, he *attends*/he's *attending* a meeting with Lisa right now.

- **Make two sentences that are true for you: one with the simple present and one with the present continuous.**

A7

1/09

Listen and take notes about Manfred Gerber and his company.

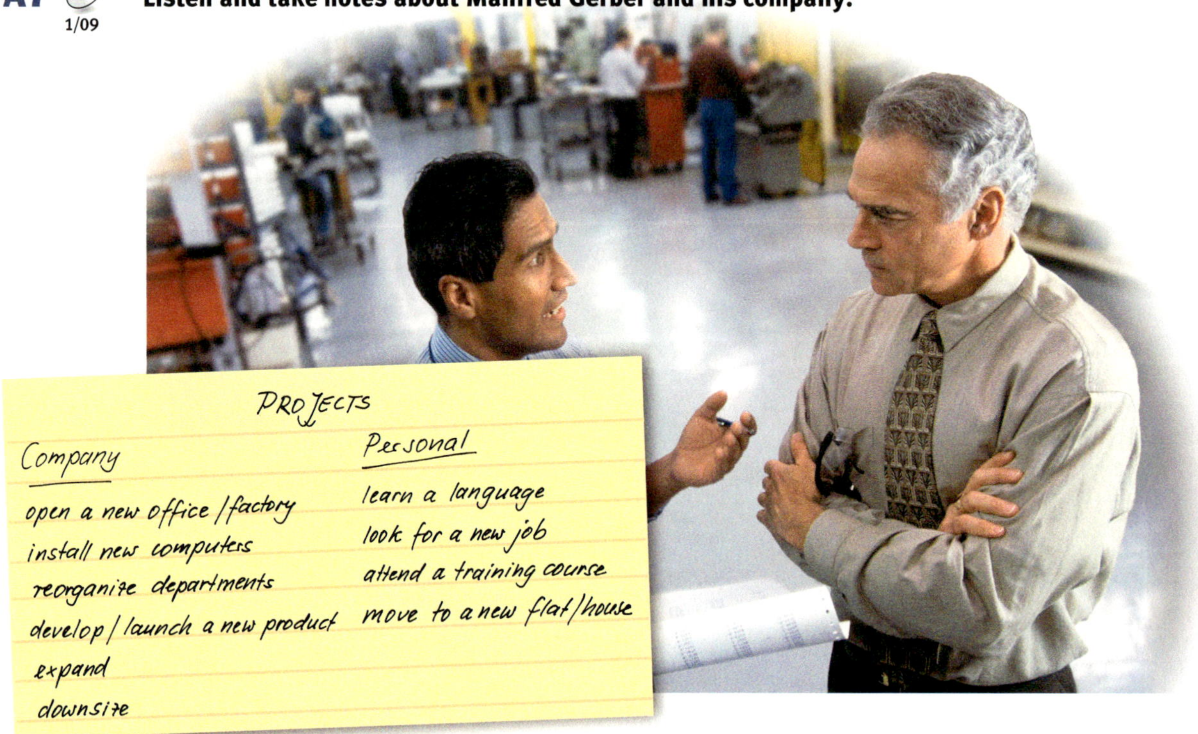

- **Now look at the list of projects above. What project(s) does Manfred's company have at the moment? What is Manfred's personal project?**

A8

Think of a project that your company, your department or a company you know has at the moment. What is it? Do you have a personal project? Tell the class.

B Where I work

WARM UP **Name the things in the room where you are at the moment.**

a door, (six) tables ...

B1

Look at this picture of Felix's office and find the things in the list. Write the numbers 1–17 below.

window .....1...	notice board	safe	briefcase ....
desk	letter rack	curtain	pens and pencils ....
office chair	telephone	plant	
waste-bin	printer	cable	
computer	cupboard	file	

- **Now ask a partner.**

What's this?

And what's that?

What are these?

What are those?

FOCUS
this, that, these, those
What's **this/that**? **It's** a ...
What are **these/those**? **They're** ...

B2

Work with a partner.

1 Make a list of the things in Felix's office. Don't look at page 21!

There's a ... There are (two) ...

2 Ask your partner.

What is there in your office (or the place where you work)?
Is there a ... ?
Are there ... ?

> **FOCUS**
>
> ***there is (there's)/there are***
>
> **There's** *a* computer. *(Singular)*
> **There are** *two* chairs. *(Plural)*
>
> **Questions and answers**
>
> **Is there** a computer in your office?
> –Yes, **there is**./No, **there isn't**.
> **Are there** two computers?
> –Yes, **there are**./No, **there aren't**. (There's only one./There are three!)

B3

Work in a small group (3–4 people).

Linz, where Lisa and Felix work, is the provincial capital of Upper Austria.

1 Test yourself. What do you know about the city? (Don't look at the brochure yet!) Try to answer these questions:

1 Linz is situated on a famous river. Which river?
2 What famous composer lived and worked in Linz?
3 What food is Linz famous for?
4 Vienna and Graz have cathedrals. Does Linz?

2 Now read the brochure and check your answers.

HERZLICH WILLKOMMEN IN

welcome to

LINZ, Austria's third largest city after Vienna and Graz, is situated on the River Danube in northern Austria. It is the provincial capital of Upper Austria, one of Austria's nine federal provinces, and has a population today of around 200,000.

Linz an der Donau

LINZ was always an important commercial and industrial city and today it is a thriving business centre with a world-class university, an exhibition centre and an international airport. It is also a historic city, with a lot of sights for the tourist: a *Schloss* (castle), a *Rathaus* (town hall), and both an old and a new *Dom* (cathedral).

LINZ is a cultural city, too. The composer Anton Bruckner lived and worked here and every autumn there is an international Bruckner Festival in the city's superb concert hall, the Brucknerhaus.

No Austrian city could be complete without its cafés, and LINZ is famous for these, too. And what do you eat with your coffee? Well, a piece of *Linzer Torte* of course!

B4 **What is the German for these cities, lakes and other places?**

North Rhine-Westphalia
Saxony
Lower Saxony
Bavaria
Thuringia
Rhineland-Palatinate
Upper and Lower Austria
Carinthia
Tyrol

Cologne
Munich
Hanover
Brunswick
Nuremberg
Basle
Geneva
Vienna

Lake Constance
Lake Geneva
the Baltic Sea
the Danube
the Black Forest

B5 **Write a text for a brochure.**

Your company (or a company that you know) is producing a brochure for foreign visitors. Work in your group again and write a text of 50–100 words about the town or city where you are located. Look at the **FOCUS** box for ideas and useful words.

Describing where you live or work

FOCUS

(My town/city) **is situated in northern/southern/eastern/western** (Austria);
in the **north/south/east/west of** (Germany)
It's **on the Danube** (Rhine/Elbe ...)

... is a **small/large/medium-sized** town
It's (Switzerland's) **largest/second largest/third/fourth** ... **largest** city
It has a **population of (around)** ...
It's a **provincial capital/the national capital**

... is a(n) **historic/industrial** city
It's a(n) **important/thriving commercial/business/cultural/media centre**

It has/There's (There are) **a lot of historic buildings/a cathedral/a castle/ a concert hall/a museum/an art gallery/a university/an airport/ a harbour/an exhibition centre/cafés** ...
It's **famous for** ...

Remember

Mit den Begriffen East Germany (GDR) *und* West Germany (FRG) *wurden die Länder* ***vor*** *der Wiedervereinigung bezeichnet. Heute sagt man* eastern *oder* western Germany.

Could I speak to ... ?

In this business file you ...
practise telephone conversations.
listen to voicemail messages.

1 1/10 **Four people are telephoning a business partner. What happens? Listen and tick (✓) the table.**

Conversation	1	2	3	4
The caller gets through to her/his business partner.				
The business partner isn't available. The caller leaves a message.				
The business partner isn't available. The caller will try again later.				
The business partner isn't available but will call back.				
The caller leaves a voicemail message.				

2 **Who said ... ?**

The phrases below were in the telephone conversations. But were they in conversation 1, 2, 3 or 4? (Listen again if necessary.)

a Just a minute. It's OK, she's free now. I'll put you through.

b Please speak after the tone.

c Just a minute, I'll get a pen. OK. Who's calling, please?

d I'm afraid Bill's in a meeting at the moment, Mr Rogers. Would you like to leave a message?

e Is Claire available at the moment?

f Try again at about 4 o'clock. The meeting should be finished by then.

g We're sorry that there's no one here to take your call at the moment.

How do I telephone a company in English?

INFO

How can I help you?

ABC Ltd.
One moment, please/Hold the line, please./It's ringing for you now.
Sales department, Michael speaking.
Who's calling, please?
I'll put you through.

Good morning/Good afternoon *(noon–6 pm)*/ Good evening.
Could I speak to ..., please?
Could I have the sales department, please?
This is/It's ... from ... .

I'm sorry ...

I'm afraid she/he isn't here at the moment/isn't in the office today/isn't available at the moment.
She/He's in a meeting/on the other line.
Would you like to leave a message?
Can she/he call you back?
Does she/he have your number?

Yes, could you say that (name) called, please? It's about ...
No, it's OK, thanks. I'll call back later/another time.
I need to speak to her/him personally.
When is a good time to call back/to reach her/him?
Do you know when she'll/he'll be back/free?
Yes, thanks. My number is ... /My name again is ...

3 **Work with a partner to make telephone calls.**

PARTNER A: Look below. PARTNER B: Look at File 2 on page 126.

PARTNER A

1 Make these telephone calls. Your partner is the telephone receptionist at ABC Ltd.
   a You're Mr/Ms White. You'd like to speak to Mr Black.
   b You're Mr/Ms Grey. You'd like to speak to Mr Redman.
   c You're Mr/Ms Teal. You'd like to speak to Mr Black.
   d You're Mr/Ms Mustard. You'd like to speak to Mrs Plum.
   e You're Mr/Ms Green. You'd like to speak to Ms Brown.

2 Now answer your partner's calls. You are the telephone receptionist at XYZ Ltd. Here's a list of people in your company with notes about whether they're available or not.
   - **Ms Baker** is ill today. If Mr/Ms Botto calls, put through to Mr Ingram.
   - **Mr Ingram** is at his desk.
   - **Mr Goodwin** is on holiday all week. He'll be back next Monday.
   - **Mrs Edwards** is on the phone. She has a meeting in ten minutes.

4 1/11 **What are your messages today?**

Listen to the three voicemail messages and note the time, the caller and the subject of each call.

TELEPHONE MESSAGE

Time:

From:

Subject:

Grammar summary

The simple present with adverbs of frequency

I **come** from Germany. (1)
Felix **often helps** his boss Lisa. (2)
I **always go** to work by bike. (2)
Lisa **is sometimes** away from the office on business trips. (3)

Die einfache Gegenwart mit Adverbien der Häufigkeit

Mit dem *simple present* werden nicht nur Fakten beschrieben (1), sondern auch routinemäßig ausgeführte Handlungen und Gewohnheiten – Dinge, die wir immer, oft, manchmal tun. Wörter wie *often, always, sometimes* usw. stehen **vor** normalen Verben (2) und **hinter** *to be* (3).

The present continuous

USE

I'**m reading** this page at the moment. (1)
My company **is developing** a new product. (2)
I'**m learning** English this year. (2)
I **think** it's a good idea. (3)
(~~I'm thinking~~)
I **like** tea but I **don't like** coffee. (3)
(~~I'm liking/I'm not liking~~)

Die Verlaufsform der Gegenwart

VERWENDUNG

Mit dem *present continuous* werden vorübergehende Vorgänge beschrieben, die entweder in dem Moment vor sich gehen, in dem man über sie spricht (1), oder auch längerfristige, zeitlich begrenzte Vorgänge – beispielsweise ein aktuell in der Firma laufendes Projekt (2). Man verwendet das *present continuous* nur mit ,Verben des aktiven Handelns' *(to do, to work, to go)*.
Es wird gewöhnlich nicht mit Verben wie *to be, to think, to like, to have* verwendet (3).

FORM

I	am	(I'm)	
he	is	(he's)	
she	is	(she's)	
it	is	(it's)	working
we	are	(we're)	
you	are	(you're)	
they	are	(they're)	

What **are** you **doing** at the moment?
I'**m not** (She **isn't**/We'**re not**) working today.
Is Tom **working** now? Yes, he **is**./No, he **isn't**.

FORM

Das *present continuous* wird mit einer Form von *to be* und der *-ing*-Form gebildet.

Bei den meisten Verben wird einfach *-ing* an den Infinitiv gehängt: *work – working; go – going*. Bei Verben, die auf -*e* enden, fällt das -*e* weg: *give – giving*. Bei kurzen Verben, die mit einem Vokal gefolgt von einem Konsonanten (außer -*y* und -*w*) enden, verdoppelt sich der Konsonant: *get – getting; say – saying.*

Fragen und Verneinungen werden im *present continuous* mit den normalen Frage- und Verneinungsformen von *to be* gebildet.

The verb *to have*

I	have	don't have
he/she/it	has	doesn't have
we/you/they	have	don't have

Do you **have** Lisa's email address?
Does your city **have** a castle?

Das Verb *to have*

In der dritten Person ist die Form von *to have* unregelmäßig *(has)*. Ansonsten verhält es sich wie ein regelmäßiges Verb.

In Ausdrücken wie *to have lunch/dinner, to have a meeting* usw. wird *to have* als ,Verb des aktiven Handelns' betrachtet (s. o.) und kann dann auch im *present continuous* verwendet werden: *We're having lunch at the moment.*

there is (there's), there are

There's a park near my office. (1)
There are ten people in my class. (2)
Is there a computer in your office? (3)
Yes, **there is**. (4)/No, **there isn't**.

there is (there's), there are

There is (There's) wird mit Substantiven im Singular verwendet (1), *there are* mit Substantiven im Plural (2). Um Fragen zu bilden, vertauscht man *there* und *is/are* (3). In Kurzantworten wird die Kurzform *there's* nicht verwendet (4).

Grammar

1 Rearrange the words to make sentences. There is one word you don't need in each sentence.

1 work/go/always/car/I/goes/to/by
2 lunch/company/has/usually/I/our/canteen/have/in
3 wears/never/tie/wear/he/a
4 drinks/she/coffee/the/morning/drink/normally/in
5 sometimes/we/goes/business/trips/go/on
6 meetings/attend/they/often/attends

2 Complete the sentences. Use the positive or negative form of the present continuous.

Trepan GmbH projects	Feder AG projects
open new office in Italy develop new products install new computer software	install new computer software work with consultant to reorganize departments downsize

1 Trepan *isn't opening* (open) a new office in France at the moment. It .... (open) an office in Italy.
2 Feder .... (move) its head office to a new city.
3 Feder .... (downsize); the personnel manager .... (put) job adverts in the newspaper.
4 A consultant .... (help) Feder to reorganize its departments.
5 Trepan and Feder .... (install) new software.
6 Trepan .... (develop) new products at the moment.

3 Choose the correct verb tense.

1 My company ~~opens~~/*is opening* a new factory in Slovakia at the moment.
2 I *learn/am learning* French at the moment.
3 He *calls/is calling* a customer right now.
4 We often *travel/are travelling* to the USA.
5 She normally *comes/is coming* to work by bike.
6 I never *drink/am drinking* coffee.

4 Each sentence has one mistake. Write the correct sentence.

1 She speaks to a customer at the moment.
2 Are you learn English for your job?
3 I not wearing a tie today.
4 We don't developing any new products at the moment.
5 I write often emails in English.
6 Do you drink usually tea or coffee?

5 Make sentences with *to have*.

1 my city/not have/a university. *My city doesn't have a university.*
2 you/have/Mike's phone number?
3 she/always/have/lunch at work.
4 I/not have/a car.
5 you/have/my email address?
6 he/not have/any plants in his office.
7 Fiona/have/a printer in her office.
8 the managers/have/a meeting/now?

6 ***Is there* or *Are there*?**

1 ……… a computer in your office?
2 ……… two computers in your office?
3 ……… a safe in your office?
4 ……… plants in your office?
5 ……… a telephone on your desk?
6 ……… curtains in your office?

■ **Now answer these questions with short answers that are true for you.**

Words and phrases

7 Complete the crossword with the English translations.

Across	
1	Bleistifte
5	Drucker
7	Sortierbox
9	Telefon
11	Ordner
12	Papierkorb

Down	
2	Schwarzes Brett
3	Tresor
4	Computer
6	Aktentasche
8	Kabel
10	Kugelschreiber (pl.)

8 Complete the text about Munich with the words in the box.

business population galleries cultural largest
museums universities famous capital historic

MUNICH

Munich is the ………[1] of Bavaria and the third ………[2] city in Germany, with a ………[3] of around 1.3 million. It is an important ………[4] centre and also has many ………[5] buildings, such as the *Altes Rathaus* and the *Isartor*. Munich is also a ………[6] city with many theatres, ………[7] and art ………[8]. It also has ten ………[9] with over eighty thousand students. Munich is ………[10] for its Oktoberfest, every year in late September and early October.

9 What are these places in English?

1 Wien 3 Genf 5 der Schwarzwald 7 Bayern
2 Köln 4 die Ostsee 6 die Schweiz 8 Nürnberg

Translating

10 **Translate into English.**

1 Er arbeitet bei BMW. (feste Stelle)
2 Ich trage oft eine Krawatte im Büro.
3 Bern ist die Hauptstadt der Schweiz.
4 Lippstadt hat keine Universität.
5 Ich kann Ihnen im Moment nicht helfen, Bill. Ich bin sehr beschäftigt.
6 Gibt es einen Laptop in Ihrem Büro?
7 Marie ist heute nicht da. Diese Woche arbeitet sie in der Zentrale.
8 Ist Berlin die größte Stadt Deutschlands? –Ja.
9 Was macht Anna gerade? –Sie telefoniert.

TYPICAL MISTAKES

1 Remember the difference:
I work for Sony. (= *Ich habe hier eine feste Stelle.*)
I'm working for Sony. (= *Ich arbeite hier nur vorübergehend.*)

2 What are you doing at the moment?
NOT What are you doing *in* the moment?

3 My boss often goes on business trips.
NOT My boss *goes often* on business trips.

4 There is a telephone on my desk.
NOT *It gives* a telephone on my desk.

5 She makes a lot of phone calls every day.
NOT She *does* a lot of phone calls every day.

6 Vienna is the capital of Austria.
NOT Vienna is the *main city* of Austria.

7 Munich is the third largest city in Germany.
NOT Munich is the third *greatest* city in Germany. (Great *hat nur die Bedeutung von ‚groß' bei einigen festen Redewendungen und Ortsnamen wie* Great Britain. *Die normale Bedeutung ist großartig oder bedeutend*: Adenauer was a great man.)

8 Osnabrück has a university.
NOT Osnabrück has *an* university. (*Viele Wörter, die mit* u *anfangen, werden mit dem Laut* [j] *ausgesprochen, z. B.* usually.)

CULTURE SPOT

British and American English

Words and phrases

British English	American English
My office is in the **city centre**.	My office is **downtown**.
I live in a **flat**.	I live in an **apartment**.
My boss is on **holiday**.	My boss is on **vacation**.
Can I use your **toilet**?	Can I use your **bathroom**?
Call me on my **mobile phone**.	Call me on my **cell phone**.
We can take the **underground**.	We can take the **subway**.
Would you like a **biscuit** with your coffee?	Would you like a **cookie** with your coffee?
The **lift** is over there.	The **elevator** is over there.
Let's see a **film** tonight.	Let's see a **movie** tonight.
I need some **petrol** for my car.	I need some **gas** for my car.
My office is on the **ground floor**.	My office is on the **first floor**.

Spellings

British English	American English
catalogue	catalog
centre/theatre	center/theater
cheque (bank)	check
colour/harbour	color/harbor
licence	license
programme (But: computer *program*)	program

UNIT 3

WORK AND LEISURE

In this unit you …

talk about your life and career:
I was born in Cologne.
I joined my company in 2002.
ask about places, people and things:
What's Denver like?
talk about your interests:
I like reading. What do you like doing?

Business file

I'm ringing about …

A Meet Eckhard Kellermann

WARM UP **Where do you live now? Were you born there? What's your job now? Was that your job five years ago?**

A1 1/12 **Listen to Eckhard Kellermann. He's talking about his career and his present job.**

"I work for a big German logistics company called Helle. We're based in Hamburg, in northern Germany, and I'm an account manager. Hamburg is where I live and work now, but I'm not from here originally. I was actually born in Cologne. That's also where I went to school and did my 'Abitur' – that's like A-Levels in the UK or the high school diploma in the USA. After school I studied for three years – still in Cologne – and got my business diploma (we call it a 'Diplomkaufmann' qualification). That was, let me see, in 1993. I got my first job in the same year. It was with a company called Richardt, a large supermarket chain in Cologne. I worked there as a management trainee first and then in 1996 I became the company's transport manager. So when did I move to Hamburg and join Helle? Well, that was in 2000."

- **Find the verbs in the simple past. Which verbs are *regular* and which verbs are *irregular*?**

The simple past FOCUS

	regular	irregular
I he/she/it we you they	work**ed**	**went**

A2 Look at Eckhard's online CV (curriculum vitae). What is the missing information?

Full name	Eckhard Heinrich ....(1).........
Profile	I am an energetic and effective Account Manager with Helle GmbH, a leading German ....(2)......... company in ....(3)......... , Germany. I have complete responsibility for the international product distribution of one of the company's biggest clients.
Education and qualifications	
1990–1993	Fachhochschule Cologne, '.........(4).........' qualification 1993
Work experience	
2000–present	Account Manager, Helle Logistics GmbH
1996–2000	.........(5)........., Richardt GmbH, a large supermarket chain in Cologne, Germany.
_(6)_-1996	Management Trainee, Richardt GmbH.
Personal details	
Languages	.........(7)......... (mother tongue), English (fluent), French (fair)
Computer skills	Microsoft Word, Excel, Dataflow 5D
Interests	Sailing, photography, reading, keeping fit

Done Internet

A3 Work with a partner.

1 Look at the verbs in the box and write down the simple past forms.

2 Then make and answer questions about Eckhard's career.

1 Where/he/be/born?
Where was he born? He was born in ...
2 Where/he/go/to school?
3 When/he/do/his *Abitur*?
4 What/he/do/next?
5 When/he/get/his *Diplomkaufmann* qualification?
6 What/be/his first job?
7 When/he/become/the company's transport manager?
8 What/he/do/in 2000?

to **be** born
to **go** to school
to **do** an exam (NOT: ~~to make~~ an exam)
to **get** a qualification/a job
to **study** at a university/college
to **become** a manager
to **join** a company
to **move** to a town

A4 Test your partner on Eckhard's career.

(Partner B: please close your book.)

Did he go to school in Hamburg?

No, he didn't. He went ...

Did he get his first job in 1993?

Yes, he did.

The simple past – questions and negatives

FOCUS

Man bildet Fragen und Verneinungen im simple past *mit* did *und* didn't.

Where **did** you **go** to school?
Did you **do** your Abitur?
– Yes, I **did**./No, I **didn't**.

Aber Vorsicht beim Verb to be:

Where **was** he born?
Were you born in ... ?
– Yes, I **was**./No, I **wasn't**.

A5 **Look and read about Eckhard.**

at the moment …
It's 3 o'clock on a Monday afternoon. At the moment Eckhard is in his office. He's working. He's talking on the phone and looking at an invoice.

this time last week …
This time last week Eckhard wasn't in his office. He wasn't working. What was he doing? He was on holiday. He was sailing his boat with a friend.

- **The forms 'was sailing' and 'wasn't working' are the *past continuous*. When do we use the past continuous?**

The past continuous FOCUS

I **was** he/she/it **was** we/you/they **were**	work**ing**

He **wasn't working** this time last week.
What **was** he **doing**?

A6 **Ask a partner.**

What are you doing at the moment?
What were you doing this time last week/this time yesterday/this time last Saturday?

A7 **What were they doing?**

The people below are Eckhard's colleagues in his office in Hamburg. What were they all doing when Eckhard arrived for work yesterday morning? Use the verbs below and make sentences.

Uta and Gertha were talking …

to talk
to discuss
to read
to make a phone call
to laugh
to drink (a cup of coffee)
to think (about)

A8 **Work with a partner.**

1 Look at the Culture Spot on page 41 and write your CV (or a short paragraph about yourself).

2 Then interview your partner and tell the class.

Jürgen/Karin was born in …

B When I'm not working

WARM UP **Ask a partner. Find out two personal details about your partner (for example: What languages does he/she speak? What are his/her hobbies?).**

B1 1/13 Listen, then answer the questions.

As an account manager at Helle, Eckhard looks after one big client. It's an American corporation based in Denver, Colorado, called Nimbus, and it manufactures sports equipment. Eckhard is having a meeting today with two people from Nimbus: Sam Engels, his regular contact (Sam works in Germany), and a visitor from the company's head office, Kay Russo. Sam, Kay and Eckhard are talking in the reception area at the moment. Eckhard is making small talk ...

Eckhard So, Kay, what's Denver like?

Kay It's OK. I like it. It's a big city so we have our problems with crime and traffic and so on but there's a lot to do there. It's really booming these days.

Eckhard How big is it?

Kay Denver itself? About half a million people, I think.

Eckhard It's in the mountains, isn't it?

Kay Everyone thinks that ... because of 'The Mile High City', right? But no, it isn't. It's actually at the foot of the Rockies. But of course the great thing is that you can be up in the mountains in about an hour.

Eckhard Do you often go to the mountains?

Kay Yes, I love skiing ...

1 Where's Kay Russo from?
2 Where does Sam Engels work?
3 What does Eckhard's client company do and what is it called?
4 How big is Denver?
5 What's the 'great thing' about Denver?

B2

Work with a partner.

1 Write down adjectives to describe the people, places and things below. Use a dictionary.

- your town/city
- the weather today
- your teacher
- your neighbours
- your flat/house

2 Now ask your partner.

What's (our/your) ... like?
What are ... like?

> **What's ... like?** FOCUS
>
> *Mit* What's ... like?/What are ... like? *kann man Beschreibungen und Meinungen über Leute, Orte und Dinge erfragen.*
>
> **What's** your office **like**? – It's big and modern. I like it very much.
>
> **What are** your colleagues **like**? – They're mostly young and friendly.

B3

What do you like doing?

Here's a list of leisure activities. Are your favourite activities on the list? Tick the things that you like doing.

- ☐ skiing/cycling/swimming
- ☐ (window) shopping
- ☐ listening to music/reading
- ☐ watching television/DVDs
- ☐ photography
- ☐ playing an instrument
- ☐ cooking/eating with friends
- ☐ going to the theatre/cinema
- ☐ keeping fit (going to a gym, attending an aerobics class ...)
- ☐ playing a sport (tennis, squash, football, snooker ...)
- ☐ travelling/going on day trips
- ☐ playing computer games
- ☐ DIY (working and repairing things in your home)
- ☐ doing absolutely nothing!

> **like, enjoy, love ... + verb + -ing** FOCUS
>
> *Im Englischen wird die -ing-Form nach Verben verwendet, die ‚Neigungen und Abneigungen' ausdrücken.*

to like	to prefer
to enjoy	to dislike
to love	to hate

> I love **eating** with friends.
> I don't like **cycling** (very much).
> I like **watching** TV but I prefer **reading**.

- **Then interview a partner.**

Do you like shopping?

– Yes, very much.

– No, not really.

– Sometimes.

– It depends.

– It's OK but I prefer ...ing.

What about you? Do you like ... ?

B4 1/14

Listen and make notes.

It's evening and Eckhard, Kay and Sam are having dinner together after the meeting. Kay is asking Eckhard and Sam what they like (or dislike) doing.

	Eckhard	Sam
likes/enjoys/loves hates/dislikes/doesn't enjoy		

B5 **Find the opposites. Use your dictionary (if necessary) to complete the table.**

~~to like~~
~~important~~
possible
to agree
happy
regular
interesting

dis	*to dislike* .... (1)
un	*unimportant* .... (2) .... (3)
ir	.... (4)
im	.... (5)

Opposites FOCUS ON WORDS

Von vielen englischen Wörtern lassen sich mit Vorsilben wie dis-, un-, ir-, und in- Wörter mit gegensätzlicher Bedeutung bilden.

I like dancing. → I **dis**like dancing.
Ich tanze gern. → Ich tanze ***un****gern.*

- **Now complete the sentences with words from the table.**

1 I like watching sport on TV but I .... playing it!
2 'To work' is a regular verb but 'to go' is ....
3 Sorry, Catherine. I .... I think you're wrong.
4 It's a good idea but I'm afraid it's .... We can't do it.
5 Larry was .... in his job here. He left the company last week.
6 Bill's presentation was very .... I fell asleep!
7 Do you really think that's .... ? I don't. I think it's extremely important.

B6 **Do a market survey for your class.**

1 First collect data on each person's top three leisure activities and list the results on the board.

2 Now analyse the results.

- What are the people in your class like? (sporty? sociable?)
- What are the top three activities in the class? Are the results different for men and women? According to age?
- What leisure products or services do you think your class likes buying?

In this business file you ...
- telephone a company for product information.
- complete an order form.

I'm ringing about ...

1 1/15 **Listen and tick the phrases that you hear.**

Jill Parsons is the office manager at Royal Oak, an insurance company in the west of England. It's part of her job to buy office supplies and furniture. Listen to Jill's phone conversation and tick the phrases you hear.

- ☐ Could I speak to someone about your advertisement ... ?
- ☐ I'm calling about ...
- ☐ I'm ringing about ...
- ☐ I understand that ...
- ☐ Could you tell me something about ... ?
- ☐ What colours do you have?
- ☐ When can you deliver ... ?
- ☐ Can you give me a discount?
- ☐ Is there a charge for delivery?
- ☐ I'd like to place an order.
- ☐ Can you send me an invoice?
- ☐ I'd like to pay by credit card.

- **Listen again and complete the order form.**

Martin's OFFICE SUPPLIES — **Telephone Orders**

ORDER NO. 12457

ITEM:	QUANTITY:	UNIT PRICE:	TOTAL
Office chairs (blue)	.... (1)	.... (2)	£1,400

DELIVER TO:	DELIVERY DATE:
Royal Oak Insurance .... (3) Bristol BS1 .... (4)	.... (5) (Note: deliver before .... (6))

METHOD OF PAYMENT:

Credit card (VISA) number: .... (7) (expiry date: .... (8))

How do I telephone for product information?

INFO

I'm calling/ringing/phoning about ...	
I understand that ...	– Yes, that's right/correct.
How much is ... ? How much are ... ?	– It's 20 euros/100 dollars/They're 20 pounds each.
Could you tell me something about ... ?	
What colours/sizes do you have?/How big are they?/... ?	– They come in black/red/.../We have two sizes.
When can you deliver?	– Is next week OK for you?
Is there a charge for delivery?	– We charge 10 euros/No, it's free.
Do you have any special offers/deals at the moment?	– Yes, we're offering .../We have a special offer/a deal at the moment on ...
Can you give me a (trade/bulk) discount?	– Yes, we can offer you 5% on orders over €1,000./No, sorry (those are our prices).
Can I pay by credit card?/Can you send me an invoice?	– Certainly./Which would you prefer?

2 **Work with a partner to make a phone call.**

You're working for a year at your company's UK branch, also in Bristol. Telephone Martin's about another offer, this time on desk lamps. Use the flow chart and add your own details.

Caller	Martin's Office Supplies
	Melden Sie sich.
Melden Sie sich und sagen Sie, warum Sie anrufen. Fragen Sie nach Einzelheiten zu dem Angebot.	
	Beantworten Sie die Frage.
Fragen Sie nach Farben und Größen.	
	Beantworten Sie die Frage.
Sie möchten zehn Lampen bestellen. Geben Sie die Daten an.	
	Beantworten Sie die Frage. Sie werden nachschauen. Ja, das geht in Ordnung. Bitten Sie um die Adresse.
Nennen Sie Ihre Adresse.	
	Fragen Sie, wie der/die Anrufer/in bezahlen möchte.
Bitten Sie um eine Rechnung.	
	Sie werden die Lampen morgen liefern.
Bedanken Sie sich und beenden Sie das Gespräch.	
	Beenden Sie das Gespräch.

3 **Work with a partner to get product information.**

PARTNER A: You work for PC Life, a computer shop. Look at File 3 on page 126.
PARTNER B: Look below.

PARTNER B

Phone PC Life about new PCs for your office.
- You need six computers.
- Your budget is 16,000 euros.
- Remember: special deals? delivery? discounts?

Grammar summary

The simple past

USE

I **left** school in 1995.
From 1995 to 1997 I **was** a secretary with a firm in Bremen.
My company **opened** its Tokyo office six years ago.

Die einfache Vergangenheit

VERWENDUNG

Das *simple past* wird verwendet, wenn man über völlig abgeschlossene Ereignisse der Vergangenheit spricht. Typische Zeitangaben mit dem *simple past* sind *in 1995/2002, six years (weeks/months) ago, last month (week/year), yesterday.*

FORM

	regular	irregular
I he she it we you they	work**ed** mov**ed** stud**ied**	**had** **went** **took**

When **did** you **move** to the UK?
Sam **didn't come** to the meeting.
Did you **study** at a college?
Yes, I **did**./No, I **didn't**.

FORM

Um das *simple past* regelmäßiger Verben zu bilden, wird meist *-ed* an den Infinitiv gehängt. An Verben, deren letzter Buchstabe ein *-e* ist, wird nur *-d* angehängt. Bei Verben, die auf *-y* enden *(to study)*, wird das *-y* zu *-i* und dann wird *-ed* angehängt.

Viele gebräuchliche Verben sind unregelmäßig. Siehe Liste auf Seite 191.

Fragen und Verneinungen sowie Kurzantworten werden im *simple past* mit *did/didn't* gebildet.

was/were

I he/she/it	**was/wasn't**
we/you/they	**were/weren't**

Where **were** you yesterday?
Was Ann at the meeting?
Yes, she **was**./No, she **wasn't**.

was/were

Die Formen von *to be* im *simple past* sind *was/were* und *wasn't/weren't*.

Um Fragen zu bilden werden Verb und Subjekt vertauscht.

The past continuous

USE

At this time last year I **was living** in London. (1)
Sally **was working** in her office yesterday morning **when** the telephone **rang**. (2)

Die Verlaufsform der Vergangenheit

VERWENDUNG

Das *past continuous* wird verwendet, um zu beschreiben, was zu einem bestimmten Zeitpunkt in der Vergangenheit vor sich ging (1). Oft kommt das *past continuous* in Sätzen gefolgt von *when* + *simple past* vor (2), um etwas zu beschreiben, das im Gange war, als sich ein zweiter Vorgang ereignete.

FORM

I he/she/it	**was/wasn't**	working
we/you/they	**were/weren't**	

FORM

Das *past continuous* wird mit *was/were* und der *-ing*-Form gebildet. Fragen, Verneinungen und Kurzantworten werden mit den entsprechenden Formen von *was/were* gebildet.

Verb + *-ing*

I **love reading**. I **don't like going** to the dentist!

Verb + *-ing*

Auf ein Verb folgt häufig ein zweites. Nach *to like, to dislike, to enjoy, to love, to hate* und *to prefer* steht das zweite Verb in der *-ing*-Form.

Grammar

1 Complete the crossword with the simple past form of the verbs.

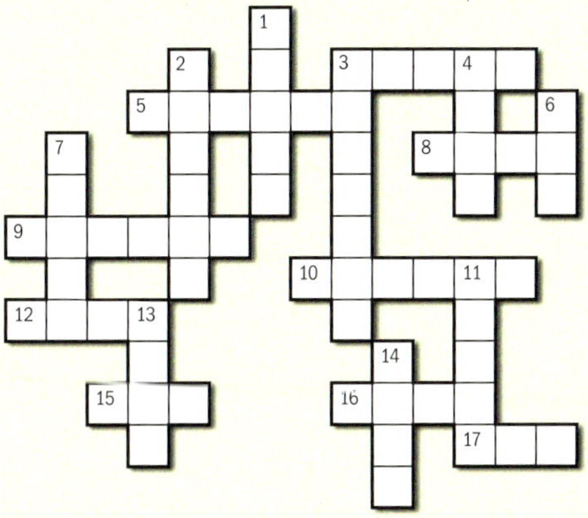

Across	Down
3 speak	1 begin
5 buy	2 join
8 go	3 study
9 work	4 know
10 become	6 eat
12 leave	7 choose
15 get	11 move
16 come	13 take
17 do	14 give

2 Katja is talking about her career. Complete the text with verbs from the box.

join become be go move work do study get (x2)

"I ....[1] born in Stuttgart. I ....[2] to school there and ....[3] my *Abitur*. After school I ....[4] for three years in Schweinfurt and in 1999 I ....[5] my business diploma. I ....[6] my first job the same year with a small company called Versero in Schweinfurt. I ....[7] first as a management trainee, then in 2001 I ....[8] the company's human resources manager. In 2002 I ....[9] to Hamm and ....[10] Zenith GmbH."

3 Make questions about Katja.

1 Where/she/go/to school? *Where did she go to school?*
2 Where/she/do/her *Abitur*?
3 When/she/get/her business diploma?
4 What/be/her first job?
5 When/she/become/the human resources manager?

■ **Now look at exercise 2 and answer the questions.**

1 She went ...

4 Complete the dialogue with the correct form of the simple past.

John Hi, Mary. How ....[1] (be) your evening? ....[2] (you/go) to the cinema?

Mary No, my friend ....[3] (not/have) time and I ....[4] (not/want) to go by myself so I ....[5] (do) nothing! What ....[6] (you/do)? ....[7] (you/play) tennis with Jim?

John No, we ....[8] (not/play). Jim ....[9] (fall) asleep at home! So I ....[10] (watch) television.

5 Make four sentences like the example.

Example: *Frank was watching television when he fell asleep.*

Frank	watch television		meet my wife
Uta	give a presentation		her mobile ring
Sarah	drive to work	when	their boss arrive
Ian and Mark	study in Bonn		she see a friend
I	discuss a new project		he fall asleep

Words and phrases

6 Match the questions to the answers.

1 What's your city like?
2 What's your office like?
3 What are your colleagues like?
4 What's your boss like?
5 What's the weather like in your country?
6 What was the conference like?

a Mostly young and friendly.
b Hot and sunny.
c Very useful.
d It's very industrial.
e It's big and modern, with a lot of plants.
f She's OK.

7 Match the extracts from a CV to the headings.

1 Full Name *f*
2 Profile
3 Education and Qualifications
4 Work Experience
5 Languages
6 Computer Skills
7 Interests

a 2002 – present Account Manager, Stork Chocolate
b I am a dynamic and successful manager with ...
c Playing the cello
d I am responsible for ...
e BA (Hons) Economics, University of London
f James Mackenzie
g Microsoft Office
h German (fluent)
i 1999 – 2001 Management Trainee, Volkswagen
j MBA University of Warwick

8 What are these leisure activities?

1 fie get pink *keeping fit*
2 pod won hip swing w i _ _ _ _ s h _ _ _ _ _ _
3 i twice nothing slave w a _ _ _ _ _ _ t e _ _ _ _ _ _ _ _
4 thin dog no gin d o _ _ _ n o _ _ _ _ _
5 i muscling it notes l i _ _ _ _ _ _ _ t _ m u _ _ _
6 chew it o king of rinds c o _ _ _ _ _ w _ _ _ f r _ _ _ _ _

9 Rearrange the words to make sentences. There is one word you don't need in each sentence.

1 friends/with/eating/I/like/eat
2 enjoy/not/doesn't/he/watching/TV
3 football/I/play/much/enjoy/playing/very
4 absolutely/I/nothing/love/did/doing
5 computer/I/not/playing/don't/games/like
6 hates/go/she/the/to/going/gym

10 **Here are five answers to the question 'Do you like cooking?', but all the vowels are missing. Can you fill in the missing letters?**

1 Y_ s, v_ ry m_ ch.

2 N_ , n_ t r_ _ lly.

3 _ t d_ p_ nds.

4 S_ m_ t_ m_ s.

5 _ t's _ k_ y, b_ t _ pr_ f_ r _ _ t_ ng _ n r_ st_ _ r_ nts.

Translating

11 **Translate into English.**

1 Wo sind Sie geboren?
2 Karin machte Ihr Abitur in Bielefeld.
3 Ich habe meine erste Stelle 1995 bekommen und wurde 1998 Verkaufsleiter.
4 Peter fing vor sechs Jahren an, bei der Firma zu arbeiten.
5 Ich gehe gern ins Kino.
6 Gestern sind wir zur Turnhalle gegangen, dann haben wir ferngesehen.
7 Sie hörten Musik als das Telefon klingelte.

TYPICAL MISTAKES

1 Susan was born in Bielefeld.
NOT Susan *is* born in Bielefeld.

2 I left school in 1990.
NOT I left school *1990*.

3 I got my first job in 1999.
NOT I *became* my first job in 1999.
(get = *bekommen*, become = *werden*)

4 She did an exam last year.
NOT She *made* an exam last year.

5 I went to a grammar school. (*Gymnasium*)
NOT I went to a *gymnasium*. (*Turnhalle*)

6 We sent the invoice two days ago.
NOT We sent the invoice *for two days*.

7 Yesterday we went to the cinema.
NOT Yesterday we went *in* the cinema.

8 Frank likes watching TV.
NOT Frank likes *looking* TV.

9 We often listen to music.
NOT We often *hear* music.

CULTURE SPOT

Education in Germany, Britain and the USA

It is very difficult to compare education and qualifications. These words and expressions are useful, but remember – they are only **approximate**!

Germany	Britain	USA
Grundschule (age 6–10)	Primary School (age 5–11)	Elementary School (age 6–11*)
Hauptschule oder Realschule oder Gymnasium oder Gesamtschule (age 10–16)	Secondary School (Almost all are Comprehensive Schools = *Gesamtschulen)* (age 11–16)	Junior High (age 11–14*)
Mittlere Reife	GCSE (or 'Standard grades' in Scotland)	
Oberstufe (age 16–19)	Sixth Form (age 16–18)	High School (age 14–17*)
Abitur	A-Levels (or 'Highers' in Scotland)	High School Diploma
Berufsbildende Schule	College of Further Education	Vocational School
Fachhochschule	Polytechnic University	College/University
Universität	University	College/University
Diplom	Diploma	Certificate/Diploma
1. Staatsexamen	Degree – BA or BSc (sometimes 'MA' in Scotland)	Bachelor's Degree (BA or BS)
2. Staatsexamen	MA or MSc	Master's Degree (MA or MS)

* *Depends on the state*

UNIT

4

A GLOBAL BUSINESS

In this unit you ...

talk about and compare global companies:

We operate in three regions.

Company A has fewer employees than B but it made more profit last year.

learn about 'global business etiquette':

In Japan you should/mustn't ...

You have to/don't have to ... in the UK.

Business file

Thanks for your email

A Helle worldwide

WARM UP **Name five global companies. What do they do? Are they German? American? Japanese? Do you know where their world headquarters are?**

A1 1/16 **Eckhard is talking about his company at an international conference this morning. Listen and find how he says these things in English:**

1 *wie Sie sicherlich schon wissen*
2 *Geschäftsaktivitäten in der ganzen Welt* operations
3 *die Regionen, in denen wir operieren*
4 *die verschiedenen Sparten unseres Unternehmens*
5 *konkrete Fallstudien*
6 *Sie können gern jederzeit Fragen stellen*

"Good morning, ladies and gentlemen. I'm Eckhard Kellermann from Germany, and I'm an account manager with Helle Logistics GmbH. As I'm sure you already know, we're one of Germany's biggest logistics companies with operations around the world. First this morning, I'd like to tell you something about our global organization, that's to say the regions where we operate and the different divisions of our company. Then I have a couple of actual case studies for you. Logistics can sometimes be a very unusual and complicated business! Please feel free to ask questions at any time, OK? Right. First then, how do we organize our company ... ?"

A2 1/17 **Eckhard is talking about the organization of his company. Listen and note the missing percentages.**

Helle Worldwide Logistics

TURNOVER BY REGION

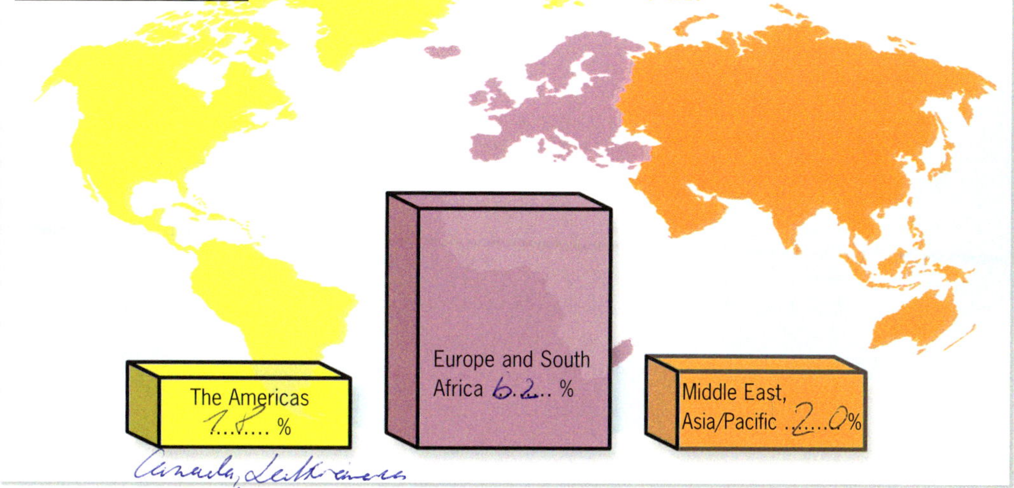

TURNOVER BY DIVISION

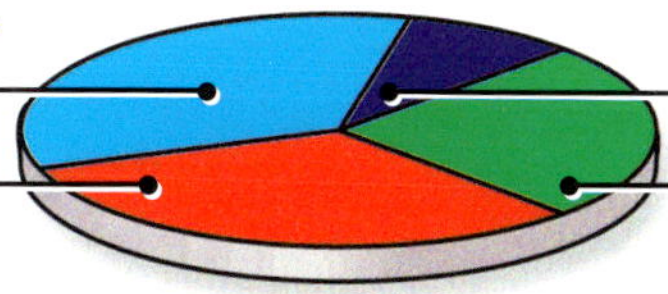

Overland freight .... %
Air freight .... %
Other (eg courier service) .... %
Sea freight .... %

- **Now check your answers with a partner.**

  What percentage of the turnover does the ... region account for?
  What percentage of sales come from the ... division?

A3 1/17 **Now listen to Eckhard again and complete this table.**

offices		turnover in € (last year)	
Germany	*40*	total turnover	.... (4)
worldwide	.... (1)	Europe/S. Africa	*1.2 billion*
employees		overland freight	*507 million*
Germany	.... (2)	air freight	.... (5)
worldwide	.... (3)	sea freight	.... (6)

- **Complete the questions with *How much*? or *How many*? and ask a partner. Then make more questions yourself.**

  1 ... offices does Helle have in Germany?
  2 ... employees does it have worldwide?
  3 ... income did it earn from sales worldwide?

> **Countable and uncountable nouns** FOCUS
> Countable: people, countries, offices, cars, books ...
> Uncountable: money, time, documentation ...
> ***How many? How much?***
> countable: How many people?
> uncountable: How much money?

A4 **Work with your partner and write a paragraph about Helle.**

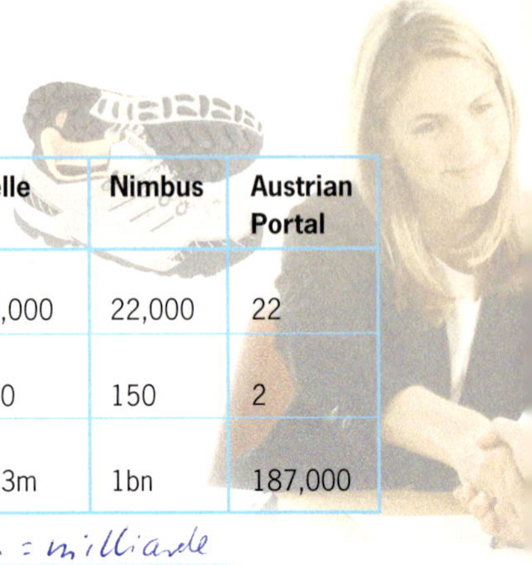

A5

Compare the companies.

The table on the right compares Helle with Eckhard's client, the American sportswear manufacturer Nimbus, and Lisa Schalk's company Austrian Portal. Look at the table and answer the questions.

1 Which company has the most employees? Which has the fewest?
2 Which company made the most profit last year? Which made the least?

- **Make sentences about the three companies.**

Helle has fewer employees than Nimbus, but it has more (employees) than Austrian Portal.

Helle made more profit last year than Austrian Portal, but Nimbus made the most profit.

	Helle	Nimbus	Austrian Portal
total employees	15,000	22,000	22
total offices	340	150	2
profit last year (€)	133m	1bn	187,000

billion = milliarde

more, less, the most, the least ... FOCUS

countable	uncountable
more (than)	more (than)
fewer (than)	less (than)
the most	the most
the fewest	the least

A6

Look at the sentences below. What do you notice about 'comparatives' and 'superlatives' in English?

1 Helle is a big company, but Nimbus is **bigger than** Helle.
2 It's one of **the biggest** companies in the world.
3 Manufacturing is a complicated business, but logistics is probably **more complicated**.
4 It's one of **the most complicated** businesses today.

- **Now complete the table in the FOCUS box.**

The comparison of adjectives FOCUS

adjective	comparative	superlative
slow	slower	slowest
quick	quicker	.... (1)
cheap	.... (2)	cheapest
large	larger	.... (3)
heavy	.... (4)	heaviest
complex	.... (5)	most complex
expensive	more expensive	.... (6)
advanced	.... (7)	.... (8)
important	.... (9)	.... (10)

A7

Complete the text with words from the FOCUS box. (There is sometimes more than one correct answer.) Compare your answers with a partner's.

The transportation of goods

Every day, from Alaska to Australia, and South America to Asia, Helle transports millions of tonnes of goods around the world. How? One of the ......(1)...... factors is size. The ......(2)...... and ......(3)...... cargoes normally go by road and/or by sea. Sea freight is much ......(4)...... than air freight (a consignment can arrive three or four weeks later), but it is ......(5)....... . Air freight is ......(6)...... (goods normally arrive the same or the next day), but it is ......(7)...... . And all this is complicated – logistics is one of the ......(8)...... businesses in the business world today and Helle uses the ......(9)...... computers and computer programs for its operations.

A8

Tell the class about your company or a company you know well.
How many employees does it have? How much profit did it make last year? Prepare and give a short presentation.

B Doing business worldwide

WARM UP **How many country names do you know in English? Can you name five (not in Europe)?**

B1 1/18 **Listen to Toshi Noguchi talking about doing business in Japan.**

"Hi. I'm Toshi Noguchi and I work for Helle in Tokyo. People often talk about doing business in my country, in Japan that is, because our customs can be, what can I say, a little different! Let me give you an example. OK, here's a story. A German businessman came to Japan on a business trip. He went to his new Japanese business partner's office and he gave a wonderful presentation in English. He spoke for an hour about Germany, about his company, about its products.
And his Japanese audience was very enthusiastic. They smiled and nodded and at the end they applauded. Then the German businessman asked for questions. The Japanese businessmen smiled, nodded and applauded again. But they didn't ask one question. Why? Well, the reason was simple: they didn't speak English!"

- **What does this story show? Look at the sentences below. Which (do you think) are true?**

A German businessmen speak very bad English.

B You must always speak Japanese in Japan.

C In Japan, 'saving face' is very important.

D Japanese businessmen are always happy.

E You should always learn about the customs of a country before you do business there.

B2 **Read Toshi's story again, then close your book. Tell the story to your partner.**

B3

In the pairs of sentences below, only one is correct. Choose the correct sentence.

1 In the USA companies sometimes have a 'dress down day'. That means:
  a you don't have to wear formal clothes.
  b you must wear formal clothes.

2 In the UK …
  a you should drive on the left.
  b you must drive on the left.

should/shouldn't FOCUS
You **should** … *Man sollte …*
You **shouldn't** … *Man sollte nicht …*
must, have to, don't have to, mustn't
You **must/have to** … *Man muss …*
! You **mustn't** … *Man **darf** nicht …*
! You **don't have to** … *Man **muss** nicht …*

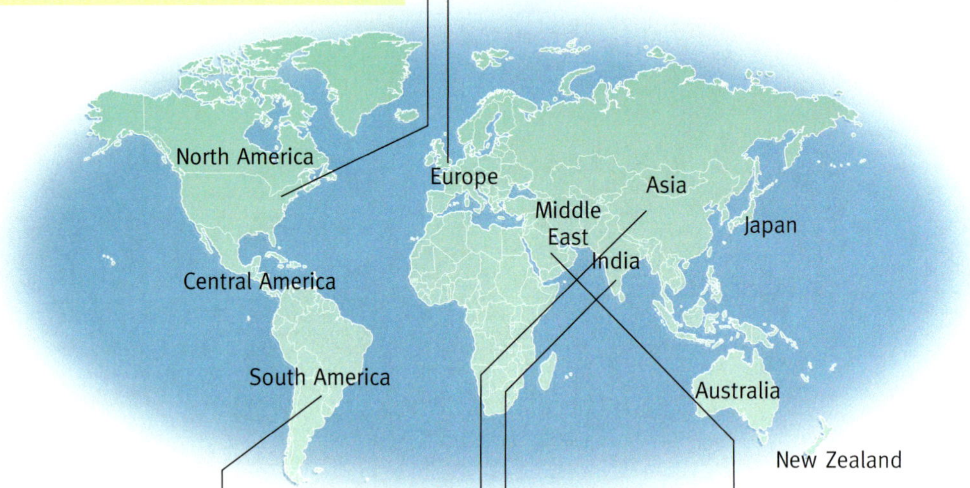

3 In Brazil it isn't polite to leave immediately after a meeting.
  a You shouldn't stay after a meeting.
  b You shouldn't go after a meeting.

4 In China gold is the colour of 'prestige' and black is 'death'.
  a You should print your business cards in black.
  b You should print your business cards in gold.

5 The left hand is 'unclean' in the Arab world.
  a You don't have to eat with your left hand.
  b You mustn't eat with your left hand.

6 In India meetings normally begin with tea, but it isn't polite to accept the first offer (only the second).
  a You have to say 'no' the first time.
  b You mustn't say 'no' the first time.

B4

Work with a partner.

1 On the next page there is a magazine article about doing business in Australia. Look quickly at the title and headings and write two questions about visiting or doing business in Australia.

2 Now read the article. Did you find the answers to your questions?

3 Read the article again and complete the table below.

In Australia you don't have to …	you must/have to/should …	you mustn't/shouldn't …
wear a jacket when it's very hot	*be honest*	*exaggerate if you give a presentation*

THE A-Z OF GLOBAL ETIQUETTE In a new series we give you our tips for doing business worldwide. Today ...

A is for AUSTRALIA

Doing business

Australian businesspeople are generally friendly and direct – and they like honesty when they do business. If you make a presentation, give the facts and *don't exaggerate*: Australian audiences will sometimes just laugh at too much exaggeration. Another thing to remember is that Australians don't generally like 'authority', so don't use formal titles like 'doctor' when you introduce yourself.

Meeting people

Meetings normally begin with a handshake. Australians use first names quickly – but wait until your Australian business partner uses your first name or suggests first names. Meetings can sometimes be a little late. Be punctual yourself, but don't be surprised if an Australian colleague doesn't arrive for two or three minutes. Remember that the summer months are September to March, and are very hot. Wear formal clothes for meetings, but if an Australian colleague takes off his or her jacket, then that's OK for you, too.

Eating out

In a lot of Australian restaurants you have to bring your own beer or wine, so telephone and ask before you go. And don't be surprised if an Australian colleague invites you for a meal and then doesn't pay for you: 'going Dutch' is normal. Australians also often invite business partners to their homes for a barbecue (or 'barbie'). Say 'yes' and be friendly – Australians love talking. But don't talk about business! For Australians work is a 'necessary evil', not a way of life!

B5 1/19 **Listen and put the names in the correct columns.**

Africa America Australia Austria Brazil Britain
Canada China Europe Germany Italy Japan

●•	●••	•●	•●••
Britain	*Germany*	Japan	....
Africa	Africa	....	....
....	....		
	....		
	....		

Word stress FOCUS ON WORDS

Wie im Deutschen ist auch im Englischen die Betonung einzelner Silben für das Hörverstehen wichtig. Aber Vorsicht: Oft wird im Englischen anders betont als im Deutschen!

B6 **Think of a country that you know well. What tips can you give a visitor there on a business trip?**

You should/shouldn't ...
It's a good idea to ...
You mustn't ...

B7 **Work in a small group.**

What are people in your country like? What is business etiquette there? What should foreign visitors know before they do business? Write 5–10 tips for foreign visitors.

In this business file you ...
write 'everyday' emails.
listen to voicemail messages.

Thanks for your email

1 1/20 **Listen and complete the emails.**

Julie Wong works in Los Angeles at the headquarters of First City Western, an American corporate bank. This morning she has four voicemail messages. Listen and take notes.

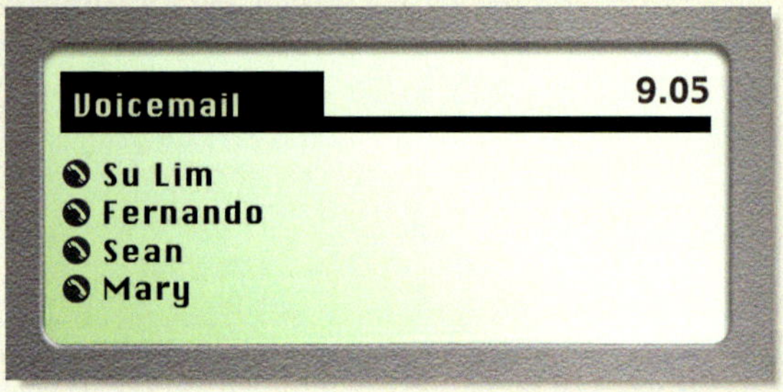

- **Julie writes four emails in reply. Complete with the correct names and the missing word or phrase.**

Hello ...... (1)
I got your message. Oh dear, I'm sorry. Here's the ...... (2) again in rich text format. Let me know if you still have problems and I'll talk to one of our IT people.
Best wishes
Julie

Hello ...... (3)
Thanks for your voicemail. It's good to hear from you. Annie's .... (4) is 664-2182.
Kind regards
Julie

Hi ...... (5)
Usual thing – hectic! Thanks very much for your message. I'm glad the ...... (6) arrived safely. Let me know if you need more.
All the best
Julie

Hi ...... (7)
Thanks for your message. I'm fine, thanks – hope you are too. Here's the ...... (8) that you wanted. Let me know if I can help further.
Best wishes
Julie

What are some common 'everyday' email phrases?

INFO

Beginning your email
Thanks (very much) for your email/your message.
This is to say thanks for …
Good to hear from you./Hope you're well.
I'm writing to ask about/to tell you that/to confirm …

Asking for things
Could you send me/let me have/tell me/let me know … ?
Do you know (if) … ?/Do you have … ?
Thanks in advance.

Replying
Here's the/Here are the … that you wanted.
I hope this helps.
Let me know if you need anything else.

Attachments
I'm sending you …/I'm attaching …
I'm afraid I can't open your file. (Could you send it again in … format?)

Apologizing
Sorry for the delay in replying.
Sorry this is so late.
Sorry, I don't know./I'm afraid I can't help you.

Ending your email
Let me know if I can help further/if you have any questions/if you have any problems.
I look forward/Looking forward to seeing you/to hearing from you soon.

FOR A GENERAL INTRODUCTION TO EMAILS → PAGE 154

2 **Work through Julie's 'to do' list.**

Write the emails on her list and reply to the two emails in her inbox. Invent all the details yourself. Remember to write a 'subject' for all the emails.

To Do:
- Email Tom Schellenberg in Atlanta. Confirm: everything is OK for his meeting here next week.
- Guy Marchand wants Alan Fournier's email address.
- Where's the monthly report from the Rome office?! Email Rosa!!!
- Is Ross Wyman still in the Melbourne office? No one here can contact him! Email Lindsay in Australia.

From: Giorgio Firente <firente.giorgio@fcw.com>
To: Julie Wong <wong.julie@fcw.com>
Subject: Milan conference

Ciao Julie
I'm attaching the details (dates, etc.) of the conference in Milan that you wanted.
Let me know if I can help further. :-)
Best wishes
Giorgio
PS: Do you have a cell phone number for either Dale Johnston or Ellen Heuer?
Thanks!

From: Ben Trull <trull.ben@fcw.com>
To: Julie Wong <wong.julie@fcw.com>
Subject: head office extension #s

Julie
Could you let me have a complete and up-to-date list of all our head office extension numbers? A pdf file would be ideal. Many thanks in advance.
Ben

3 **Write an email to your partner.**

PARTNER A: look at File 4 on page 127. PARTNER B: look at File 24 on page 137. Use the role cards to write an email to your partner. Then exchange emails and write a reply.

Grammar summary

Comparing people and things

USE

Company A is (much) **bigger than** company B. In fact it's one of **the biggest** and **the most successful** companies in Europe.

FORM

adjective	comparative	superlative
quick (1)	quick**er**	quick**est**
large (2)	large**r**	large**st**
big (3)	bi**gg**er	bi**gg**est
easy (4)	eas**ier**	eas**iest**
modern (5)	**more** modern	**most** modern
good (6)	better	best
bad (6)	worse	worst

Vergleiche anstellen

VERWENDUNG

Menschen und Dinge können mithilfe der Steigerungsformen von Adjektiven verglichen werden.

FORM

Bei einsilbigen Adjektiven (1, 2) werden die Steigerungsformen durch Anhängen von *-(e)r* und *-(e)st* gebildet. Bei Adjektiven, die auf einen Vokal gefolgt von einem Konsonanten enden (3), verdoppelt sich der Konsonant. Bei Adjektiven, die auf *-y* enden (4), wird das *-y* vor den Endungen *-er* und *-est* zu -i.

Bei allen Adjektiven mit zwei oder mehr Silben werden mit wenigen Ausnahmen die Steigerungsformen mit *more* und *most* gebildet (5).

Good und *bad* werden unregelmäßig gesteigert (6).

Quantifiers

countable	uncountable
a lot of/lots	a lot of/lots
more	more
how many	how much
fewer	less
the fewest	the least

How many offices do they have?
How much time do you need?
We sent **a lot of** brochures/information.
They have **fewer** employees than we do.
Company C made **the least** profit.

Mengenangaben

A lot of/Lots of (eine Menge) und *more* (mehr) werden mit allen Substantiven verwendet. Die Verwendung anderer Mengenangaben ist davon abhängig, ob das zugehörige Substantiv zählbar *(people, cars, offices)* oder nicht zählbar *(time, profit, documentation)* ist. In Fragen und Verneinungen wird *many* mit zählbaren und *much* mit nicht zählbaren Substantiven verwendet.

Anzahl und Mengen werden mit *fewer/the fewest* und *less/the least* verglichen.

should(n't), must(n't), (don't) have to

I he/she/it we you they	should shouldn't must mustn't	speak English

I think you **should** find a better job. (1)
You **shouldn't** work so hard! (1)

I'm sorry. I **have to/must** go. I **have to/must** be in London at 3 o'clock. (2)

You **mustn't** park your car here, it's illegal! (3)
You **don't have to** drink the coffee if you don't like it, Mike. (4)

should(n't), must(n't), (don't) have to

Should und *must* bleiben in allen Personen unverändert. Die verneinten Formen sind *shouldn't* und *mustn't.*

Should(n't) drückt aus, dass etwas ‚richtig' oder ‚ratsam' ist. Es wird deshalb oft verwendet, um Ratschläge zu geben (1).

Must und *have to* haben die gleiche Bedeutung und drücken Verpflichtung und Notwendigkeit aus (2).

Mustn't heißt ‚nicht dürfen' (3), *don't have to* heißt ‚nicht müssen' (4).

Grammar

1 Seven of the comparatives and superlative forms below are incorrect. Can you correct them?

1	more interesting	✓	7	famousest	....
2	~~more new~~	*newer*	8	more small	....
3	oldest	....	9	heavyest	....
4	niceer	....	10	more younger	....
5	importanter	....	11	most effective	....
6	most complicated	....			

2 Complete the sentences with the correct form of the adjective.

1 (*large*) The USA is larger than Germany.
2 (*easy*) My boss has the .... job in the company!
3 (*quick*) Air freight is much .... than sea freight.
4 (*good*) Our new software is .... than the old one.
5 (*big*) At the moment Microsoft is the .... software company in the world.
6 (*modern*) Our new office is .... than the old office.
7 (*bad*) This is the .... hotel in the world!
8 (*important*) They are one of our .... customers.

3 *Many* or *much*?

1 How .... clients does your company have?
2 How .... crime is there in your city?
3 How .... cafés are there in Linz?
4 How .... invoices did you send yesterday?
5 How .... food do we need?
6 How .... coffee do you drink every day?

4 Choose the correct form.

1 We don't have *many/much* time.
2 Japan is one of the countries with the *least/fewest* crime.
3 There aren't *many/much* chairs in my office.
4 There is *less/fewer* traffic today.
5 My new company has *less/fewer* employees than my old company.
6 We bought *a lot of/much* food for the office party.

5 Choose the correct alternative.

1 You *don't have to/mustn't* eat with your left hand in the Arab world.
2 In the UK you *don't have to/mustn't* drive on the right-hand side of the road.
3 You *don't have to/mustn't* wear a jacket when it's hot in Australia.
4 On a 'dress down' day in the USA you *don't have to/mustn't* wear formal clothes.

6 **Look at the company guidelines and complete the sentences with *must, should, shouldn't, don't have to* and *mustn't*.**

company guidelines	necessary	good idea	bad idea	not necessary	not allowed
jacket & ties (men)	X				
personal phone calls					X
speak English		X			
start work at 9 am				X	
smoke in the office					X
take more than one hour for lunch			X		

1 Male employees .... wear ties.
2 Employees .... make personal phone calls.
3 Employees .... speak English.
4 Employees .... start work at 9 am.
5 Employees .... smoke in their offices.
6 Employees .... take more than one hour for lunch.

Words and phrases

7 **Find the words and complete the puzzle.**

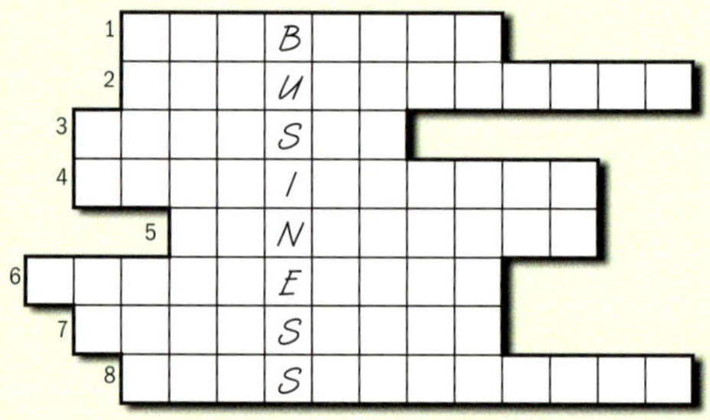

1 A meal cooked on a grill
2 Another word for 'maker': sportswear ...
3 Always telling the truth
4 We sent the goods to you yesterday: We sent your ... yesterday.
5 People normally shake hands at the beginning of a meeting: Meetings normally begin with a ... .
6 To say that something is bigger or better than it is: to ...
7 To send goods to another place, by road, sea or air: to ...
8 He told them about his company's new products: He gave a ... of his company's new products.

8 **What are the nationalities? Use your dictionary if necessary.**

Country	Nationality
Brazil	*Brazilian*
China	
Germany	
Canada	
Austria	
Japan	
Australia	
Italy	
USA	

- **Complete the sentences with words from the table.**

1 The .... flag is black, red and gold.
2 Toronto and Quebec are .... cities.
3 Ferrari is an .... car manufacturer.
4 The japan flag is white with a red circle.
5 Tsingtao is a .... beer.
6 Graz is an important .... city.

Translating

9 **Translate into English.**

1 Visitenkarten sind in Japan sehr wichtig.
2 Wie viele Leute arbeiten in Ihrem Unternehmen?
3 Sie haben viel Geld, aber sie haben nicht sehr viele Ideen.
4 Wo ist mein Kugelschreiber? – Er liegt auf Ihrem Schreibtisch.
5 Sie müssen nicht um 8.00 Uhr im Büro sein.
6 Wie war Ihre Geschäftsreise?
7 Wir verkaufen nicht viele Produkte in Deutschland, aber in Belgien und den Niederlanden machen wir gute Geschäfte.

TYPICAL MISTAKES

1 How many people were at the meeting?
NOT How *much* people were at the meeting?
2 He has a lot of money.
NOT He has *much* money.
3 You don't have to wear a jacket when it's hot.
(= Sie müssen nicht)
NOT You *mustn't* wear a jacket when it's hot.
(= Sie dürfen nicht)
4 My boss went to Japan on a business trip.
NOT My boss went to Japan on a business *travel*.
(*Das Substantiv* travel = *Reisen*: My hobbies are reading and travel.)
5 Can I give you my business card?
NOT Can I give you my *visiting* card?
6 My company does a lot of business in Australia.
NOT My company *makes* a lot of business in Australia.
7 Remember the difference between *its* and *it's*.
It's *(= it is)* a Canadian company.
Its head office is in Toronto.

Countries and nationalities

CULTURE SPOT

Do you know the difference between Great Britain and the UK?

Great Britain = England, Scotland and Wales, the three countries on the island of Britain.

The United Kingdom (UK) = England, Scotland, Wales and Northern Ireland.

Remember that not all the people in Great Britain are 'English'! Don't call people from Scotland or Wales 'English' – they are 'Scottish' or 'Welsh'. And people from southern Ireland, that is the Republic of Ireland, are not British at all. They are Irish and their name for their country is 'Éire'.

UNIT 5

IT'S URGENT!

In this unit you ...

talk about facts in the future:
The package will be in London this evening.
make 'spontaneous decisions':
I'll call you tomorrow.
talk about websites and the Internet:
People use our website for getting information.

Business file

What are your terms?

A An urgent phone call

WARM UP **What are the days of the week in English? Can you spell them? Do you have a favourite day? Why?**

A1 1/21 **Find suitable words to complete this text. Then listen to the text and the telephone conversation.**

Helle Logistics is based in Hamburg in .... (1) Germany. It .... (2) goods all over the .... (3) by truck, air and sea. Eckhard Kellermann is an account manager, that is to say he works with one big .... (4), Nimbus, an American sportswear manufacturer. Eckhard's regular .... (5) person there is Sam Engels. It's 6 o'clock on a Monday evening ...

Eckhard	Kellermann.
Sam	Hi, Eckhard. It's Sam Engels.
Eckhard	Oh, hi Sam. How's business?
Sam	Hectic!
Eckhard	How can I help?
Sam	I have a package for our London office. It isn't very big, but it's, well, urgent! Can you deliver it this evening? It must be on my boss's desk before 9 o'clock this evening!
Eckhard	Er, right. I'll call you back in ten minutes, Sam, OK?

***

Sam	Eckhard?
Eckhard	Yes, hi. OK. I have a courier for you and a flight to London. With the time difference, your package will be there at about 8.30 this evening. The courier's on the way to you now, by the way. She'll probably be there in a quarter of an hour.
Sam	Thanks, Eckhard. You're a genius.

A2

If all goes well, what will happen after Eckhard's phone call to Sam?
Use the *will* or *'ll* forms of the verbs in the box to complete the sentences. (You can use the verbs more than once.)

to arrive ✓ to catch ✓ to collect
to deliver ✓ to fly ✓
to go to land to stay ✓

if FOCUS

Man verwendet oft if (wenn/im Falle, dass/solange) in Sätzen, die im will-future stehen.

If all goes well, the plane will land at 7.45.

If + simple present	*will + verb*
*If all **goes** well,*	*the plane **will land** at 7.45.*

If all goes well, ...

1 the courier *will collect* the package from Sam's office at about 6.30.
2 she .... to the airport in Hamburg.
3 she .... the plane to London at 7.10 pm and she .... at Heathrow at 7.45 local time, 8.45 in Germany.
4 she .... by taxi from Heathrow to central London.
5 the courier .... to Nimbus's London office. She .... there at about 8.30.
6 she .... the package and then she .... overnight at a hotel.
7 the courier .... back to Hamburg tomorrow morning.

A3

Test your partner. Ask him or her questions about the courier's journey.

When will she ... ?

How will she ... ?

Where will she ... ?

What will she do then/next?

A4

What if all *doesn't* go well with the courier's journey? Match the sentence halves below.

1 If the courier is late at the airport,
2 If she doesn't catch the plane to London,
3 If she doesn't deliver the package,
4 If Sam's company doesn't get the important contract,
5 If Sam doesn't get his bonus this month,

a Sam won't get his bonus this month.
b ... ????? (*You decide!*)
c she won't catch the plane to London.
d Sam's company won't get an important contract.
e she won't deliver the package.

A5

What are the missing pronouns?

1 Do you know Lisa Schalk?
– Yes, I know .... very well.
2 Those faxes are on your desk, Mary.
– OK, thanks. I'll read .... tomorrow.
3 Do you have your report?
– Yes, I have .... here.
4 You should phone Peter.
– Yes. I'll call .... now.
5 Can you help .... , please? We're looking for the Royal Hotel.

Object pronouns FOCUS

Do you know Sam Engels?
– Yes, I know **him** very well.
Do you have those sales figures?
– Yes, I have **them** here.

I	me
he	him
she	her
it	it
we	us
you	you
they	them

A6

1/22

Amber Lee is a busy investment banker in New York. She gets phone calls, meets colleagues, ... Listen to the conversations and choose what (you think) Amber says next.

Conversation 1 ..C..
Conversation 2 ..C D..
Conversation 3 ..E..
Conversation 4 ....
Conversation 5 ..B..

A I'll finish it for you as soon as possible.
B Great! I'll see you tomorrow at ten.
C I'll find out and call you back.
D I'll send them by courier this afternoon.
E Thanks. I'll come down.

REMEMBER *Man verwendet das* will-future *für spontane Entscheidungen und Versprechungen.*

I'**ll call** you back. *Ich rufe Sie zurück.*
NICHT: ~~I call you back~~.

B Our website

WARM UP **How important is the Internet for you (at work or personally)? Give an example of one thing you do on the Internet.**

B1 **Match the people and what they say.**

Arnold is a stockbroker.

Diana is a journalist with a business newspaper.

Chris runs his own small company.

Marianne is a PA and her boss travels a lot.

Claudia is learning English in Germany.

a I use the Internet for reading English newspapers.

b When I'm not in my office, I use the Internet for getting the latest share prices.

c I use the Internet for doing research into companies, people and so on.

d I use the Internet for promoting my business.

e I use the Internet all the time for booking flights and hotels.

for + verb + -ing FOCUS

Man verwendet for + verb + -ing, *um den Zweck einer Handlung anzugeben.*

I use the Internet **for reading** newspapers.

*Ich benutze das Internet **um** Zeitungen **zu** lesen.*

- **Ask a partner.**

  Who uses the Internet for booking hotels? – Marianne.
  What does Chris use the Internet for? – He uses it for ...
  What do you use the Internet for?

B2

Here's Helle's international home page. Find the English for ...

1 *globale Dienstleistungen*
2 *Stichwortsuche*
3 *bitte wählen Sie*
4 *unser Service umfasst*
5 *Lagerung*
6 *Beratung*
7 *was auch immer Ihr Unternehmen erfordert*
8 *Lösungen*

B3

1/23

Listen to Jo MacKenzie talking about her company's website.

1 Jo works in Helle's Calgary office in Canada. Listen and complete the sentences.

1 Like all companies, Helle uses its website for ....
2 Jo uses the website every day for ....
3 The most important feature for customers is ....
4 They use it for ....

2 Listen again and take careful notes. Then summarize what Jo says. Use phrases like *first*, *second*, *the most important thing is* ... .

B4

Work with a partner.

If you point your mouse at the buttons on the Helle web page, you'll get 'dropdown menus'. On the right you can see the dropdown menu under the 'Company' button.

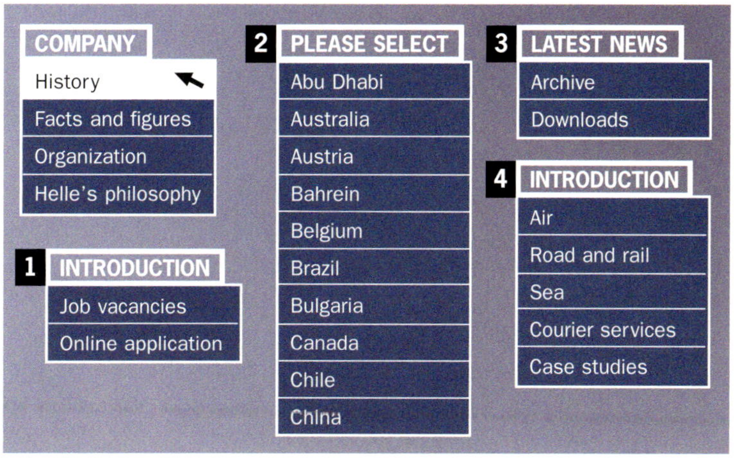

1 Where do the other dropdown menus 1–4 come from?

2 Look at the menus and the example on the right. Then ask and answer questions with your partner.

How can you ...

- get information about Helle's air transport services?
- see a case study?
- read the latest news?
- visit the Canada website?
- ... ?
- ... ?

How can you get information about the company's history?

Well, first, you click on 'Company', then you (just) click on/select 'History' on the dropdown menu.

B5

Work in a small group (3–4 people).

In File 5 on page 127 you will find short profiles of three small companies and 'Tips for Designing a Website'.

1 In your group, choose one company and design a simple home page for it.

2 Now show your web page to the class. Use these expressions.

- *This is a home page for the ... company.*
- *Our website is mainly for (promoting the company/...)*
- *What can you use our website for? Well, first ..., second ..., next ...*
- *These are the buttons/links to other pages. There's a ... button, a ...*
- *How do you ... ? Well, for example, if you ...*

B6

Choose the correct forms.

1 How do you get *information/informations* about careers with the company?

2 The news today *isn't/aren't* very interesting.

3 The letter contains a very important *information/piece of information:* the date of the next meeting.

4 I have one *piece of good news/good news* and two *pieces of bad news/bad news*.

FOCUS ON WORDS

news, information

News *und* information *stehen im Englischen im* ***Singular***.

What **is** the latest company news?

NICHT: ~~What are the latest company news~~?

How can I get **this information**?

NICHT: ~~How can I get these informations~~?

Um zu sagen ‚eine Nachricht', oder, eine Information' verwendet man **a piece of** *oder* **a bit of** *(umgangssprachlicher).*

That's **an** interesting **piece of information**.

In this business file you ...

talk about trading terms.

compare prices and terms.

What are your terms?

1 1/24 **Listen and choose the correct answer.**

Willi Becker runs an engineering company in Hanover, Germany. He builds reproduction classic British sports cars and today he's talking to a new supplier for automotive paints. It's an English company called Rolac and its European sales representative is Brian Ledger. Listen and choose the correct answer a, b (or c).
Sometimes more than one answer is correct!

1 The prices of the paints ...
 a are ex-works.
 b include delivery to Willi's factory in Hanover.

2 The terms of payment are ...
 a payment in advance (before delivery).
 b COD (cash on delivery).
 c payment in full within 30 days.

3 Willi can pay by ...
 a credit card.
 b bank transfer.
 c cheque.

4 Willi can return the paint ...
 a but he must pay the transport costs.
 b and Rolac will pay the transport costs.

5 Brian offers Willi ...
 a no discount.
 b a 10% discount.
 c a rebate of 5% after 6 months.

6 Willi ...
 a places his first order straight away with Brian.
 b decides against Rolac paints.
 c will order next week.

2 **Write notes.**

After the meeting, Willi made notes of what they agreed. Write his notes (or a short summary) of the most important points.

How do I talk about prices and terms?

INFO

Asking about prices and terms

What do your prices include?/Are these the ex-works prices?/Do these prices include delivery (taxes)?

What are your terms of payment?/What method(s) of payment do you accept?
What discount(s) can you offer us?

Quoting prices and terms

The prices are ex-works./They (don't) include delivery/taxes.
Our terms of payment are 30 days/payment in full within 30 days.
We ask for payment in advance./Payment is COD (Cash On Delivery).

You can pay by credit card./We accept cheques/bank transfers.
We can give/offer you a 5% volume discount./I'm sorry, we don't give a discount on a first order./We can give you a rebate after six months.

3 **Work in a group of 4 to 8 people to discuss terms at a trade fair.**

1 First find a partner and choose one of the companies in File 7 on page 128. (But make sure you choose a different company from the others in your group.) Look at the role card, decide your prices and terms and fill in the company form.

2 Now you and your partner find a place in your classroom and make your 'stand'.
PARTNER A: You stay on the stand and answer visitors' questions.
PARTNER B: You go round the 'trade fair' and find out about the other companies and their products. Make careful notes about prices and terms.

Company: Alba bros engineering
Products: motor boats
Prices: 12.000 - 100.000
Prices include ... ex works
Terms of payment are ... bank transfer
Discounts? by paying cash you will have a discount of 5 percent

4 **Discuss as a class.**

1 Check with the companies that you visited. Did you get the correct information?
2 Are there two (or more) companies with the same products? Who has the best prices and terms?

Grammar summary

Talking about the future: *will*

USE

In ten years from now technology **will be** very different. (1)
Thanks for a good meeting, Tom. I'**ll call** you next week, OK? (2)

Über Zukünftiges sprechen: *will*

VERWENDUNG

Will wird verwendet, wenn man über nicht beeinflussbare künftige Tatsachen spricht oder subjektive Vorhersagen macht (1). *Will* wird auch verwendet, um eine gerade getroffene Entscheidung bekannt zu geben (2). Beachten Sie, dass dies im Deutschen anders ausgedrückt wird!

Ich **rufe** Sie nächste Woche an, OK? ≠ ~~I call you next week, OK?~~

FORM

I he she it we you they	will	(I'll) (he'll) (she'll) (it'll) (we'll) (you'll) (they'll)	won't	be in London tomorrow

When **will** you **arrive**?
How **will** Susan **travel** to the airport?
Will you **be** there? Yes, I **will**./No, I **won't**.

FORM

Will bleibt in allen Personen unverändert. Die verneinte Form ist *won't*. In der Umgangssprache wird normalerweise die Kurzform von *will* verwendet: *'ll*. Nach *will* und *won't* wird der Infinitiv eines zweiten Verbs ohne *to* verwendet.

Fragen werden durch Vertauschen von *will* und Subjekt, Kurzantworten mit *will/won't* gebildet.

When/If

When you see Mr Brownstone, please say 'hello' from me! (1)
If you see Mr Brownstone, please say 'hello' from me! (2)

When/If

Verwechseln Sie nicht *when* und *if*, denn beide können mit ‚wenn' übersetzt werden. *If* entspricht dem deutschen ‚falls/im Falle, dass ...' und drückt eine Bedingung aus. *When* hat einen zeitlichen Bezug. Vergleichen Sie die Sätze (1) und (2). Im ersten Satz weiß der Sprecher, dass Sie Mr Brownstone treffen werden. Im zweiten Satz weiß er es nicht. Sie können ihn nur grüßen, falls Sie ihn treffen.

Sentences with *if*

If I **have** time, **I'll come** to the meeting.
I **won't come if** I'**m** busy.

if + simple present	will/won't
If I **have** time, If I'**m** busy,	I'**ll come** to the meeting. I **won't go**.

Sätze mit *if*

Die sogenannten *if*-Sätze Typ 1 werden mit *if* + *simple present* und *will* oder *won't* gebildet. Steht der *if*-Teil am Anfang des Satzes, muss danach ein Komma stehen.

for + verb + *-ing*

You can use a dictionary **for finding** the meanings of words.
I use my mobile mainly **for sending** text messages.

for + Verb + *-ing*

Mit *for* + der *-ing*-Form eines Verbs lässt sich der Zweck einer Handlung angeben – beispielsweise um zu sagen, wozu man etwas benutzt.

Grammar

1 Complete the dialogue. Use the verbs from the box and the *will* future.

send do collect come call be (x2) arrive

Helen Hi Mike, this is Helen from ETA GmbH. I have a small problem. One of our customers wants some spare parts by 8 o'clock tomorrow morning. Can you deliver them for us?

Mike Sure. That ....[1] (not) a problem. With our 'early bird' service, the parts ....[2] before 8 o'clock.

Helen That's great. When .... you ....[3] the parts?

Mike Let me see. It's 4 pm now. Our courier ....[4] at 6, if that's OK.

Helen That ....[5] fine.

Mike Good. If the courier is late, I ....[6] you, OK?

Helen That's fine. And .... you ....[7] the invoice to me as usual?

Mike Yes, I ....[8] that.

Helen Thanks very much, Mike. Bye now.

Mike You're welcome, Helen. Bye.

2 What does person B say? Complete the sentences with verbs from the box.

find give write send get help collect open

	PERSON A	PERSON B
1	It's hot in here.	I*'ll open* the window.
2	My flight arrives at 9.	I......... you at the airport.
3	I need the report by tomorrow.	I......... it to you later today.
4	I can't do this alone.	I......... you.
5	Who is responsible for this?	I......... out for you and call you back.
6	Jack needs the document.	I......... it to him.
7	My pen is broken.	I......... you a new one.
8	The letter is urgent.	I......... it as soon as possible.

3 Rearrange the words to make sentences starting with *if*.

1 if/the contract/I'll give/I see her/her *If I see her, I'll give her the contract.*
2 call you/if/you're busy/later/I'll
3 on time/the plane/won't arrive/if/is late/the package
4 if/we'll give/a big order/a discount/you place/you
5 the report/Alison/she'll write/has time/if/today
6 she'll/today/send it/she finishes/if/the report/by email/to you

4 Complete the sentences with *for* + one of the verbs below.

do find go promote ~~read~~ send

1 I use the Internet *for reading* newspapers.
2 I use my dictionary .... the meanings of new words.
3 They use the Internet .... research.
4 She uses her computer .... emails.
5 I use my car .... to work.
6 We use our website .... our business.

5 Complete the sentences with the correct object pronouns.

me you her him it us them

1 'Are you free this evening?' — 'Yes – would you like to have dinner with me?'

2 'You work with foreign companies. What do you do exactly?' — 'We help .... do business in Germany.'

3 'When can you give me an answer?' — 'I'll call .... tomorrow.'

4 'Are you seeing Bob today?' — 'Yes, I have a meeting with .... at 4 pm.'

5 'Was your meeting a success?' — 'Yes. They want to do business with ....'

6 'Jill is having problems with the project.' — 'Maybe I can help ....'

Words and phrases

6 One phrase in each pair is correct. Which is it?

1 A deliver the package ✓
B deliver the business

2 A transport the contract
B transport goods

3 A catch a plane
B catch a message

4 A get the contract
B get a business

5 A do goods
B do research

6 A visit our address
B visit our website

7 A promote our business
B promote a report

8 A book a hotel
B book a lunch

7 Complete these sentences with the correct form of the phrases above.

1 I have a meeting next week in London. Can you .... for me, please?
2 Helle can .... all over the world.
3 I use the Internet for .... for my university course.
4 I hope we will .... – then I'll get a bonus!
5 I'm driving to the airport. I have to .... at 1 pm.
6 We use our website for .... We want to find new customers.
7 Helle needs to .... to their customer in London – and it's urgent!
8 You can .... at www.helle.com.

8 Complete the crossword with the English translations.

Across
2 Partner (pl.)
3 weltweit
4 Dienstleistungen
8 Versand
9 führend

Down
1 Bedürfnisse
2 Anbieter (pl.)
5 Verfrachtung
6 reichen (von ... bis)
7 Ratschlag

- **Now complete the dialogue using the words from the crossword.**

Phillip So tell me something about Helle.

Jo Well, we're one of the ....[1] logistics ....[2] in the world and offer a lot of services. They ....[3] from classic ....[4] by truck, air and sea, to warehousing and also specialized courier ....[5] . So you see, Phillip, we can offer you a full logistics solution, and we would work together with you as full business ....[6] .

Phillip So how big is Helle exactly?

Jo Well, we have 340 offices ....[7], so we're a real global player. We provide our customers with expert ....[8] around the world. And with our tracking and tracing service you can locate your ....[9] wherever it is in the world. But maybe you can tell me something more about your company's logistic ....[10]?

Phillip OK. As you know, we're a car parts manufacturer and so it's very important that we ...

Translating

9 Translate into English.

1 Wenn alles gut läuft, bekommen wir den Vertrag.

2 Die Maschine ist jetzt zum Einsteigen bereit. (*ready for boarding*).

3 Danke für das gute Meeting, Harry. Wir sehen uns nächste Woche.

4 Was macht Jürgen?
– Er hat eine eigene Firma in Magdeburg.

5 Wenn ich Zeit habe, komme ich zu dem Treffen.

6 Gute Reise! – Danke. Ich rufe an, wenn ich angekommen bin.

7 Ich denke, dass Jeannettes Idee sehr gut ist.
– Ich bin mir nicht sicher. Wir brauchen mehr Informationen.

TYPICAL MISTAKES

1 If the package is late, we won't get the contract.
NOT If the package *will be* late, we won't get the contract.

2 If the courier is late at the airport, she won't catch the plane.
NOT *When* the courier is late at the airport, she won't catch the plane. (When *steht für eine Zeitangabe, ‚if' für eine Bedingung.*)

3 The plane landed ten minutes ago.
NOT The *machine* landed ten minutes ago.

4 I'll see you tomorrow.
NOT I see you tomorrow.

5 I'll see you tomorrow.
NOT *We* see *us* tomorrow.

6 Chris needs more information before the meeting.
NOT Chris needs more *informations* before the meeting. (Information *ist im Englischen immer Singular.*)

7 Ulrike runs her own business.
NOT Ulrike runs *an* own business.

Abbreviations

CULTURE SPOT

Here are some useful English abbreviations.

am	ante meridiem = before noon
pm	post meridiem = after noon
ie	id est = in other words (*bzw.*)
eg	exempli gratia = for example (*z. B.*)
re	regarding (*betr.*)
asap	as soon as possible
attn	for the attention of (*z.Hd.*)
vs	versus
ca	circa
approx	approximately
cc	carbon copy (used to send copies of an email)
encl	enclosed (used at the end of a *letter*)
pp	per procurationem (*i.A.*)
RSVP	répondez s'il vous plaît (*U.A.w.g.*)
VAT	value added tax (*MwSt.*)
FAQ	frequently asked questions (often used on websites)
BTW	by the way (used in emails)
FYI	for your information (*zur Kenntnisnahme*)

UNIT

6 A NEW BOSS

In this unit you ...

talk about your experiences:

Have you ever been to the USA?
– Yes, I was there last year.

talk about arrangements:

What are you doing next Tuesday?
– I'm flying to London for a meeting.

practise making arrangements:

Have you booked a taxi to the airport?
– No, not yet.

Business file

Can we find a time?

Chief executive officer

A The new CEO of BlueSky

WARM UP **Can you name three famous company bosses? What do you know about them?**

A1 2/02 **Listen to this excerpt from a radio programme.**

"And now, software news. Portland, Oregon, in the north-western United States, is the home of BlueSky Software. A global company, BlueSky produces business software – specialist packages for financial, marketing and other applications, and complete systems for office networks and company intranets. BlueSky began in the late 1980s, and it is now one of the largest business software producers worldwide. As from today, the company has a new CEO, Lee Mazry. Mazry is an interesting man. He has managed a number of successful companies in the States. He has travelled widely (he speaks Spanish and Japanese). Plus, and this is amazing in a busy career like his, he has even written a book. It's called 'The Bottom Line' and in Mazry's words, it's a business thriller. OK. Let's see what time it is on Lee Mazry's first day at work. It's coming up for 8.30. You're listening to 'The Business World Today' and here are the news headlines ..."

- **True, false or 'don't know'?**

1 The BlueSky Corporation makes business software.
2 This isn't Lee Mazry's first job as a CEO. He has managed other companies.
3 He managed his first company in 1985.
4 He has travelled to South America a lot.
5 He wrote his book in 1999.

A2

Work with a partner.

1 Find the past participles of the verbs below (→ page 191).

to eat *eaten*
to be ....
to read ....
to play ....
to manage ....
to lose ....
to make ....
to sing ....

> **The present perfect** — FOCUS
>
> Lee Mazry **has managed** a number of companies.
> He **has** (He's) **travelled** widely.
> He**'s written** a book**.**
> **Has** Lee Mazry (ever) **managed** other companies? – Yes, he **has**.
> **Have** you (ever) **managed** a company? – Yes, I **have**./No, I **haven't**.

2 Now use the verbs above to make questions and ask your partner.

Have you ever eaten Japanese food?
Have you ever been to (= visited) ... ?

Have you ever ... ?

1) Japanese food

2) The United States

3) a karaoke bar

4) golf or beach volleyball

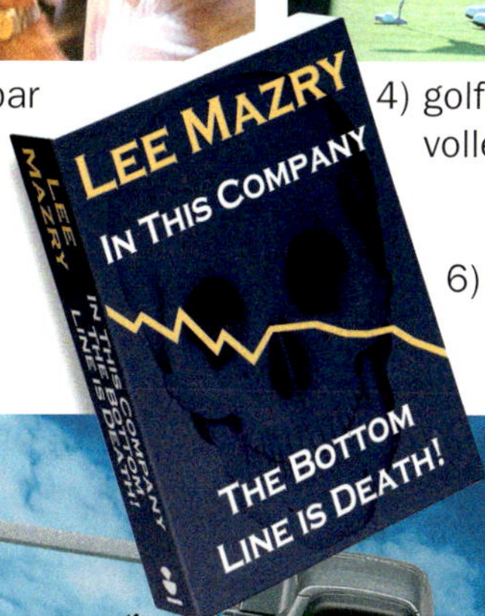

6) a thriller

5) your car keys or wallet

7) a company

8) a home movie

A3

Here's the beginning of an article from the BlueSky company magazine about Lee Mazry. Read the article and answer the questions.

Meet Lee Mazry

BlueSky welcomes its new CEO

We welcome today our new CEO, Mr Lee Mazry. Lee comes to us with an impressive CV. From 1985 to 1996 he managed a number of successful companies in the States, and then from 1996 to January this year he worked in Japan and Chile (where he learned Japanese and Spanish). Lee even found time in 1999 to write an international bestseller!

Full interview page 2
Feature article page 3
Read an extract from 'The Bottom Line' pages 9–11!

1 When did Lee manage the companies in the USA?
2 Where did he work from 1996 to January this year?
3 What languages did he learn there?
4 When did he write his book?

A4

Work with a partner.

1 Write down the names of four cities in your country. Ask your partner:

Have you ever been to Berlin/... ?

Yes, I have./No, I haven't. (No, I've never been to Berlin/... .)

2 If the answer is 'yes', ask again:

When were you there?

What did you do?

Was it a business trip?

Did you like it?

FOCUS

The present perfect
He **has worked** in Japan.
(zu einem nicht näher angegebenen Zeitpunkt bis hin zum jetzigen Augenblick)
Have you ever **been** to the USA?
(zu irgendeinem Zeitpunkt bis hin zum jetzigen Augenblick)

The simple past
He **worked** in Japan from 1996–2000.
Yes, I **was** in the States two years ago.
(bestimmte Ereignisse, die in der Vergangenheit zu einem genau angegebenen Zeitpunkt stattfanden)

A5

Who has done what in your class?

1 Think of an interesting experience from your life and write it on a slip of paper. For example: *I have run in a marathon. I've been to Kenya. I've ...*
2 Give the paper to your teacher/trainer. She/He will read out the papers. Can you guess the person?
3 Now tell the class about your experience.
I ran in the London marathon in 2001. I was 605th! It was a hot day. I saw ...
I enjoyed it very much ...

B My diary

WARM UP **Describe your normal day. What time do you usually get up, leave your house or flat, have lunch ... ?**

B1

Look at the diary and answer the questions.

Munich is the home of BlueSky's biggest overseas subsidiary, BlueSky Deutschland GmbH. Holly Beretti and Martin Schiller work together in the sales department there. Here's Martin's diary for this week.

1 What days does Martin have free?
2 When does he have a personal appointment?

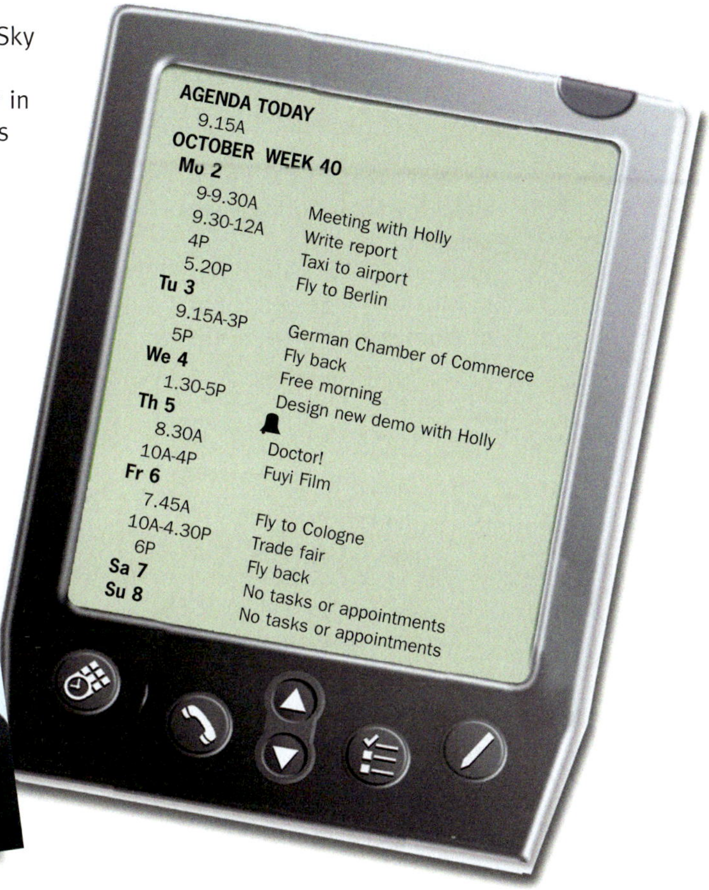

B2

2/03

It's lunchtime on Monday, and Martin and Holly are talking to a British colleague. Use the diary to find the missing information, then listen and check.

Tony So what are you two doing this week?
Martin We're giving a lot of demonstrations, basically. We're flying to .... (1) this afternoon and giving a demonstration tomorrow morning at the .... (2).
Tony When are you coming back?
Holly Tomorrow evening.
Tony So, Martin, are you taking Wednesday off? Did that work out?
Martin Well, yes, but only in the morning. Unfortunately, we're designing a .... (3) in the afternoon.
Tony What about Thursday and Friday?
Martin Let's see. I think we're going to .... (4) here in Munich on Thursday ...
Holly ... and on Friday we're flying to the trade fair in .... (5) for the day.
Tony Sounds like a busy week! Glad it's you and not me. Well, good luck with your demos ...

B3

Work with a partner.

1 First write five questions about Martin's and Holly's arrangements this week.

2 Then ask your partner (Partner B close your book!).

What are they doing at ... ?

When/Where are they ... ?

The present continuous for future arrangements — FOCUS

Martin and Holly **are flying** to Cologne on Friday morning.
When **are** you **having** lunch with Mr Perry?

Time expressions

on	Monday/Tuesday morning/ Thursday evening
at	three o'clock
in	the morning/afternoon/evening

at night

B4

2/04

Listen to Martin and Holly. They are checking their arrangements for the trip to Cologne.

What things have they done? What things haven't they done yet? Listen and put ticks ✓ or crosses ✗ on their 'to do' list.

To do
- Book flights to Cologne ✓
- Order taxis to airport on Friday morning
- Reserve a projector for the presentation at the trade fair
- Phone Gerhard in Cologne

The present perfect with *yet* — FOCUS

Have you phoned Mike **yet?**
–Yes, I have./Yes, I've done that. (I did it last week.)
–No, not **yet.**/No, I haven't done that **yet.** (I'll do it now.)

- **Complete the phrases below from the dialogue, then listen and check.**

1 Holly: .... you booked the flights to Cologne yet?

2 Martin: Yes, I have. I .... them two weeks ago. Taxis. .... someone .... them for Friday morning yet?

3 Holly: No, not yet. I .... that tomorrow.

4 Martin: .... you .... a projector yet?

5 Holly: Yes, I .... that last week. .... you .... Gerhard in the Cologne office yet?

6 Martin: Oh no, I .... that yet. I .... him now.

B5

Work with your partner again.

Next week, you and your partner are having a meeting with five important clients from around the world. Unfortunately, your secretary is ill, so you have to make all the arrangements yourselves!

1 Look at the pictures below and make a 'to do' list for the meeting (invent the details yourselves).
2 Tick three or four things on your list (but not all).
3 Now check your arrangements with your partner. Make a dialogue like Holly's and Martin's on page 70.

B6

Find the verbs in Box A that go together with the nouns in Box B. (There is often more than one answer.) Then choose three collocations and write sentences.

A

to manage   to provide   to give   to send
to read   to deliver   to speak   to produce
to join   to have   to sell   to book

B

a company   a package   a demonstration
an email   a report   a service   a language
a product   lunch   a letter   a flight
dinner   a presentation

Collocations — FOCUS ON WORDS

Ausdrücke wie to book a hotel, to have a meeting *und* to make arrangements *sind Kollokationen, d. h. Wörter (beispielsweise Verben und Substantive), die oft miteinander kombiniert werden.*

In this business file you ...

practise making and changing appointments.

write an email to confirm an appointment.

Can we find a time?

1 **Try this quick test with a partner.**

TEST YOURSELF

1 The 12-hour clock

Say the times (or write them down in words), then check your answers on page 138.

A B C D E F

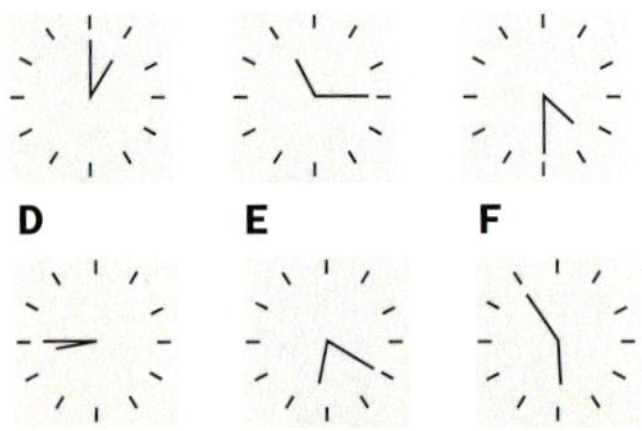

2 ***'half past one'* or *'half past two'*?**

3 ***in, on* or *at*?**

A ____ Monday
B ____ 5 o'clock
C ____ Tuesday morning
D ____ the evening
E ____ noon
F ____ 2003

2 2/05 **Listen and write a new diary page.**

Joscelyn Taylor is a busy lawyer with a law firm in Melbourne Australia. Here's her diary for the week. It's 8.30 Monday morning and Joscelyn is on the phone. She has to change some of her appointments. Listen and write the new diary page after the changes.

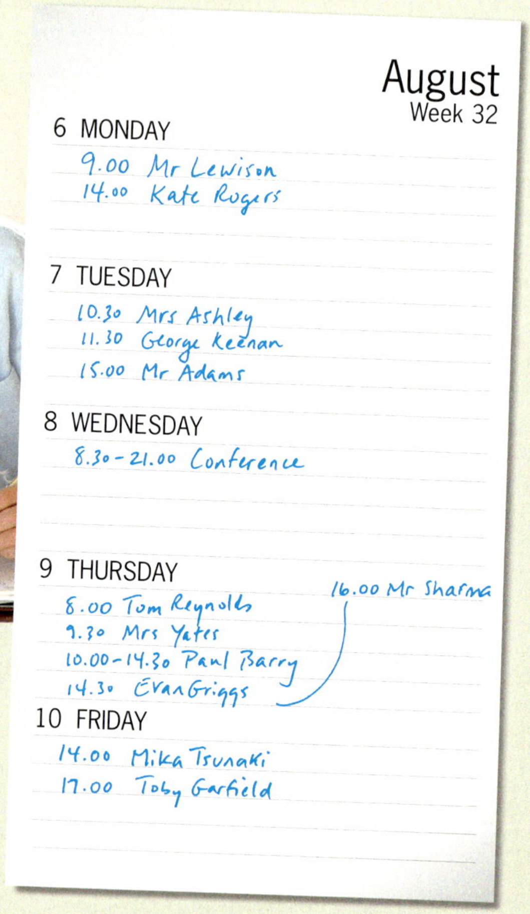

- **Listen again. In which conversation (1–4) does Joscelyn ...**

a make a (new) appointment? Mr. Yates
b cancel an appointment? Tom Reynolds
c postpone an appointment?
d bring forward an appointment?

How do I make and change appointments?

INFO

Making an appointment

Can we find/fix a time for a meeting?
What are you doing on Monday?/How about Monday?/Does Monday suit you?
– Yes, that's fine./No, I can't make that./I'm tied up all day on Monday.
– How about Tuesday instead?/I'm free on Tuesday./Tuesday is OK, though.

Cancelling, postponing and bringing forward an appointment

I'm sorry but I have to cancel our appointment next Wednesday.(Something unexpected has come up.)
I'm afraid I can't make/keep our appointment next Wednesday.
Could we postpone/bring forward our meeting next Wednesday?
I apologize for this./I'm (really) sorry about this.
Can we find an alternative time?/Can we make an alternative arrangement?
– That's OK./Never mind./Don't worry. Do you want to find another time?

Confirming an appointment

I'm just ringing/writing to confirm that our meeting next week will take place on/will be on Monday, 5 May (Monday the fifth of May) at 3.15 pm.
I look forward to seeing you then./See you then!

3

Work in a group of 3. Find a time for a meeting and write emails.

A British construction firm is building a new factory for your company, and you and your partners are your company's 'Project Team'. You need to find a time next week (Wednesday, Thursday or Friday) when the three of you can meet three colleagues from the British firm – all six of you together. You'll need about *two hours* for the meeting.

1 First look at your file where you'll see an extract from your diary and an email from a member of the British team. (Partner A: File 8 on page 129; Partner B: File 12 on page 131; Partner C: File 17 on page 133.) Work together to find the best time for the meeting.
2 Now write the British colleagues an email to confirm the arrangements.
3 What about the appointments that you had in your diary before? Do you have to cancel or postpone appointments now? If so, write emails to say you are sorry and suggest alternative times.

Grammar summary

The present perfect

USE

Have you ever **played** golf? (1)
I'**ve been** to the USA but I **haven't been** to Canada. (1)

I **played** golf last week. (2)
I **went** to the the USA two years ago. (2)

Present Perfect

VERWENDUNG

Das *present perfect* (1) verwendet man ohne genaue Zeitangabe, um über ein Geschehen in der Vergangenheit zu sprechen, wobei der Zeitpunkt des Geschehens keine Rolle spielt.

Vergleichen Sie dies mit dem *simple past* (2), das mit einer Zeitangabe verwendet wird, um über ein vergangenes Geschehen – und dessen genauen Zeitpunkt – zu sprechen.

FORM

	to have		past participle
I	have	(I've)	
he she it	has	(he's) (she's) (it's)	**worked** in the UK **been** to the USA
we you they	have	(we've) (you've) (they've)	

Have you (ever) **been** to Japan?
Has George (ever) **eaten** Japanese food?
No, I **haven't been** to Japan.
No, George **hasn't eaten** Japanese food.
Have you ever **played** golf?
Yes, I **have**./No, I **haven't**.

FORM

Das *present perfect* wird für alle Verben mit *to have* und dem Partizip Perfekt (3. Form) gebildet. Oft wird eine verkürzte Form von *to have (I've, he's, she's* usw.) verwendet. Das Partizip Perfekt regelmäßiger Verben entspricht der Form des *simple past*: work – worked. Viele gebräuchliche Verben haben unregelmäßige Partizip-Perfekt-Formen. Siehe Liste auf Seite 191.

Um Fragen im *present perfect* zu bilden, werden *have/has* und das Subjekt vertauscht. Die verneinten Formen von *have* und *has* sind *haven't* und *hasn't*. Kurzantworten werden mit einer Form von *have* gebildet.

Talking about the future: the present continuous for arrangements

What **are** you **doing** tomorrow?
I'**m meeting** Sylvia Rogers at 9.00 and I'**m having** lunch with Ted Wilson at 12.30.

Über Zukünftiges sprechen: die Verlaufsform der Gegenwart für Vereinbarungen

Das *present continuous* wird verwendet, wenn man über bereits fest verabredete Vereinbarungen hinsichtlich zukünftiger Vorhaben sprechen will – beispielsweise im Terminkalender eingetragene Termine.

Time expressions

at	3 o'clock
on	Monday (afternoon) 3 March
in	the morning/afternoon/evening 1998/2005

Zeitangaben

At wird bei Uhrzeiten, *on* bei Wochentagen und Datumsangaben und *in* bei Tageszeiten und Jahresangaben verwendet.

The present perfect + *yet*

I'**ve booked** the flights. (1)
I'**ve reserved** the hotel rooms. (1)
Have you **sent** an email to Clive Mitchel about our visit **yet**? (2)
No, I **haven't done** that **yet**. (3) I'll email him now.

Present Perfect + yet

Das *present perfect* wird häufig verwendet, um deutlich zu machen, dass gegenwärtig ein Ergebnis dessen vorliegt, was man bereits erledigt hat (1).

Yet wird in Fragen (2) und verneinten Sätzen (3) mit der Bedeutung ‚schon' bzw. ‚noch (nicht)' verwendet.

Grammar

1 Complete the sentences using the present perfect.

1 *Have you ever lost* (you/ever/lose) your mobile phone?
2 I .... (never/be) to Russia.
3 .... (she/ever/work) in logistics?
4 They .... (not/open) the new factory yet.
5 .... (we/receive) the contract yet?
6 He .... (book) the room for the meeting.
7 You .... (not/attend) the training course yet.

2 Make questions. Use the words and phrases in the boxes.

1 Have you ever *worked with Americans?*
2 Have you ever ....?
3 Have you ....?
4 Have ....?
5 ....?
6 ....?

~~work~~	on the left
use	squash
give	SAP software
drive	a flight on the Internet
book	a presentation in English
play	~~with Americans~~

■ **Now match these answers to the questions above.**

a Yes, when I was in Britain three years ago on business. I found it very difficult!
b Yes. Actually I played it last week, with a business partner.
c Yes. I did that last year, for my trip to Italy.
d No, I haven't. But my company is planning to install it on all our computers.
e Yes, when I was in San Francisco last year. They were very friendly.
f No. I'm glad I've never done that! I don't think my English is good enough.

3 Complete the text with the verbs below. Use the present perfect or the simple past.

speak travel live be (x2) learn (x2) work (x2)

I ....[1] a lot in my life. I ....[2] to many different countries, including China, Zimbabwe and Suriname. And I ....[3] in two different countries. In 1998 I ....[4] in Mexico for an American company. I ....[5] Spanish while I was there. Then in 2001 I ....[6] in France, in Paris. But I'm afraid I ....[7] (not) French – I ....[8] English all the time! But my dream is to go to Russia – I ....[9] (never) there.

4 Make sentences using the present perfect and *yet*.

1 you/book/the hotel room? *Have you booked the hotel room yet?*
2 I/not send/the email *I haven't sent the email yet.*
3 he/tell you/the date of the meeting?
4 we/not find/the solution
5 you/see/the new website?
6 they/not do/the research

5 **Complete this dialogue with the present continuous forms of the verbs in brackets.**

Charles So Anita, what are your plans for tomorrow?

Anita Let me see – first of all, I'*m meeting*[1] (meet) a client at 9 am.

Charles OK. What ....[2] (you/do) after that?

Anita Well, at 12 I ....[3] (see) a representative from our Frankfurt office. The meeting will probably last the rest of the day.

Charles Oh, I see. Well, ...[4] (you/do) anything in the evening?

Anita Yes, my father ....[5] (come) to dinner. Then we ....[6] (go) to the cinema together.

Charles What about Friday? Are you free then?

Anita Yes, I am. I ....[7] (not/do) anything then.

Charles Fantastic. Would you like to have dinner with me?

Words and phrases

6 **Complete the sentences with the correct form of verbs below.**

deliver give manage provide put read send speak

1 My boss .... four languages.
2 My company .... financial and insurance services to large firms.
3 I .... him an email yesterday, but he hasn't replied yet.
4 I .... the report on your desk yesterday. .... you .... it yet?
5 Before I started work here, I .... my own company.
6 .... UPS .... the package yet?
7 I .... a demonstration of our software yesterday.

7 **Complete the puzzle with the missing words from these sentences.**

Sarah So Fraser, is everything ready for your trip to the trade ....[1] in London?

Fraser Yes. I've booked the ....[2], and I've arranged to meet our ....[3] at the ....[4] – hmm, that's Heathrow. Then we're having ....[5] together at a nice restaurant.

Sarah How long is the ....[6] to London?

Fraser I'm not sure – my secretary made the ....[7]. I think it's two hours.

Sarah And what about equipment? Have you reserved a ....[8] for your ....[9]?

Fraser No, they don't have one. They only have a ....[10] – can you believe it?

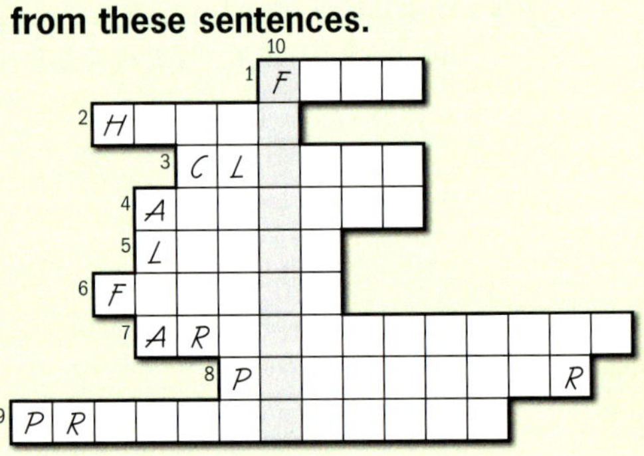

8 ***At, in* or *on*?**

1 .... three o'clock
2 2001
3 .... the afternoon
4 .... the evening
5 .... Friday evening
6 .... Monday
7 .... 4 January
8 .... the morning
9 .... Tuesday morning

9 **What did they say? Complete these sentences.**

sounds luck glad out see off

1 Are you taking Wednesday .... ?
2 Did that work .... ?
3 Let's ....
4 .... like a busy week.
5 .... it's you and not me.
6 Good .... with your demos.

Translating

10 **Translate into English.**

1 Ich habe diesen Film letztes Jahr gesehen.
2 Ich fliege nächste Woche nach New York.
3 Die Firma hat eine Tochtergesellschaft in Frankreich.
4 Mögen Sie Ihren Chef? – Er ist in Ordnung.
5 Von 1990 bis 1998 war Michel Koch in einem Hotel in Paris.
6 Was machen Sie morgen, Paula? – Ich bleibe zu Hause. Ich nehme mir morgen frei.

TYPICAL MISTAKES

1 What's your boss's name?
NOT What's your *chef*'s name? (= *Koch*)
2 I read a good book last week.
NOT I *have read* a good book last week.
(*Verwechseln Sie nicht ‚ich habe gelesen/gemacht' mit den Formen des* present perfect!)
3 We're flying to London tomorrow.
NOT We *fly* to London tomorrow.
4 We're flying to London tomorrow.
NOT We're flying *tomorrow to London*.
5 BlueSky Deutschland is a subsidiary of the BlueSky Corporation.
NOT BlueSky Deutschland is a *daughter company* ...
(*Den Ausdruck* daughter company *(Tochtergesellschaft) gibt es im Englischen nicht. Muttergesellschaft bedeutet* parent company.*)*
6 Are you taking tomorrow off?
NOT Are you taking tomorrow *free*?

CULTURE SPOT

Job titles and company forms

Lee Mazry is the CEO (Chief Executive Officer) of BlueSky Software. Here are some other job titles you may hear:

CFO	Chief Financial Officer (responsible for financial planning and record-keeping)
CIO	Chief Information Officer (responsible for a company's internal information)
COO	Chief Operating Officer (responsible for the day-to-day management of a company)
CRO	Chief Risk Officer (analyses major business decisions to check the risks)
CTO	Chief Technology Officer (responsible for R&D and sometimes for new product plans)

Holly and Martin work for BlueSky Deutschland GmbH. The table below shows the equivalents to the German GmbH and AG forms in different countries.

UK	Ltd (Limited Company)	This form is similar to the German GmbH. These companies are owned privately by up to 50 shareholders.
	plc (Public Limited Company)	These companies sell shares to the public. They are similar to the German AG form.
USA	Inc./Corp. (Incorporated)	These companies can be 'closed corporations' (similar to GmbH) or 'open corporations' (similar to AG).
Australia/South Africa	Pty Ltd (Proprietary Limited Company)	Similar to GmbH.

UNIT

7

LOOKING AHEAD

In this unit you ...

talk about company plans for the future:
We're going to launch a new product.
describe future products:
It will be a software package.
You'll be able to buy it next year.
talk about careers and career plans:
I've been with my company for five years.
I want to be a manager.

Business file
Have I got that right?

A Skyline

WARM UP

What type of company do you work for? (A car manufacturer? A bank?) Think of more types of companies. Use your dictionary if necessary.

A1 **Look at the two companies below. They each have plans for next year. Which plans are MaxMedien's and which are Impact Pharmaceuticals'? What do you think?**

MaxMedien is a small, Leipzig-based film company. It makes documentary films for television.

Impact Pharmaceuticals is an Anglo-Dutch multinational. It manufactures drugs for sale worldwide.

- We're going to spend €500 million on new product development. ....
- We're going to spend around €50,000 on new equipment. ....
- We're going to make a product for the BBC in London. ....
- We're going to show one of our products at the Cannes film festival. ....
- We're going to open a new sales office in Singapore. ....
- We're going to launch a new range of weight-control products. ....
- We're going to spend a lot more money on advertising. ....
- We're going to hire two new people. ....

A2

Compare your answers with your partner's.

MaxMedien is going to ...
Impact Pharmaceuticals is going to ...
They're perhaps both going to ...

- **What aren't the two companies going to do? Find two examples.**

MaxMedien isn't going to ...

Plans for the future

FOCUS

I'**m** He'**s** She'**s** It'**s** We'**re** You'**re** They'**re**	**going**	**to launch** a new product next year.

A3

2/06

Listen to Holly Berretti. She's talking about BlueSky's history and its plans for a new software package: Skyline.

1 First look at the Skyline box in the picture. What do you learn about the software package from the box?

2 Now listen to Holly and find the answers to these questions:

1 When did the BlueSky company begin?
2 What did it do in 1998?
3 What was Skynet?
4 When did the company bring out the second version of Skynet?
5 When is it going to launch Skyline?
6 How will Skyline be different from Skynet?

"Hi. I'm Holly Berretti and I work for BlueSky in Germany, in the sales department. As you already know, BlueSky sells business software. What does that mean exactly? Well, the company began in 1991 but the story really starts, so to speak, in 1998. That's when we brought out the first version of our Skynet software. Skynet was a *complete* package for small to medium-sized businesses. You went into a shop, bought the box, and the software did everything for your company – your accounting, your stock control, whatever. The software was very user-friendly so that you could adapt it to your business – a retail company, for example – and it was fantastically popular. We produced a second version two years ago and now next month we're going to launch the third version. We're going to call it Skyline. It'll do all the things that Skynet did but this version will give you a lot more help with e-business and websites. We're all very excited about it!"

A4

Will or *going to*?

In the pairs of sentences below, one sentence is a 'plan' and one is a 'future fact'. Which is which? Complete the sentences.

1a We*'re going to launch* (launch) a new product next year.
1b It .... (be) a software package.

2a We .... (open) a new sales office next year.
2b It .... (be) in Singapore.

3a Our new range of office furniture .... (go) on sale from next January.
3b We .... (call) the range 'The Executive Suite'.

4a The research .... (cost) $5m.
4b But we .... (develop) the product anyway.

Describing a future product FOCUS

Um ‚Zukunftsaussagen' über ein neues Produkt zu machen, verwendet man will.

Skyline **will give** you a lot more help with e-business.

will be able (to)

Die Zukunftsform von can *ist* will be able (to).

With Skynet you **can** already control all your business activities but with Skyline you**'ll be able to** build a professional website, too.

A5

With Skyline software even small businesses will be able to have a 'virtual storefront' – sell their products online. Make sentences with *will be able to*. Here are some keywords to help:

to promote/to display (products) – to find bigger markets – to increase profits – web/Internet shopper – to purchase – (to pay by) credit card – to process orders – to control stock

Companies will be able to ...
Web shoppers will be able to ...

A6

Write a press release.

Companies often produce press releases about their plans for the future and their new products or services. Write a press release (about 100 words) for your company or one of the companies in exercise A1 (invent the details).

B Career plans

WARM UP **How many jobs can you name in English (eg accountant, manager)? Can you find ten? Use your dictionary if necessary.**

B1 **Look at the expressions below. Which are in the past and which are in the future? Make two lists.**

~~10 years ago~~	next week
8 years ago	tomorrow
last year	yesterday
next year	in 5 years from now
in 1999	when I was younger
last October	from now on

Past	Future
10 years ago	

B2 2/07 **Listen to Martin Schiller and find the missing time expressions.** (Hint: they were in the list in exercise B1.)

"Hi. I'm Martin Schiller and I work for BlueSky Software in Germany. I guess I'm one of the 'old hands' there now. I joined the company .... (1). My first job was in technical support – I answered people's questions about their software on the hotline. But then I think it was .... (2), I got a job in the sales department and that's where I still work now. Do I like the job? Well, the good things about it are that I meet a lot of interesting people, I work with a really nice colleague, Holly, and our software is good, so it's not hard to sell. But the bad thing is that I travel a lot. My wife and I had a baby .... (3) and I'd like to have a job now where I can be at home more. In this job I often spend half my life in hotels and I don't want to do that .... (4). BlueSky Software is a good company, but early .... (5) I'm going to look for a new job."

B3 **Work with a partner.**

1 First a little arithmetic! Martin joined BlueSky ten years ago. What year was that? (1994? 95? 96? ...?)

2 Write the year from above in sentence B below and look at the two sentences.

How long has Martin worked for BlueSky Software?
A He's worked for the company **for** ten years.
B He's worked for the company **since** ....

3 Now give two answers to this question: How long has Martin been in the sales department?

B4

***For* or *since*?**

1 Martin has lived in Munich .... 15 years.
2 His wife Heidi has lived there .... five years.
3 She's been a teacher .... 1991.
4 They've been married .... 1993.
5 Martin's colleague Holly has worked for BlueSky .... four years.
6 She's worked in sales department with Martin .... May last year.

- **Ask a partner.**

  How long have you lived in the town/house/flat where you live now? Do you have a car? How long have you had it?

FOCUS

The present perfect + *for* and *since*.

How long has Martin **worked** for his company?
– He**'s** (He **has**) **worked** for the company **for** ten years/**since** 1995. *NICHT:* ~~He works for the company for ten years/since 1995~~.

for	+ Zeitspanne
since	+ Zeitpunkt

***to want, to hope, would like* + infinitive**

verb	+ infinitive
I want	**to get** a better job.
I hope	**to become** a manager.
I'd (= I would) like	**to run** my own company.

B5

Work with your partner again.

PARTNER A (Kathy): Look below.
PARTNER B (Derek): Look at File 10 on page 130.

PARTNER A

You and Derek both work for BlueSky. Where does Derek work? What's his job? How long has he been with the company? And what are his ideas and plans for the future? Interview 'Derek' and complete the form. Then answer Derek's questions.

Name	Kathy Fischer
Job	Computer programmer
Place of work	Head office, Portland Oregon
How long with company?	Joined 2001
Good thing(s) about job?	Nice colleagues, good salary, challenging
Bad thing(s)?	It's sometimes a bit monotonous
Ideas about future?	Would like to have my own business (as a computer consultant)
Plans?	Going to buy a house next year

Name	Derek Carter
Job	
Place of work	
How long with company?	
Good thing(s) about job?	
Bad thing(s)?	
Ideas about future?	
Plans?	

B6

Try this personality test.

What's the right job for you? Are you in the right job now? What's your 'personality type'?

1 Look at the test below and check that you understand all the job titles.

2 Then do the test and look at File 11 on page 130 for the answers.

Which jobs interest you?

Below you can see 30 jobs. Tick (✓) the boxes (or write down) all the jobs that *interest* you – that you find attractive in some way. Don't choose jobs where you are unsure or that you would dislike.

- actor ☐
- auctioneer ☐
- bank clerk ☐
- book editor ☐
- bookkeeper ☐
- bus driver ☐
- chemist ☐
- clothes designer ☐
- counsellor ☐
- electrical technician ☐

- estate agent ☐
- farmer ☐
- graphic artist ☐
- lawyer ☐
- librarian ☐
- mechanic ☐
- musician ☐
- nurse ☐
- pharmacist ☐
- pilot ☐

- police officer ☐
- postman/postwoman ☐
- salesperson ☐
- secretary ☐
- social worker ☐
- surveyor ☐
- teacher ☐
- travel agent ☐
- typist ☐
- vet ☐

B7

Complete the sentences with words from the FOCUS box.

1 If you don't know an English word, you can look it .... in your dictionary.
2 All good companies make plans and look ....
3 Please look .... page 23.
4 Two important visitors are looking .... our factory tomorrow. Could you look .... them?
5 Your report is very good, Jim. I'll look .... your ideas.
6 She doesn't like her boss! She's going to look .... a new job.
7 Thanks for your phone call, Sally. I'm looking .... our meeting next week.

Phrasal verbs with *look*

FOCUS ON WORDS

Man kann viele nützliche englische Verben bilden, indem man ein zweites Wort hinter das Verb setzt.

to look ...	
after	*sich kümmern um*
ahead	*vorausschauen*
at	*ansehen*
for	*suchen*
forward to	*sich freuen auf*
into	*in etwas sehen/untersuchen*
round	*sich umschauen/ansehen*
up (a word)	*(ein Wort) nachschlagen*

Have I got that right?

In this business file you ...
- practise being clear about numbers, prices, etc.
- write and check an invoice.

1 **Work with a partner. What are the product codes and prices?**

You work in your company's New Orleans office. You're interested in buying promotional gifts for your clients and you get a catalogue from a company called Logos-To-Go. It sells things like polo shirts, pens and travel bags, and prints your company's logo on them. Here's a page from their catalogue. Work with a partner to make a phone call.

PARTNER A: look below. PARTNER B: please look at File 15 on page 132.

PARTNER A: Ask your partner for the missing prices and product codes, and answer her/his questions about the items at the bottom of the page. If you have a problem understanding, use the phrases on page 85.

How can I be clear about names, numbers, prices, etc.?

INFO

Sorry. I didn't catch that. Could you say it again/repeat it, please?
Was that ... ? (or ... ?)
So that was ... . Is that right?
Have I got that right?
I'll just read that back to you. B for bravo, A–2–5 ...

The international spelling alphabet

A	Alpha	H	Hotel	O	Oscar	V	Victor
B	Bravo	I	India	P	Papa	W	Whisky
C	Charlie	J	Juliet	Q	Quebec	X	X-ray
D	Delta	K	Kilo	R	Romeo	Y	Yankee
E	Echo	L	Lima	S	Sierra	Z	Zulu
F	Foxtrot	M	Mike	T	Tango		
G	Golf	N	November	U	Uniform		

2 2/08 **Listen and make notes.**

Rick Simonette is also interested in Logos-To-Go. He's calling them now. Listen and make notes.

- How do you send your logo to the company?
- Do the prices in the catalogue include printing the logo?
- How much does it cost to develop the logo?
- What are the terms of payment?
- What are the shipping and handling costs?
- What does Rick order?

3 **Write an invoice. Then check it with a partner.**

1 Look at your notes and the catalogue page again and complete Rick's invoice below.

2 Now compare your invoice with Logos-To-Go's. (Partner B: look at File 25 on page 137.) Their invoice has six mistakes in it. Can you find them?

Logos-To-Go
601 Poydras Street,
New Orleans, LA 70130-4114

Invoice No. 1001999
Invoice Date: August 20, 20..

INVOICE

To: Rick Simonette
WAFB-TV
844 Government Street
Baton Rouge, LA 70802-6030

Ship to (if different address)

Qty.	Cat. no.	Description	Unit price	Amount

Terms

SUBTOTAL
SHIPPING AND HANDLING
ONE-TIME LOGO DEVELOPMENT CHARGE
AMOUNT DUE

Signature *(if required)*

Thank you for your business

Grammar summary

Talking about the future: *going to* for plans

USE

What **are** you **going to do** when you finish your studies, Kelly? (1)
I'm going to get a better job. (1)

We**'re going to launch** a new product. (1)
It **will be** more expensive than our old product but it **will be** much better. (2)

Über Zukünftiges sprechen: *going to* für Pläne

VERWENDUNG

Going to wird verwendet, wenn man über feste Pläne und Absichten im Hinblick auf die Zukunft sprechen will (1).

Vergleiche dazu das *will-future*, das verwendet wird, um über künftige Tatsachen zu sprechen (2).

FORM

am/is/are going to		infinitive
I'm he's/she's/it's we're/you're/they're	going to	work abroad next year

When **is** your company **going to launch** its new range of products?
I'm not going to attend the conference. I'm too busy.

Are you **going to employ** new staff in your new office? Yes, **we are**./No, **we aren't**.

FORM

Das *going-to-future* wird mit der Form des *present continuous* von *to go* und dem Infinitiv mit *to* gebildet.

Fragen und Verneinungen werden mit den Frage- und Verneinungsformen von *I'm going, you're going* usw. gebildet. In Kurzantworten mit dem *going-to-future* muss die entsprechende Form von *to be* verwendet werden.

The future form of *can: will be able to*

I don't have time today. **Can** we **meet** tomorrow instead? (1)
Our customers **will** soon **be able to shop** online on our new website. (2)

Die Zukunftsform von *can: will be able to*

Das Verb *can* wird nur begrenzt für die Zukunft benutzt, um z. B. etwas für die Zukunft anzubieten oder vorzuschlagen (1). Sonst wird *will be able to* benutzt und hat die Bedeutung von ‚dazu fähig sein/in der Lage sein' (2).

The present perfect + *for/since*

I've lived in the USA but **I've** never **been** to Chicago. (1)
I've worked for my company **for** ten years. (2)
I've lived in Aachen **since** 1991. (3)

How long has Tom **been** a sales manager?
Well, he**'s been** in the sales department **for** five years, but he**'s** only **been** the manager **since** last year.

Present Perfect + for/since

In Unit 6 wurde dargestellt, dass das *present perfect* für Ereignisse in der Vergangenheit verwendet wird, ohne einen Zeitpunkt zu erwähnen (1).

Das *present perfect* wird auch für Vorgänge verwendet, die in der Vergangenheit begannen und bis zum jetzigen Augenblick andauern. Um zu sagen, ‚wie lange' diese Vorgänge bereits andauern, verwendet man *for* mit Angabe der Zeitspanne (2) und *since* mit Angabe eines Zeitpunktes (3).

Verb + *-ing*/verb + infinitive

verb + *-ing*		verb + infinitive	
to like to dislike to enjoy to hate to love	**doing**	to want to hope I'd like	**to do**

Verb + *-ing*/Verb + Infinitiv

Auf viele englische Verben folgt oft ein zweites Verb. Nach bestimmten Verben (z. B. to *(dis)like, to enjoy)* steht das zweite Verb in der *-ing*-Form. (Siehe auch Unit 3, Seite 38.) Nach anderen Verben (z. B. *to want, to hope* und nach dem Ausdruck *I'd like*) steht der Infinitiv.

Grammar

1 Each sentence has one mistake. Correct the mistakes.

1 We going to start a new project next week.
2 He are going to look for new clients.
3 Do will it be more expensive?
4 The goods will to arrive tomorrow.
5 They are not going make a profit this year.
6 The party not will be on Saturday.
7 I not going to go to my English class this week.

2 Complete the sentences with *can, can't, will be able to* or *won't be able to* and the verbs in brackets.

1 Today our factory .... (produce) more than 500 units per day. When we build our new factory, we .... (produce) up to 5000 units per day.
2 .... (you/send) me the information tomorrow? – No, sorry, I'm away tomorrow. I .... (not/send) it until next week.
3 .... (you/purchase) our products online in the future?
4 I'm afraid she .... (attend) the meeting tomorrow. She's ill.

3 *For* or *since*?

1 I've worked here .... ten years.
2 He's been on holiday .... two weeks.
3 I've lived in a small town near Nuremberg .... 1996.
4 She's been my boss .... last May.
5 We've been married .... six years.
6 Fiona has worked in our department .... January last year.

4 Make sentences about Prentice Associates. Use *since*.

1 The main office/be/in London *The main office has been in London since 1979.*
2 Prentice Associates/produce/country reports
3 Prentice Associates/work/Alpha Consulting
4 Prentice Associates/offer/IT services
5 Prentice Associate/sell/financial data
6 Kevin Turner/be/CEO

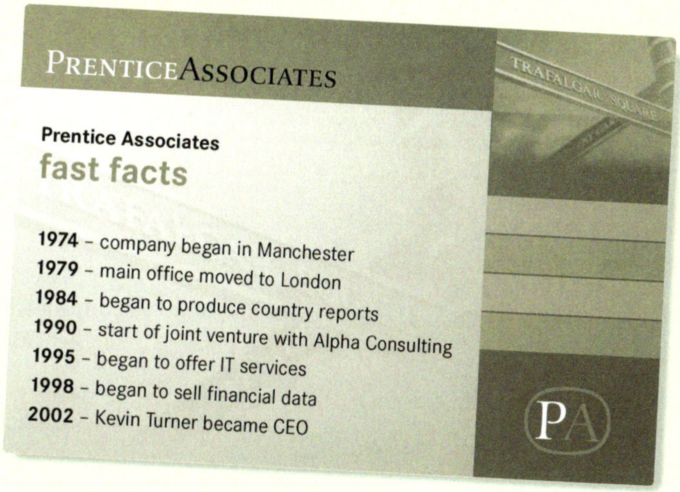

5 Complete the text using the correct form of the verbs in brackets.

My partner Ruth works in the sales department of a large company. She likes ....[1] (work) there, because she has friendly colleagues, but she has to go on a lot of business trips and she hates ....[2] (travel). She wants ....[3] (get) a better job in the company so that she doesn't have to travel so much. We hope ....[4] (get) married next year, and I'd love ....[5] (have) a baby, but she's not so sure. She loves ....[6] (have) an active social life, you see, and that will be difficult if we have a baby.

Words and phrases

6 Complete with the missing vowels to identify the jobs.

1 p o l i c e o f f i c e r
2 _ s t _ t _ _ g _ n t
3 s_ c_ _ l w_ rk_ r
4 cl_ th_ s d_ s_ gn_ r
5 _ l_ ctr_ c_ l t_ chn_ c_ _ n
6 s_ cr_ t_ ry
7 b_ _ kk_ _ p _ r
8 m_ ch_ n_ c

7 Choose the correct word.

1 Mr Mendes will look *after/~~at/for~~* you during your stay in Los Angeles.
2 We're looking *ahead/at/round* to next year so that we can plan our strategy.
3 Can you look *round/at/forward* this report for me, please?
4 I'm looking *into/up/for* a new flat at the moment.
5 I look *forward/ahead/after* to hearing from you.
6 One of our customers has a problem. I have to look *round/forward/into* it.
7 Can we look *after/ahead/round* the factory before we leave?
8 I don't know that word – I'll have to look it *at/up/into.*

8 Match words from A and B to make phrases.

	A	**B**
1	open	a new company
2	launch	a new range of products
3	spend	a new sales office
4	hire	interesting people
5	increase	money
6	process	new employees
7	meet	orders
8	join	profits

■ **Now complete these sentences with the phrases above.**

a Our company is going to .... next year. We are designing them for the Asian market.
b With this new software we can .... from our customers very quickly.
c We aren't going to .... on advertising this new product. It'll only be in our sales catalogue.
d My company is going to .... in the next few months – we need more people!
e I'm a clothes designer. I love my job because I often .... from all over the world.
f We need to .... or we're going to go bankrupt!
g I want to .... soon – I hate working at my present company!
h My company is going to .... in San Francisco next month – the American market is very important for us.

9 **Put the time expressions into the right order on the time line.**

1 six years ago
2 from now on
3 in two years from now
4 next year
5 last year
6 next week
7 tomorrow
8 last month
9 when I was young
10 yesterday

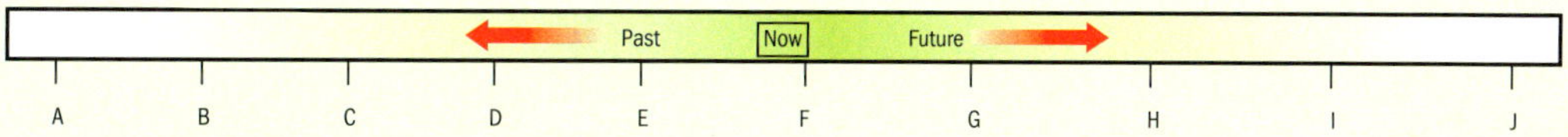

Translating

10 **Translate into English.**

1 Ich mag meine Arbeit, weil ich gern reise.
2 Sie haben vor, 1 Million Euro für die neue Fabrik auszugeben.
3 Sie können bald bei uns direkt bestellen. Wir werden nächstes Jahr unseren eigenen Online-Katalog haben.
4 Ich lebe seit acht Jahren in Frankfurt.
5 Wir werden das Produkt nicht in der Schweiz verkaufen.
6 Alice ist seit 2001 Sekretärin.
7 Sie wollen ein neues Produkt für den amerikanischen Markt entwickeln.
8 Dieses Jahr haben sie nicht viel Geld für Werbung ausgegeben.

TYPICAL MISTAKES

1 We aren't going to meet the client this week.
NOT We *don't* going to meet the client this week.

2 We're going to spend a lot of money on advertising.
NOT We're going to spend a lot of money *for* advertising.

3 We'll be able to deliver the package before 8 am.
NOT We will *can* deliver the package before 8 am.

4 I've worked for my company for five years.
NOT I *work* for my company for five years. (*In solchen Sätzen benutzen wir das* present perfect *und nicht das* simple present *wie in Deutschen.*)

5 He's lived in Essen for ten years.
NOT He's lived (or He lives!) in Essen *since* ten years. (*for* + Zeitspanne, *since* + Zeitpunkt, z. B. *since 1994*)

6 I enjoy playing sport.
NOT I enjoy *to play* sport.

7 My brother wants to find a new job.
NOT My brother wants *find* a new job. (*Nicht vergessen: Nach Verben wie* want *benutzen wir den Infinitiv mit* to.)

8 I want to buy a new car.
NOT I *will* buy a new car. (*Verwechseln Sie nicht ,wollen' mit dem englischen* will.)

Careers in the UK and USA

CULTURE SPOT

British and American careers are often very different from German, Swiss or Austrian careers. First, British and American people often begin their careers when they are younger. For example, it's normal for British people to finish university and begin working at the age of 21. Also, in Britain and America a lot of employers think that practical experience is more important than university qualifications, so many young people prefer finding a job to studying.

Another difference is that it is much easier for employers to hire and fire workers in the UK and the USA than in Germany, so workers often have less job security. German workers also generally have better benefits than British or American workers – better company pension schemes, for example.

Another difference between Britain and the USA and German-speaking countries: it is much easier to change career. A lot of British and American people have two (or even more!) completely different careers in their lives. You can always make a new start – it's never too late!

UNIT 8 SALES

In this unit you ...

talk about sales figures:

Sales fell/went down slightly last year.

But this year they have risen/have gone up dramatically.

practise 'hotel language':

Would you like some tea or coffee, madam?

I'm afraid I don't have any towels in my room.

Business file

Arranging a business trip

A A sales meeting at Amsel AG

WARM UP **Is your town or city famous for a product – like chocolate, cars, ... ? Can you think of three towns or cities in your country that are famous for a product?**

A1 **Look at the front page of the company brochure below and answer these questions.**

1 What does Amsel AG do?
2 Where is it based?
3 How long has it been there?
4 Who founded the company?
5 Who runs it now?
6 How many people work there?
7 How do you know from the brochure that Amsel also exports its products?
8 What type of people are its products for (eg professional chefs)?

AMSEL
Solingen Germany

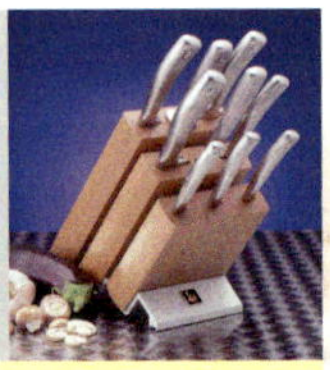

SOLINGEN in Germany has been famous for its blades since the 14th century, and the AMSEL company has been part of the Solingen tradition for over two hundred years. AMSEL'S founder, Otto Weber, first registered the famous blackbird trademark in 1796. Still a family concern today, AMSEL is now one of the world's leading manufacturers of precision knives and employs around 300 people in its modern production facilities in Solingen.

AMSEL steel kitchen knives mean one thing: quality. Around the world, professional chefs and enthusiastic amateurs recognize the AMSEL logo as a symbol of excellence.

A2 **What's the English for ... ?**

1 *Klingen*
2 *Jahrhundert*
3 *Warenzeichen*
trade mark
4 *Konzern*
5 *(an)erkennen*
6 *stehen für*

A3 2/09 **Listen and say which sales graph Steve is describing: A, B or C.**

Amsel sells its products around the world and its European Sales Manager is Andrea Graf. Andrea holds two sales meetings every year with her European representatives. It's June, and she's holding the first of the two today.

Andrea OK, let's move on to the second point on the agenda: the review of the year so far. Steve, would you like to start? How have things been in the UK?

Steve Hi everybody. Before I talk about my sales this year, I'd like to put them in context a bit – so here are my quarterly sales figures for *last* year. As you can see, the first two quarters were fine. First quarter sales were around €750,000, and in the second quarter they rose to €850,000. But then the third quarter wasn't so good. Sales fell sharply. They went up again in the fourth quarter but only slightly. So overall, the year was, well, a bit disappointing ...

A

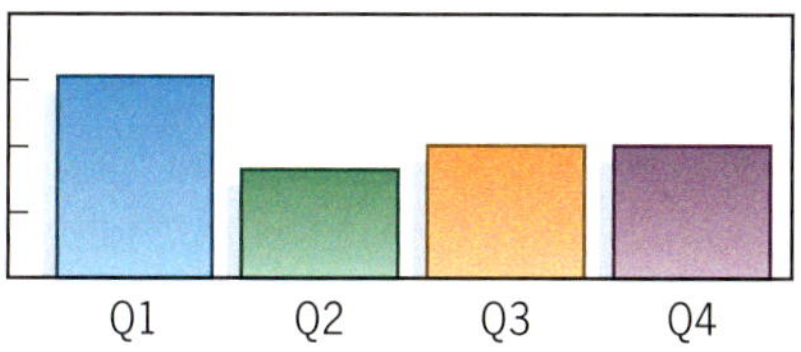

B

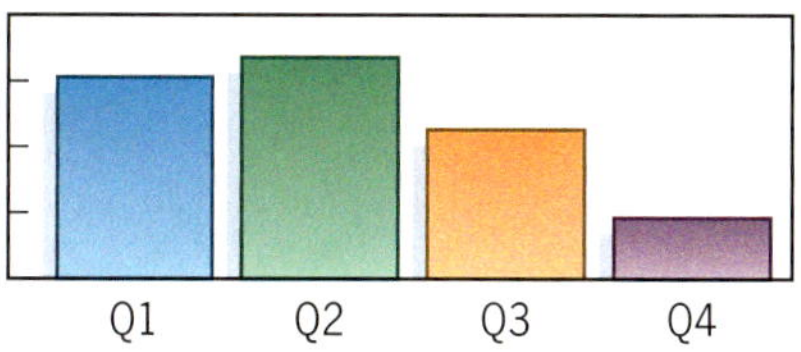

C

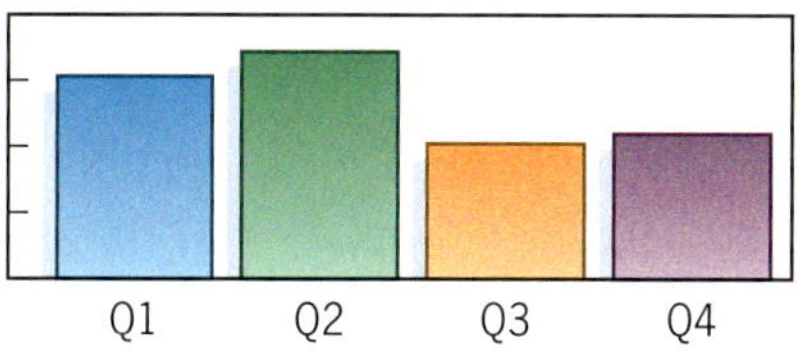

Talking about sales FOCUS

to rise to go up to increase ↑	to fall to go down to decrease ↓
→ to remain stable	↗ to level off

Adverbs

Adverbien wie slightly, dramatically, sharply *und* steadily *werden verwendet, um auszudrücken wie Dinge verlaufen – beispielsweise wenn wir über Absatzzahlen sprechen.*
Sales fell. (How?) **Sharply!**

A4 **Work with a partner.**

1. Describe the other two graphs in A3. Use words from the FOCUS box.
2. Partner A: make a simple graph of a different company's quarterly sales last year (invent the details yourself). Describe the graph to your partner. Partner B: draw the graph.

A5 Listen and complete the sentences.

2/10

Steve is talking now about his sales *so far this year*. Remember – it's still June, so just *before* the end of the second quarter.

1 First quarter sales this year were ...
2 But this quarter has been '...'
3 So far sales have already reached ...
4 Steve thinks that ...
5 Delia Smith is a ...
6 A couple of months ago Delila ...
7 Since then, sales of Amsel knives ...

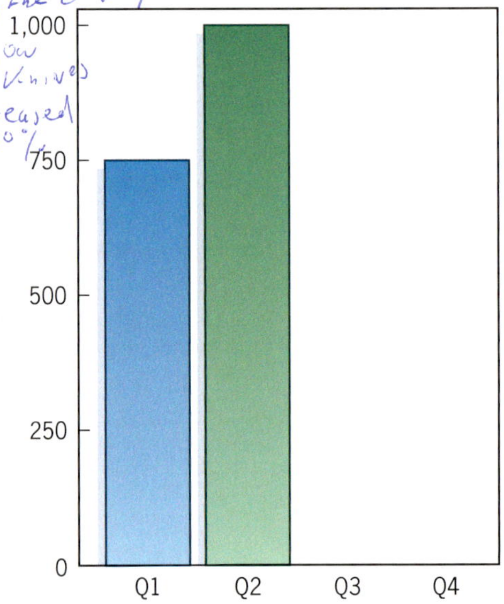

The simple past or the present perfect?

FOCUS

Simple past
*Man verwendet das simple past für ‚**abgeschlossene Zeiträume**' (Zeiträume, die eindeutig in der Vergangenheit endeten).*

last year
two years ago
yesterday
NOW

Present perfect
*Man verwendet das present perfect für ‚**Zeiträume bis zur Gegenwart**' (Zeiträume, die bis zum **gegenwärtigen Augenblick reichen**).*

so far this year/quarter
since yesterday
for/over the last two years
NOW

A6 Simple past or present perfect? Choose the correct form.

1 Last year Steve's sales *were/have been* disappointing.
2 His first and second quarter sales *were/have been* good, but then sales *fell/have fallen*.
3 But so far this year, sales *were/have been* much better.
4 In the first quarter they *rose/have risen* to 750,000 again – back 'on target'.
5 And so far this quarter they *were/have been* 'sensational'.
6 Two months ago, an English chef *started/has started* using Amsel knives on her TV programme.
7 Since then Steve's sales *increased/have increased* by 100 per cent.

A7 Look at File 14 on page 131 or File 16 on page 132. Work in a small group and present 'your' company and its finances to the others.

B Travelling on business

WARM UP **Do you sometimes go on business trips? What do you like and dislike about being on a trip?**

B1

2/11

Listen and answer the questions.

Andrea Graf is in Manchester in the north of England for a trade fair. These three conversations take place during her first half an hour in the hotel.

At the reception desk

1 How many nights is Andrea staying?
2 What's her room number and which floor is the room on?
3 There's a message for Andrea when she arrives. Who's it from?

In the hotel room

4 In her room, Andrea picks up her phone and makes a call. Who answers?
5 Why is Andrea phoning?

In the lobby

6 Who (do you think) Andrea is talking to?
7 What questions does he ask her?
8 What does he bring her?

B2

Complete the sentences with *some* or *any*. (Listen again if necessary.)

1 Are there .... messages for me?

2 I'm afraid I don't have .... towels in my room.

3 Would you like .... tea or coffee, madam?

4 Could I have .... cake or biscuits with that?

some and *any*

FOCUS

Man verwendet some *und* any *mit zählbaren und nicht zählbaren Substantiven.*

some

Aussagen:
There's **some** hot water in this pot.
There are **some** chairs in the lobby.

Höfliche Angebote:
Would you like **some** tea?

Um etwas bitten:
Could I have **some** coffee, please?

any

Fragen:
Are there **any** messages for me?

Verneinungen:
I don't have **any** soap in my room.

B3

***Some* or *any*?**

1 Here's your bill, Mr Richards. Did you have .... drinks from the mini bar?
2 Would you like .... more coffee?
3 There are .... 'What's On?' brochures in your room. You'll find .... cinemas in there.
4 I'm sorry, the restaurant's completely booked at the moment. We don't have .... free tables until about 9.30.
5 Are there .... non-smoking rooms in the hotel?
6 Yes, there are .... on the first floor.
7 Waiter! Could I have .... mineral water, please?
8 Oh, and I'd like .... more bread, please.

B4

2/12

Three people are complaining in a hotel. Listen and complete the table.

	Customer	Problem	Solution
1	Mr Black	he can't watch TV	
2	Mrs White		
3	Mr Green		

- **Now match these apologies to the conversations. What were the speakers referring to?**

Oh, I'm sorry about that. I'll send someone up straight away.

I'm terribly sorry. I've made a mistake.

Again, I'm sorry about this. There won't be a charge for your order.

Being polite – complaining

FOCUS

I wonder if you could help me?
I'm afraid I have a problem with …
I'm afraid I don't have any … (in my room).
The … in my room isn't working.
I think you've made a mistake (with my bill).
I don't think this is right.
Could you check that again, please?

B5

Work with a partner.

PARTNER A: Look at File 9 on page 129.
PARTNER B: Look at File 13 on page 131. Use the information on the role cards to make conversations. Then write down one conversation and read it to the class.

B6

Read the article on page 95 from an American in-flight magazine and make notes about what Bob says under the following headings:

- flying
- the advantages and disadvantages of being a 'constant flyer'
- how he uses modern technology like a laptop and a cell phone
- his tips and 'golden rules'

Travelers' Tales

As a troubleshooter with a multinational oil company, last year Bob Bukowski flew over 8m miles. Bob isn't so much a frequent flyer as ... a constant flyer

HIGHLIGHT What does that mean, Bob, a 'constant flyer'?

BOB For me, it means that when I get up in the morning, I don't usually know where I'll be in the evening. I can spend a week in the office, at other times I'm away for two weeks. I guess on average I'm 'somewhere else' four days a week.

HIGHLIGHT Do you have any 'golden rules' when you're flying?

BOB Yes, one, I never talk to the person in the seat next to me. Traveling time for me is working time. I always take a laptop and work on the papers that my p.a. has prepared. When I'm not doing that I'm sleeping.

HIGHLIGHT Do you actually enjoy traveling?

BOB I wouldn't say I actually enjoy being on airplanes much, and when I visit a place I very often see only the inside of a hotel or an office, but yes, sure, I've been to some great places. I always try to eat local food when I'm in a country. I've had some wonderful eating experiences.

HIGHLIGHT And the disadvantages?

BOB Well, obviously being away from home so much. I have two daughters, 4 and 6, and I really hate not seeing them grow up. But I must say that modern technology is a great help. I always have a cell phone with me, so I can call home regularly, and I send pictures home with it from all over the world. You know: 'Here's me in front of the Taj Mahal!' The kids love that. And a couple of years ago I began faxing bedtime stories.

HIGHLIGHT How does that work?

BOB Well, I have this story in which the kids are the main characters and every night when I'm away I send a bit of the story home. The scene is the place where I am at the time. It's the first thing I do as soon as I arrive at my hotel.

HIGHLIGHT What about packing? Any tips?

BOB For me, it's easy. When I shop I buy two of everything and keep a bag permanently packed.

Compound nouns

FOCUS ON WORDS

Im Gegensatz zur deutschen Sprache werden Begriffe im Englischen, die sich aus zwei Wörtern zusammensetzen, nicht immer zusammengeschrieben. Leider gibt es dafür keine klaren Regeln – sehen Sie in Ihrem Wörterbuch nach!

B7 **Match the words in boxes A and B to make things that you often take on a business trip. (Be careful! Sometimes the new word is one word, sometimes two.)**

A

brief laptop alarm tooth
mobile rain paperback
phrase credit pass suit

B

clock card computer
phone case port
coat brush book

B8 **What do you take with you when you travel? What are your 'tips and golden rules' for successful travel? Write a short text in English for your company intranet.**

Arranging a business trip

In this business file you ...

- talk about flight times and book a flight.
- get information about hotels and book a room.

1 **Try this quick test with a partner.**

TEST YOURSELF

Say the times and dates (or write them down in words), then check your answers on pages 138–139.

1 The 24-hour clock

A	B	C	D	E	F
17:15	05:20	18:05	15:00	23:16	00:00

2 Dates

A The meeting is on 19 February, isn't it?
B No, now it's on 23 March.
C The date on this letter from our American office is July 14.

3 What are these dates in the USA and in the UK?

A 11/3 **C** 2/2 **E** 7/4
B 8/9 **D** 6/8 **F** 1/6

2 2/13 **Listen and make notes.**

You work for an international company in Düsseldorf and your boss, Alastair Graham, has to go on a business trip to the east of England. Your job is to make all the arrangements. He's giving you the details of what he wants and when. Listen and make notes.

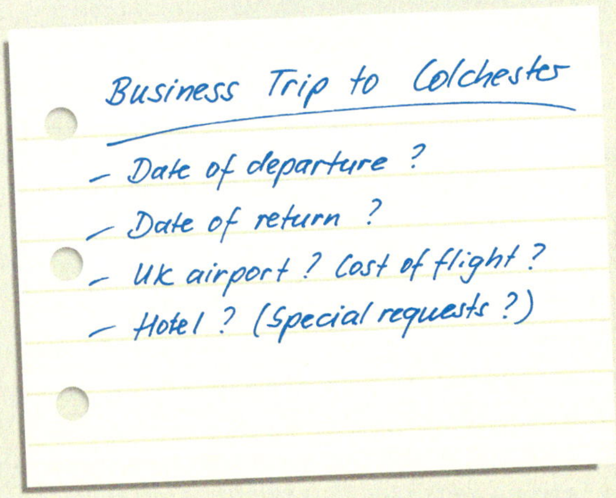

3 **First work with a partner to check flights.**

1 Look at this online screen. What information from your notes (on page 96) goes where?
2 What flights are available? Are they on the days that you want? What are the flight times and numbers? Ask your partner! (PARTNER B: Look at File 18 on page 133 for information.)
3 Now, with your partner, decide which flights are best.

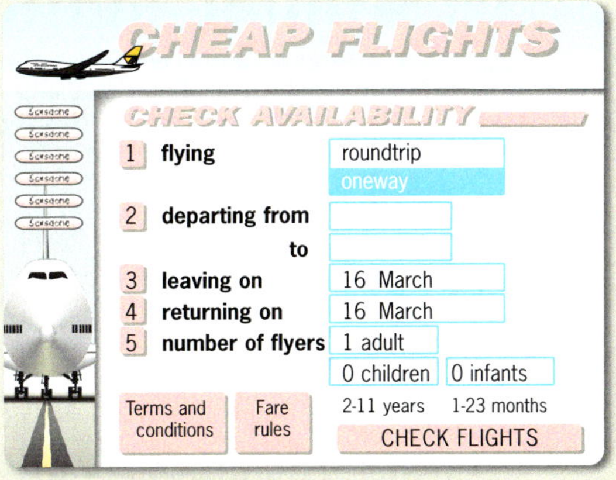

How do I talk about flight times?

INFO

Über persönliche Pläne sprechen wir normalerweise im present continuous:
What are you doing next week? I'm going to a meeting in England.
Geht es aber um Abflugzeiten (und alle anderen Arten von Fahrplänen), die bereits feststehen, benutzen wir das simple present:
The flight leaves at 18.05.

4 **Now work with your partner again to choose a hotel. Here are three possible hotels in (or near) Colchester.**

1 PARTNER A: You are arranging Mr Graham's trip. Telephone the three hotels and get information. (Do the hotels have rooms available on the dates that you need? What are their prices? And how convenient/quiet/big/small, etc. are they?)
PARTNER B: You are the receptionist at the hotels above. Look at File 19 on page 134 and answer the questions.
2 With your partner, choose one hotel for Mr Graham.
3 PARTNER A: Telephone the hotel you have chosen
PARTNER B: Look at File 20 on page 134 and complete the booking form.

5 **Write an email to your boss with the details.**

Grammar summary

The present perfect for 'time up to the present' and the simple past for 'finished time'

Sales **this year have been** good.
We'**ve sold** a lot of new products **this month**.
So far today I'**ve received** over 80 emails!

Sales **last year were** not as good.
We **didn't sell** as many new products **last month**.
Yesterday I received 100 emails!

Present Perfect für ‚bis in die Gegenwart reichende Zeiträume' und die einfache Vergangenheit für ‚abgeschlossene Zeiträume'

Zur Beschreibung von Vorgängen, die sich in einem Zeitraum ereigneten, der die Gegenwart mit einschließt *(this year, this month, today, so far, this week)*, verwendet man das **present perfect**.

Zur Beschreibung von Vorgängen, die sich in einem Zeitraum der Vergangenheit ereigneten, der jetzt abgeschlossen ist *(last year, last month, yesterday, last week)*, verwendet man das **simple past**.

Adjectives and adverbs

USE

Marina is a **competent** manager. (1)
She manages her department **competently**. (2)
Sales in 2003 fell **sharply/dramatically/steadily/slightly**. (3)

Adjektive und Adverbien

VERWENDUNG

Adjektive beschreiben Substantive: Personen, Orte, Dinge (1). Adverbien beschreiben, *wie* sich etwas ereignet hat und beziehen sich auf ein Verb (2).

Mit Adverbien wie *sharply, dramatically, steadily* und *slightly* werden oft Veränderungen der Absatzzahlen beschrieben (3).

FORM

This is an **automatic** door.
It opens **automatically**. (1)

Phil's boss was **angry**.
He spoke to Phil **angrily**. (1)

He has a **fast** car.
He drives **fast**. (2)

Gerhard is a **good** tennis player.
He plays tennis **well**. (3)

FORM

Adverbien und Adjektive haben im Englischen unterschiedliche Formen. Fast alle Adverbien werden durch Anhängen von *-ly* (manchmal *-ally* oder *-ily*) an ein Adjektiv gebildet (1).

Ein paar Adverbien (wie *fast*, *early* und *late*) haben die gleiche Form wie ein Adjektiv (2).

Das Adverb von *good* ist *well* (3).

some and *any*

There are **some** biscuits in the conference room, and there's also **some** coffee. (1)

Are there **any** pencils? Is there **any** coffee? (2)
No, there aren't **any** pencils and there isn't **any** coffee. (2)

Would you like **some** tea? (3)
Could we have **some** markers for the flipchart, please? (4)

some und *any*

Some wird verwendet, um über eine ‚bestimmte Menge oder Anzahl' an Personen oder Dingen zu sprechen: ‚etwas', ‚einige'. Es wird mit zählbaren und nicht zählbaren Substantiven verwendet (1). In Fragen und Verneinungen wird *some* durch *any* ersetzt (2).

Some wird statt *any* verwendet, wenn man etwas höflich in Frageform anbietet (3) und wenn man nach etwas fragt (4).

Talking about the future: the simple present for timetables

What **are** you **doing** tomorrow? (1)
I'm flying to London. (1)
My flight **leaves** Düsseldorf at 10.00 and **arrives** in London at 10.30. (2)

Über Zukünftiges sprechen: die einfache Gegenwart für Zeitpläne

Während mit dem *present continuous* persönliche Vereinbarungen beschrieben werden (1), wird in der Regel das *simple present* für Flug- und andere Zeitpläne verwendet, die extern festgesetzt werden (2).

Grammar

1 Choose the correct sentence.

1A Sales have been bad so far this year.
1B ~~Sales were bad so far this year.~~
2A Sales have risen in the fourth quarter of last year.
2B Sales rose in the fourth quarter of last year.
3A I've given a sales presentation yesterday.
3B I gave a sales presentation yesterday.
4A Sales last year have been around 1 million euros.
4B Sales last year were around 1 million euros.
5A Amsel has sold a lot of products so far this month.
5B Amsel sold a lot of products so far this month.

2 Complete the table.

	adjective	adverb
1	....	well
2	quick	....
3	permanent	....
4	....	possibly
5	....	fluently
6	urgent	....
7	....	easily

3 Adjective or adverb? Choose the correct alternative in each sentence.

1 Can you type this for me *quick/quickly*, please?
2 He's travelled *wide/widely*.
3 Jürgen speaks *fluent/fluently* English.
4 We're talking about a *possible/possibly* joint venture between our companies.
5 Marilyn plays tennis *good/well*.
6 I'm glad the package arrived *safe/safely*.

4 Complete the sentences with phrases from the box.

to decrease slightly | to fall sharply | to go up steadily | to increase dramatically | to level off | to remain stable

So, as you can see, sales ...1 in January.

They then ...2 in February, and ...3 in March.

They ...4 in April.

But then they ...5 in May, and in June they actually ...6.

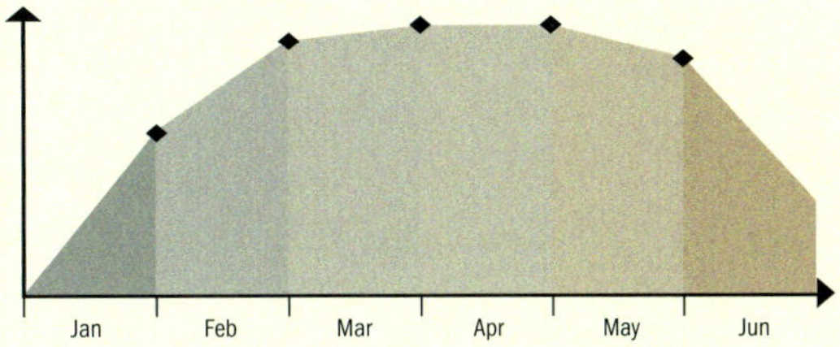

5 Complete the sentences using *some* or *any*.

1 Would you like .... tea or coffee?
2 I'd like .... more sugar, please.
3 Do you have .... dictionaries in your office?
4 There are .... new email programs on the market.
5 Are there .... good restaurants near your office?
6 I'm sorry, but she doesn't have .... time this month.

6 **Simple present for timetables or present continuous for personal arrangements? Complete the dialogue with the correct form of the verbs.**

arrive (x2) be do fly get leave (x2)

Craig Hey Lilly, what ……… you ……… [1] tomorrow?

Lilly Actually, I ……… [2] to New York.

Craig Really? What time ……… [3] your flight?

Lilly It ……… [4] Berlin at 9 am and ……… [5] in Frankfurt at 10.30. The flight to New York ……… [6] at 11.30.

Craig And what time ……… you ……… [7] to New York?

Lilly I'm not sure. I think the plane ……… [8] at about 5 pm New York time. I'll have to check.

Words and phrases

7 **Match words from A and B to make words or phrases from this unit.**

A

1 business	6 golden
2 cell	7 hotel
3 company	8 local
4 first	9 sales
5 frequent	10 trade

B

brochure	mark
figures	phone
flyer	quarter
food	rule
lobby	trip

■ **Now complete these sentences with the words or phrases above.**

a Can I use your ………, please? I need to call my family.
b I always try to eat ……… when I'm travelling.
c I'll meet you in the ……… at 8 pm. Then we can go out for dinner.
d Our ……… is a picture of an apple.
e Sales rose in the ……… of last year.
f I fly almost every week – I'm a ……… .
g This graph shows our ……… for last year.
h One ……… of travel is to take as little luggage as possible.
i Hilda is going on a ……… to Singapore next week.
j You can find more information about our products in our ……… .

8 **What did they say? Rearrange the words to make sentences.**

1 you I wonder me could if help
2 telephone have with I seem problem to a my
3 towels room afraid don't any in I'm I have my
4 in working my room the light isn't
5 made my mistake you've with I bill think a
6 don't this right I is think
7 that check please again you could?

9 **Complete with the missing vowels to make hotel words and phrases.**

1 r_c_pt_ _n d_sk	5 r_ _m s_rv_c_
2 r_g_str_t_ _n f_rm	6 m_n_b_r
3 r_ _m k_y	7 r_ _m n_mb_r
4 t_w_ls	8 m_ss_g_

10 **Complete the crossword with the English translations of things you might take on a business trip.**

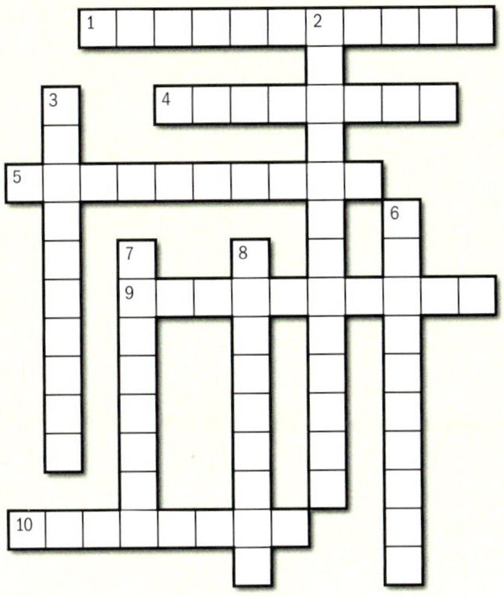

Across	Down
1 Handy	2 Taschenbuch
4 Reisepass	3 Sprachführer
5 Kreditkarte	6 Zahnbürste
9 Wecker	7 Regenmantel
10 Koffer	8 Aktentasche

Translating

11 **Translate into English.**

1 Wo ist Ihr Firmensitz? – In Manchester.
2 Gibt es Kaffee im Konferenzraum? – Ja, und es gibt auch Tee.
3 Ich fürchte, es gibt ein Problem mit meiner Rechnung.
4 Guten Morgen. Kann ich bitte Ihren Pass sehen?
5 Ich suche mein Handy. Wissen Sie, wo es ist?
6 Klaus spricht sehr gut Englisch.

TYPICAL MISTAKES

1 My partner speaks English well. (adverb)
NOT My partner speaks English *good*. (adjective)
(Aber wir können auch sagen: My partner speaks good English. = ... *spricht (ein) gutes Englisch.)*

2 This is an automatic door *(*adjective*)*. It opens automatically *(*adverb*).*
NOT It opens *automatic*.

3 There is some coffee in the conference room.
NOT There is *any* coffee in the conference room.

4 Where is Amsel based?
NOT Where *is based* Amsel?

6 I'm afraid I don't have any hot water in my room.
NOT *I'm afraid but* I don't have any hot water in my room.

7 I use my mobile/cell phone every day for my job.
NOT I use my *handy* every day for my job.
(‚Handy' bedeutet auf Englisch ‚praktisch'.)

8 Don't forget your passport when you go on your business trip!
NOT Don't forget your *pass* when you go on your business trip!

Being polite

CULTURE SPOT

Being polite is very important in British and American cultures. Here are some tips on how to be polite in English.

- Say sorry if you complain about something, even if the problem is not your fault. Start by saying 'I'm sorry, but ...' or 'I'm afraid ...'. State the problem objectively ('I'm afraid there are no towels in my room'); don't blame the person ('You forgot to put towels in my room'). Use phrases like 'I think' or 'it seems' to soften your complaint.
- If you want someone to do something for you, ask a question ('Could you check this again?'); don't give an order ('Check this again.'). Use words like 'maybe' and 'possibly' to make your request more polite: 'Could you possibly send me the report by 3 pm?' is more polite than 'Could you send me the report by 3 pm?'.
- Don't use the phrase 'Would you be so kind as to ...' when asking for something – it is so polite that it can sound ironic.

UNIT 9

AT A TRADE FAIR

In this unit you ...

practise 'trade fair' language:

I'd like some information about your products.

describe and compare products:

They're easy to use and less expensive than our competitors'.

look at an invoice and do some office work:

checking voicemail, writing an email, making a phone call

Business file

Please compare ...

A The International Food Industry Show

WARM UP

Have you ever been to a trade fair? Where was it? When did you go? Tell the class. Name three things companies do at trade fairs.

A1 **Andrea Graf from Amsel AG is at the International Food Industry Show in Manchester. Companies from all over the world have stands there. Look at the trade fair scene below and find the best replies (1–10) for what the visitors to the stands are saying (a–j).**

1 Of course. How can I help?
2 Oh yes, very. I'll show you.
3 Here we are. Please help yourself.
4 Great. I'll look forward to it.
5 Yes, they're our latest range.
6 €2,000 each.
7 That's him over there.
8 A special new kind of plastic.
9 12 months.
10 In Munich in southern Germany.

A2 2/14 **Andrea has an important visitor at her stand. Paul Hornby is a buyer for a large hotel chain. Listen to the first part of their conversation and answer these questions.**

1 How many hotels does Paul's chain own?
2 Where does Paul normally buy knives? Why hasn't he bought Amsel knives before?
3 How much more expensive are Amsel knives than the knives Paul is buying at the moment?
4 Does Andrea say that it *is easy* or *isn't easy* to see the difference between an Amsel knife and an 'ordinary' knife?
5 What happens if you break a knife?
6 What kind of guarantee comes with an Amsel knife?

A3 2/15 **Now listen to the second part of Paul and Andrea's conversation and complete these sentences.**

1 Amsel knives are popular with chefs because ...
2 The handles are ergonomically designed so the knives won't ...
3 The main thing about the blades is that ...
4 Amsel knife blades are made of ...

A4 **Make a summary.**

1 Look at the FOCUS box. What phrases did Andrea use in the conversation?
2 Make a short summary ('bullet points') of the features and benefits of an Amsel knife.

Describing the features and benefits of a product

FOCUS

It's made of (steel, glass, wood, plastic ...)
It's made from (the best available materials, the finest ingredients ...)
It's (very, extremely, completely) **safe, sharp, attractive, durable ...**
It's very **good value for money, cost-effective ...**
It's **expensive,** it's **an excellent investment,** it **will last a lifetime ...**
It comes with full **instructions,** a year's (a two-year, a lifetime) **guarantee ...**

ADJEKTIV + INFINITIV
It's **easy to use, simple to understand, comfortable to hold ...**

ADVERB + PARTIZIP PERFEKT
It's **beautifully made, perfectly balanced, technically advanced ...**

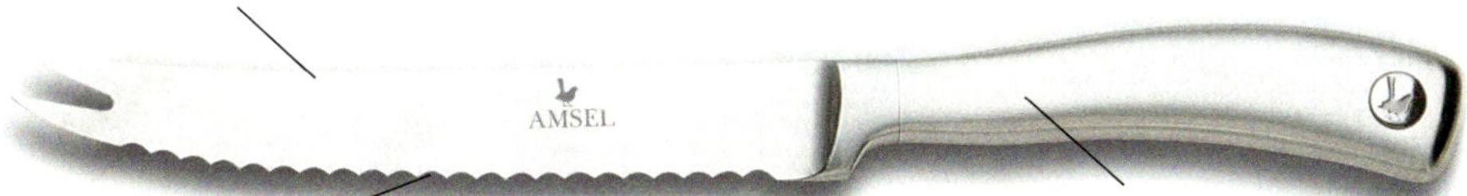

A5 **Find an object in the classroom. Make one or two sentences about it.**

(What's it made of? Is it sharp? heavy? fragile? Is it easy to use? Expensive? ... ?)

A6

Work with a partner. Match the words and expressions with the same meaning.

A	B
<u>cheaper</u>	the least expensive
easier	less difficult
harder	more difficult
nicer	<u>less expensive</u>
the cheapest	the most difficult
the easiest	the least difficult
the hardest	more attractive
the nicest	the most attractive

- **Use the words from the table and make six positive statements for describing products. Try to find more than one way to say the same thing.**

Our products are much less expensive than our competitors'. They aren't as ...

Making comparisons

FOCUS

not as ... as

Man verwendet **not as ... as** *mit allen Adjektiven:*
Product A **isn't as big/as good/as expensive as** product B.

less, (the) least

Bei Adjektiven, die den Komparativ und Superlativ mit more *und* (the) most *bilden, kann man auch* less *und* (the) least *verwenden:*
Product A is **less expensive** than B or C.
It's **the least expensive** of the three.

(MEHR VERGLEICHENDE ADJEKTIVE → UNIT 4, SEITE 44)

A7

Work with your partner again.

Are you a good salesperson? Look at these products (and the service) and choose one.

PARTNER A: You are the 'potential customer'. Ask Partner B questions about the product or service.

PARTNER B: Look at the notes in File 22 on page 136. Greet partner A at your trade fair stand, then try to sell him or her your product or service.

1

Elexis e-Book

Potential customer: 'keen reader' at a book fair

2

PRONTO office-size espresso machine

Potential customer: office manager of a magazine publisher

3

Arnie the walking-talking robot

Potential customer: CEO of a big multinational

4

INTERLANG International Translating and Interpreting Service

Potential customer: owner of a small family firm

B Back in the office

WARM UP **What do you think is easiest and hardest: talking in English face-to-face with someone, talking in English on the phone or writing an email (or a letter) in English? Why?**

B1 2/16 Listen to voicemail messages.

Jan Zielinski is Andrea's assistant and he is taking care of things in the Solingen office while Andrea is in Manchester. It's Tuesday morning. Jan has just arrived for work, and he's listening to his voicemail messages. There are four. Listen. What does each person want?

- **Here are some extracts from the messages. Can you give the missing words?**

Hello Jan. It's Paula Morris from Cookshops Ltd. in England. I've got .... (1) about your last invoice.

Jan, hi, it's Lucia in Rome. [...] I'm going to the Milan trade fair the week after next, so could you send them .... (2) possible?

Hello. I hope I'm ringing the right number. I've had a set of Amsel knives for five years now and I've .... (3) the blade of one of them.

My name's Claude Lebon [...] Do you have a representative in the Netherlands and .... (4), how can I contact him or her?

The present perfect + *just* FOCUS

I've just faxed you the invoice.
Ich habe Ihnen eben gerade die Rechnung gefaxt.

I've just seen your website.
Ich habe eben gerade Ihre Website gesehen.

B2 Complete Jan's 'TO DO' list. (Listen again to the messages if necessary.)

TO DO

- *Check Paula's .... and phone her back or .... her.*
- *Send .... company brochures (......... version) to .... asap.*
- *Ring Claude Lebon on .... with Antje van Eeden's phone number.*
- *Contact David Roberts about ....*
- *Phone: .... or email: ....*

B3 Work with a partner. Can you do Jan's job for him this morning?

Look again at his 'TO DO' list on page 105 and the **FOCUS** box on page 107. Then work with a partner to complete the activities below.

1 PAULA MORRIS'S INVOICE

Here's part of Paula's fax with her comments. Check the invoice against Amsel's price list and Paula's last invoice (Partner B: please look at File 21 on page 135), then finish Jan's email.

Do you have two sizes of bread knives? The knives I received this time are slightly smaller.

Cat. No.	Quantity	Description	Unit price (euros)	Amount (euros)
3038	10	Peeling knife 7cm	31.00	310.00
3527	10	Tomato knife 14cm	39.00	390.00
3157	5	Bread knife 20cm	60.00	300.00
3819	30	Chef's knife 20cm	75.00	1,500.00
3063	10	Oriental chef's knife 17cm	70.00	700.00
9338	20	5-piece knife set	320.00	6,400.00
			SUBTOTAL	9,600.00
			WITH 5% DISCOUNT	9,120.00
			SHIPPING	20.00
			Please Pay This Amount:	€9,140.00

Don't want to pay extra (!) but I'm sure the list price was 75.

On my last order I got 10%

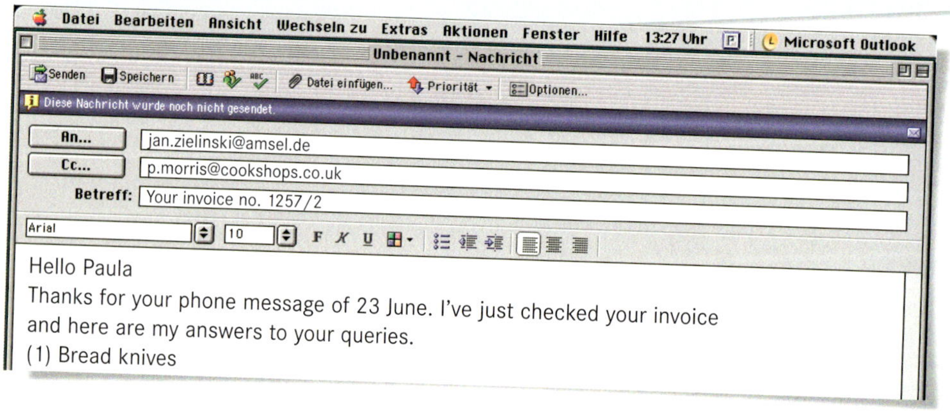
Datei Bearbeiten Ansicht Wechseln zu Extras Aktionen Fenster Hilfe 13:27 Uhr Microsoft Outlook

Unbenannt – Nachricht

Senden Speichern Datei einfügen... Priorität Optionen...

Diese Nachricht wurde noch nicht gesendet.

An... jan.zielinski@amsel.de

Cc... p.morris@cookshops.co.uk

Betreff: Your invoice no. 1257/2

Hello Paula

Thanks for your phone message of 23 June. I've just checked your invoice and here are my answers to your queries.

(1) Bread knives

2 LUCIA'S BROCHURES

You ring Lucia in Rome but she's out. Leave a voicemail message: you've just sent the brochures. They should arrive in about two days.

3 CLAUDE LEBON'S QUESTION

Ring Claude Lebon at his restaurant in Amsterdam. Antje's (Amsel's Dutch representative's) phone number is: 020 5117869.

4 DAVID ROBERTS

Write an email to David Roberts. Include the following points:

- Pots 'n' Pans (a kitchen equipment shop) at 23 Cathedral Street, Durham, are stockists of Amsel knives.
- If he prefers, he can send his knife directly to Amsel in Solingen (address on the guarantee) and will receive a free replacement in five days.

Beginning and ending …

FOCUS

a phone call

Good morning/afternoon.
Could I speak to …, please?
(S)he's in the … department/works in …
This is/It's … (here) from …
I'm ringing about …
I'm returning your call about …
…
I hope this helps.
Don't hesitate to ring me again if you have any problems, OK?
(Thanks very much.) You're welcome.
Goodbye/Bye/Bye now.

an email

Hello Jan/Hi Karen
Dear Mr/Ms …
Thanks very much for your email/message/fax/phone call about …
Here are my answers to your queries/questions.
You asked about/wanted to know about …
…
Let me know if you have any further questions/if you have any problems.
I look forward to hearing from you soon.
Best wishes/All the best/Kind regards

B4 **Find the missing nouns in the table. Use your dictionary if necessary.**

Verb	Noun
to **reply** to	to send/write a *reply* (a) to
to **enquire** about	to make an ……… (b) about
to **query** something	to have a ……… (c) about something
to **invoice** someone	to send someone an ……… (d)
to **order** something	to place an ……… (e) for something
to **pay** a bill	to make/send a ……… (f)
to **invest** in	to make an ……… (g) in
to **deliver**	to make a ……… (h)
to **offer**	to make a ……… (i)

- **Now complete the second sentences below with a verb or noun from the table. The coloured words in the first sentence will help you.**

1 Have they **replied** to our letter yet? — Have they sent us a *reply* to our letter yet?
2 Please **pay** the bill immediately. — Please send us your ……… immediately.
3 The company made a huge **investment** last year in new machinery. — The company ……… a lot of money last year in new machinery.
4 I'd like to **order** ten computers. — I'd like to place an ……… for ten computers.
5 When can we expect **delivery**? — When can you ……… them?
6 A&C made us a good **offer**. — A&C ……… us a good price.
7 Could you send me an **invoice**? — Could you ……… me?
8 Yes, hello. I'd like to **query** one of the items on my hotel bill. — Yes, hello. I have a ……… about one of the items on my hotel bill.

Word families

FOCUS ON WORDS

Achten Sie beim Vokabeln lernen auf ‚verwandte' Substantive und Verben. Leider gibt es im Englischen wenig feste Regeln zur Bildung verwandter Wörter – schlagen Sie deshalb die jeweilige Schreibweise in Ihrem Wörterbuch nach!

Please compare ...

In this business file you ...
- look at sales figures and compare products.
- write a report.

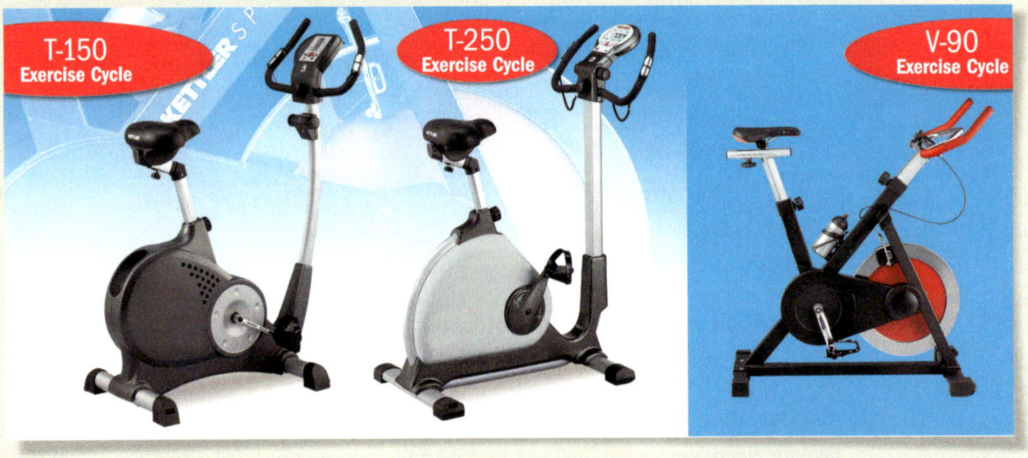

1 **Read the email below.**

Your company manufactures and sells fitness equipment – like the exercise cycles above. You work in the sales and marketing department and you get the email below from your Commercial Director, Richard Hanley.

Look at the email now. What information will you need for your report? Tick the boxes.

- sales figures for all your company's products ☐
- sales figures for exercise cycles from two years ago ☐
- customer ratings for exercise cycles from last year and this year ☐
- the sales figures of your major competitors ☐
- a price list for all your company's products ☐
- sales figures for exercise cycles from last year and this year ☐

Product review

From: Richard Hanley
Sent: Wednesday, 17 December 10.35
Subject: Product review

Over the next three weeks I propose to undertake a complete review of our products and I want to start with our range of Exercise Cycles.

I'd like a report on the sales performance of the six models in the range, i.e. the T-10, T-20, T-150, T-250, V-80 and V-90. Please compare the sales figures from last year and this year. Take into account the customer ratings from our market research too.

In your report, make it clear where:
- Sales have increased this year compared to last year
- Sales have decreased this year compared to last year
- Customer ratings have risen or fallen over the two years.

I also want your recommendations about which cycles, in your opinion, we should continue or possibly discontinue.

Please let me have your report by 22 December at the latest.

2 **Work with a partner to complete the chart.**

Here is the basic information for your report. Partner A: look below. Partner B: look at your chart in File 23 on page 136. Ask your partner for the missing information and answer his or her questions.

How many did we sell last year?

How many have we sold this year?

What was the customer rating last year?

What's the customer rating been this year?

MODEL	Units sold last year (000s)	Customer rating last year*	Units sold this year (000s)	Customer rating this year*
T-10	10	●●●●○	………	………
T-20	………	………	9.5	●●●●○
T-150	………	●●●●●	………	●●●●●
T-250	3	………	1.8	………
V-80	………	………	11	●●●○○
V-90	11	●●●○○	………	………

Customer ratings:
very poor ●○○○○
poor ●●○○○
average ●●●○○
good ●●●●○
very good ●●●●●

*in terms of reliability and price

3 **Write a report.**

With your partner again write the report for Richard Hanley. Make sure that you cover all the points in his email. Organize your report into three sections:

- Aim: Why you are writing
- Findings: The facts and figures
- Conclusions and recommendations: Your opinions and suggestions

How do I write a report?

INFO

Aim

The aim of this report is to compare/review/examine/contrast …

Findings

Our findings are as follows./We found that …
Sales (of …) have increased/decreased compared to last year.
Customer ratings (for …) have risen/fallen compared to last year.
Sales/Customer ratings have remained the same/remained stable.
Two/Three/Four out of six products … (but two products …)

Conclusions and recommendations

It is clear from these findings that …
The best-selling/most successful product is/products are …
The worst-selling/least successful product is/products are …
Product B has performed particularly well/badly.
On the one hand … . On the other hand …
Based on the above findings we recommend that …
In the light of these findings we suggest that …

Grammar summary

Adjective + infinitive

It's **easy to use**.
The instructions are **simple to understand**.
The product isn't **expensive to buy**.

Adjektiv + Infinitiv

Mit der Kombination von Adjektiv + Infinitiv mit *to* werden oft Merkmale eines Produkts oder Services beschrieben wie ‚einfach zu bedienen', ‚leicht zu verstehen' usw.

Adverb + past participle

This coffee cup is **broken**. (1)
Sent emails. (1)
It's **complicated**. (1)

Our products are **beautifully made**. (2)
They're **ergonomically designed**. (2)
And our production methods are **technically** very **advanced**. (2)

Adverb + Partizip Perfekt

Das Partizip Perfekt (3. Form) dient meistens der Bildung des *present perfect*, aber es kann auch allein als Adjektiv verwendet werden (1), z. B. ‚zerbrochen', ‚versandte', ‚kompliziert'.

Eine andere geeignete Möglichkeit, Produkte und Servicemerkmale zu beschreiben, ist die Verwendung eines Partizip Perfekt als Adjektiv, dem ein Adverb vorausgeht (2).

Comparing people and things

A is **bigger**. (1)
B is **more expensive**. (1)
C is **the biggest** and **the most expensive**. (1)
B is**n't as big as** A. (2)
A is**n't as expensive as** B. (2)
A is **less expensive than** B. (3)
A is **the least expensive** of all the products**.** (3)

Vergleiche anstellen

In Unit 4 wurde dargestellt, wie Personen und Dinge mit den Steigerungsformen des Adjektivs verglichen werden können (1). Vergleiche lassen sich auch anstellen mit *not as ... as* und *less than/the least.* Man verwendet *not as ... as* (nicht so ... wie) mit kurzen und längeren Adjektiven (2). *Less* und *the least* werden mit längeren Adjektiven verwendet, deren Steigerungsformen mit *more* und *the most* gebildet werden (3).

The present perfect + *just*

I've just read your letter.
Marianne **has just phoned**.
Mr Rogers isn't in his office, I'm afraid – oh, wait a moment, he**'s just come** in.

Present Perfect + just

Um etwas zu beschreiben, das sich ‚gerade eben erst' ereignet hat, verwendet man das *present perfect* mit *just*. *Just* steht zwischen einer Form von *to have* und dem Partizip Perfekt.

Verbs and nouns

Did you **reply** to their letter? (verb)
Did you send a **reply**? (noun)

I'll **confirm** your order. (verb)
I'll send you a **confirmation**. (noun)

Substantivierte Verben

Viele englische Verben lassen sich zu Substantiven machen, indem man sie auf unterschiedliche Weise verändert – oder manchmal auch nicht verändert. Leider gibt es keine eindeutigen Regeln für diese Veränderungen. Hier einige Beispiele:

verb	noun	verb	noun
to confirm	confirmation	to reimburse	reimbursement
to enquire	enquiry	to receive	receipt
to deliver	delivery	to complain	complaint
to pay	payment	to insure	insurance
to advertise	advertisement	to invoice	invoice
to ship	shipment	to offer	offer
to invest	investment	to cost	cost

Grammar

1 **Rewrite these sentences as in the example. Use an adjective + infinitive.**

1 Manufacturing mobile phones is expensive. *Mobile phones are expensive to manufacture.*
2 Understanding his English is easy. *His English ...*
3 Finding the location for the factory was easy. *The ...*
4 Transporting the goods is difficult.
5 Organizing the meeting was complicated.

2 **Match the adverbs to the adjectives. (More than one answer is sometimes possible.)**

1 beautifully	advanced
2 perfectly	designed
3 technically	safe
4 ergonomically	balanced
5 completely	made

- **Now complete this text with phrases from above.**

a This new mouse is .... See how well it fits your hand.
b Our factory is .... We use the latest production technology.
c This sports equipment is .... Nothing bad can happen.
d Can you feel how this knife is .... ? You won't get tired when you use it.
e What a nice tie you're wearing! It's ....

3 **Find the words and expressions which have the opposite meaning.**

1 harder	a not as expensive
2 the hardest	b the most difficult
3 easier	c the most expensive
4 the easiest	d not as difficult
5 not as easy	e the least difficult
6 the cheapest	f less difficult
7 not as cheap	g more difficult

4 **Complete the sentences with *just* and the present perfect.**

1 *I've just read* (read) your letter and I have a couple of questions.
2 They .... (see) our website on the Internet.
3 She .... (phone) him to ask about the order.
4 We .... (fax) a copy to you.
5 I .... (come) into the office – I haven't had time.
6 My boss .... (broke) my favourite pen!

- **Now match the sentences above to questions (a–f).**

a Can you send us the contract? ☐
b How did they find out about us? ☐
c What can I do for you? 1
d Have you read your emails yet? ☐
e Why are you so angry? ☐
f Has she spoken to Bob yet? ☐

5 **Complete the table.**

	verb	noun
1	advertise	*advertisement*
2	complain	
3	deliver	
4	enquire	
5	insure	
6	invest	
7	invoice	
8	reimburse	

- **Now complete the sentences with the correct form of words from the table.**

a Have they paid our .... yet? We sent it four weeks ago.
b I'm afraid the .... will arrive a day late. The truck broke down in France.
c How much does it cost to .... in your magazine?
d I'm sorry, but I have to .... about your customer service.
e We made a large .... in IT last year, so we can't spend so much this year.
f Do we have .... for fire damage?
g Can you .... me for the expenses from my business trip?
h I'm writing to .... about your range of office furniture.

Words and phrases

6 **Make questions you could hear at a trade fair. Start at the numbered word, then move one square at a time (left, right, up or down).**

①Do	you	these?	with	do	guarantee	of	use?
these?	have	a	give	you	②What	kind	to
are	brochures?	minute?	③Where	are	kind	of	easy
much	any	based?	actually	you	④What	quantities	they
⑤How	have	mind?	in	have	you	did	⑥Are
all?	you	you	using	any	have	any	plans
at	⑦Do	⑧Are	our	of	you	⑨Do	for
help	I	⑩Can	products	at	the	moment?	lunch?

1 Do *you have a minute*?
2 What ....?
3 Where ....?
4 What ....?
5 How ....?
6 Are ....?
7 Do ....?
8 Are ....?
9 Do ....?
10 Can ....?

7 **Rearrange the words to make telephone and email sentences.**

1 speak Could Jane please I to?
2 your I'm about delivery call the returning
3 again Don't me have hesitate any you problems to ring if
4 helps hope I this
5 your for Thanks phone our call meeting very much about
6 answers Here my are your queries to
7 you let questions if any further Please me know have
8 forward I soon to hearing you look from

8 Complete the text with the words in the box.

expensive
materials
investment
guarantee
lifetime
instructions
durable

KarryRite suitcases are made from the best available ....[1]. They are extremely ....[2] and will last a ....[3]. KarryRite suitcases are a little more ....[4] than other ordinary suitcases, but they are an excellent ....[5] for the future. They come with full ....[6] and a lifetime ....[7].

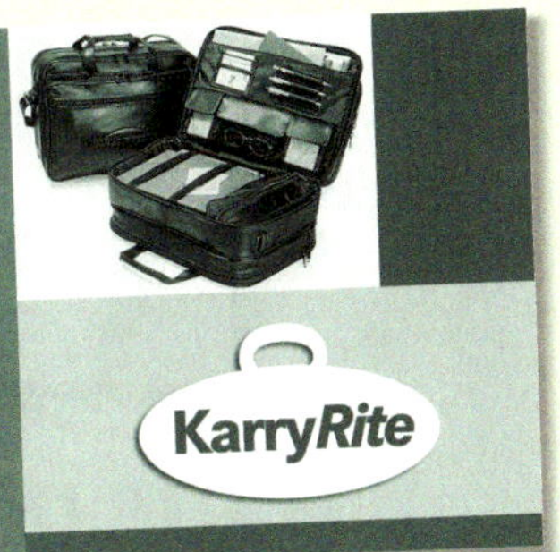

Translating

9 Translate into English.

1 Meine Präsentation war absolut furchtbar. Ich fühlte mich total blöd!

2 Mein Büro ist nicht so groß wie mein altes Büro, aber es ist viel schöner.

3 Diese Software ist von den dreien am wenigsten kompliziert.

4 Wir haben auf dieser Messe immer einen Stand.

5 Wann ist Ihre Verabredung mit Frau Fischer?

6 Alle unsere Produkte haben fünf Jahre Garantie.

7 Was für ein Handy haben Sie? – Weiß ich nicht mehr, ich habe es gerade gekauft!

TYPICAL MISTAKES

1 The software is technically advanced.
NOT The software is *technical* advanced.

2 This hotel isn't as nice as the other hotel.
NOT This hotel isn't *so* nice *like* the other hotel.

3 This car is the least expensive of the three.
NOT This car is the *less* expensive of the three.

4 We were at a trade fair last week.
NOT We were *on* a trade fair last week.

5 I've got an appointment with Mr Jones at 10 am.
NOT I've got a *date* with Mr Jones at 10 am. (= *Rendezvous*)

6 It comes with a two-year guarantee.
NOT It comes with a two-*years* guarantee.

7 What kind of a knife is that?
NOT What *for* a knife is that?

Small talk in the UK and USA

CULTURE SPOT

Small talk is extremely important when doing business with British or American people. British and American business people normally expect a period of small talk before talking about business. This is also true on the telephone if you are speaking to someone you know. Listen for signals that your business partner wants to change from small talk to doing business; these signals can be words like 'OK', 'so', 'well', or 'right'.

Safe topics for small talk in both the UK and USA include the weather, business in general, entertainment (for example books and films), travel and sports. Family and children are also acceptable topics when you know a person better. Don't talk about topics such as health and personal matters; normally nobody expects a real answer to the question 'How are you?' Politics is a relatively safe topic in the UK, but not in the USA. British people often use jokes and sarcasm when making small talk, and this sometimes seems aggressive to people from other countries – don't take it personally!

UNIT

10 MADE IN GERMANY

In this unit you ...

describe to a visitor some typical processes in your company:
Our products are made by skilled workers.
explain a menu to a visitor:
It's a kind of roast pork. It's a local speciality.
make friendly conversation and talk about topics of general interest:
That's interesting. How long have you lived there? What makes a good manager? Well, ...

Business file
Thanks for everything

A A visitor

WARM UP **Why do business people sometimes visit their business partner's company? What sort of things happen during a typical visit?**

A1  2/17 **Here are some typical questions for a visitor. Listen and find the missing words.**

At the trade fair in Manchester, Andrea invited Paul Hornby to Solingen and today, two weeks later, he has just arrived at the Amsel works. Andrea is welcoming him and introducing Paul to her colleagues.

1. How was .... ?
2. Did you .... OK?
3. Can I offer you a .... ?
4. Is this your .... here?
5. How long .... ?

- **How does Paul answer the questions?**

A2 **Look at the two sentences below.**

*Amsel **makes** knives.*
*Amsel knives **are made** in Germany.*

The second sentence is a 'passive' sentence. Look at the Amsel brochure on page 115 and find eleven examples of the passive.

The passive FOCUS

Amsel knives	**are** **were** **have been** **will be** **can be**	**made/ used**	**by ...**

Das deutsche ‚von' heißt in englischen Passivsätzen by:
The company was founded **by** Otto Weber.

AMSEL KNIFE MAKERS TO THE WORLD.

AMSEL is one of the world's leading manufacturers of precision forged knives. All our products are made in Solingen, Germany's 'knife capital', but they are used all around the world by professional chefs and enthusiastic amateurs. The AMSEL logo is recognized worldwide as a guarantee of excellence.

A PROUD TRADITION

AMSEL knives have been made in Solingen for over two hundred years and we are proud of our long tradition. The company was founded in 1796 by Otto Weber and the first factory on our current site was opened 50 years later. AMSEL has remained a family concern right up to the present day and the company is still run by members of the Weber family.

TRADITIONAL CRAFTSMANSHIP MEETS 21ST CENTURY TECHNOLOGY

We are proud of our tradition but we are also famous for our innovation. An AMSEL knife can pass through 40 or more different processes before it is ready to leave the factory. Every step in the production process is performed by skilled workers but in today's hi-tech world they are helped by the latest technology, from computer-guided equipment to powerful robots. At AMSEL, traditional craftsmanship meets 21st century technology. The result is a knife that can be used for a lifetime and that will remain as good as the day when it was bought.

AMSEL

Precision forged knives.
Since 1796

AMSEL PRECISION THROUGH TRADITION AND INNOVATION

A3

What's the English for ... ?

1 *überall auf der Welt*
2 *das Logo wird (an)erkannt (als)*
3 *stolz (auf)*
4 *das Unternehmen wurde gegründet*
5 *bis auf den heutigen Tag*
6 *Innovation*
7 *Stufe (des Produktionsprozesses)*
8 *computergesteuerte Geräte*

Asking questions with the passive

FOCUS

Are all the knives **made** in Solingen?
– Yes, they are.

Where	are	the knives	used?
Who	are	they	used by?
When	was	the company	founded?

A4

Paul asks a lot of questions during his visit. Look at the brochure and give the answers.

1 Are all the knives made here in Solingen?

2 Where are the knives used?

3 Who are they used by?

4 How long have they been made here?

- **Now you. Work with a partner. Take it in turns to make and answer questions about the information in the brochure.**

A5

These people work in a typical manufacturing company. Match the people and their departments.

Purchasing Marketing Sales Accounts Distribution
Research and Development (R&D) Customer Support Quality Control

1 We buy raw materials and equipment.
2 We develop and test new products.
3 We sell the products.
4 We do market research and organize advertising campaigns.
5 We deal with customers' problems.
6 We check the products before they leave the factory.
7 We oversee the company's finances and write an annual report.
8 We transport the products to retailers and wholesalers.

- **One very important department isn't here – it *makes* the products. What's it called?**

A6

Work with a partner. Look at the departments in A5 and write a short description about how products are made. Begin like this:

First, raw materials (for the products) are bought by the Purchasing Department ... Next, they're made by the ... After that ... Finally ...

- **Can you describe how a *new* product is developed and sold?**

A7

Work in a small group.

One of you is a visitor to your company (or a company that you know).

1 Welcome your visitor and introduce colleagues.
2 Give a short presentation about the company and its products or services.

B In a restaurant

WARM UP

What region of your country do you live in? What do other people normally say about your region – its people, food and drink, scenery and lifestyle?

B1

2/18

Listen and answer the questions.

It's evening, and Paul, Andrea, Gerd Haase and Karin Josef are in a traditional *Gaststätte* in the old part of Düsseldorf.

Andrea Well, Paul. Here's to a long and happy partnership! Cheers!

Paul Cheers! How do you say that in German? 'Cheers', I mean.

Andrea We say 'Prost!'

All Prost!

Gerd So, what do you think of the *Altbier*?

Paul I'm not sure yet! It's a bit, well, unusual.

Gerd Have another. It'll get better.

Paul So is this, you know, a typical German pub?

Andrea Well, put it this way, Paul: it's a typical *traditional* Düsseldorf pub. It's the sort of place that visitors often like.

Paul Ah, I see. Well, I find it very interesting so thanks for suggesting it.

Gerd I'm glad you like it. I've never been to England, but I always imagine that English pubs are a bit like this.

Paul Hmm, yes, maybe in some ways. But we don't have waiters in our pubs, of course.

Gerd Really?

Paul Yes, you have to go to the bar yourself and buy your drinks.

Gerd I'll remember that if I'm ever in England.

Andrea Speaking of waiters, do we know what we want to order? They serve traditional food here, Paul, but if you don't like it, they have other things on the menu, too.

Paul No, I'd like to try something new. But you'll have to help me with the menu!

1 How do you think the meeting in the afternoon went? Why do you say that?
2 What impression do you get of Paul Hornby? Is he a friendly, open-minded person or a bit conservative? Why do you say that?
3 In what important way is an English pub different from a German one?

B2

What's the English for ... ?

1 *Auf eine gute Zusammenarbeit*
2 *Was halten Sie von (dem Bier)?*
3 *Sagen wir mal so ...*
4 *Ich stelle mir immer vor, (dass)*
5 *in gewisser Hinsicht*
6 *Ich werde daran denken, wenn ich in England bin*

B3 Can you help Paul?

Use phrases from the **FOCUS** box (below) and your dictionary, if necessary, to help explain the menu to Paul.

SPEZIALITÄTEN

Rinderbrühe mit Gemüse und Fleischeinlage

Hausgemachte Gulaschsuppe
Sauerbraten ‚Rheinische Art' mit Kartoffelklößen und Apfelmus

Herzhafte Rinderroulade mit Erbsen-Möhren und Salzkartoffeln

Gekochtes Kasseler mit Kartoffelpüree und Sauerkraut

Geräucherte Fischspezialitäten mit Dill- und Meerettichsauce

Brat-, Bauern- oder Fleischwurst mit hausgemachtem Kartoffelsalat

Tatar vom Rind und Schweinemett, angemacht mit Zwiebeln, Brot und Butter

Roher und gekochter Schinken mit Brot und Butter

KLASSIKER

‚Himmel und Erde':
Kartoffelpüree und Apfelkompott mit gebratener Blutwurst

Schweinehaxe, kross gebraten, mit Krautsalat und Treberbrötchen

Explaining a menu

FOCUS

These are cold dishes/hot dishes/starters/main courses/desserts/salads/soups/snacks.

It's a sort of/kind of … beef/pork/lamb/veal/chicken/duck/turkey/liver/fish/sausage/vegetable.

It's made from …/it's cooked in (wine)/it comes with a sauce/it's covered in syrup.

It's fried/roasted/boiled/pickled/baked (in an oven)/smoked.

It's spicy/salty/sweet/creamy/delicious.

It's a local speciality/It's a speciality of the restaurant/It's cooked 'house style'.

B4 Making 'small talk' – talking about family, jobs, where people live, interests and hobbies, etc. – is important in business.

1 First, make a list of questions. (You can look back over the course book for ideas.)
2 Then work with a partner and ask and answer the questions. Like this:

Ask a question.
(Where do you live?)

Answer the question.
(I live in Düsseldorf, in Western Germany.)

Make a comment and ask another question.
(Oh, that's interesting. How long have you lived there?)

Answer the question and give new information. Then ask a (related) question.
(Well, I've lived there for five years now but I was born in Dresden. What about you? Where do you live?)

The verb *to get*

FOCUS ON WORDS

to get *(bekommen)*
We **got** a letter from A&C yesterday.

to get *(werden)*
It will **get** better.
I'm **getting** hungry.
He **got** very angry.

to get to know *(näher kennen lernen)*
He **got to know** his new colleagues.

Phrasal verbs with *get*

get across	*verständlich machen*
get down to	*in Angriff nehmen, kommen zu*
get on (well) with	*sich gut verstehen mit*
get out of	*um etwas herumkommen*
get over	*sich erholen von*
get up	*aufstehen*

B5 **Complete the sentences. Then make three more sentences with *get*.**

1 OK. Let's get .... business!
2 In Düsseldorf, Paul got .... the people from Amsel.
3 He got .... very well .... them. They had a good working relationship.
4 I still feel terrible. I haven't got .... my cold yet.
5 I don't want to go to the meeting but I can't get .... it now.
6 Let's eat. I'm .... hungry!
7 Wonderful presentation, Ann! You really got your ideas ....
8 We .... ten email enquiries yesterday.

B6 **Work in your group again.**

Choose one of the topics below (or think of your own) and prepare a short talk (two to three minutes). Then give your talk to the people in your group.

Why learn English?

Local specialities – where I live

What makes a good manager?

Computers – do you love them or hate them?

BUSINESS FILE

In this business file you ...
- write a letter after a company visit.
- plan a visit schedule for a foreign visitor.

Thanks for everything

1 2/19 **Listen. Which situations do you hear?**

Werner Held is a German businessman who is currently on a week-long business trip in the UK. His company manufactures power cables and he's finalizing an important contract with Southern Power, a British electricity supply company.
Listen to the five conversations and say where they take place.
Write the situations (a–h) in the table.

a He's saying goodbye to his British colleagues.
b He's just arrived in Britain and is at an airport.
c He's having a meal with his British colleagues.
d The British company is entertaining Werner with a day at the races.
e One of the British colleagues is introducing Werner to others.
f Werner is in a meeting.
g He's having a one-to-one discussion with a British colleague.
h He's giving a presentation.

	situation
Conversation 1	
Conversation 2	
Conversation 3	
Conversation 4	
Conversation 5	

• **In which conversations did you hear these phrases?**

I like your optimism, Werner.

Our tests have shown that this increases the life of the cable.

The car's just outside, sir.

Good. I'm glad you like it.

How do I write an email (or a letter) after a meeting?

INFO

About the meeting

I'm glad that/I'm pleased that/I'm delighted that we were able to agree ...
I'm enclosing/I'm attaching my notes of the meeting.
Please also find enclosed/I'm also attaching the figures/details/extra information that you asked for/that I promised.
I'm (very) pleased that you are satisfied with our products/with our service.
I look forward to our next meeting on (date)/to hearing from you shortly/to seeing you again (soon).

Saying thank you

On a (more) personal note I'd like to say thank you (very much indeed) for your hospitality/for your kindness while I was visiting you.
I enjoyed/I really appreciated the (delicious) meals/the visit to the theatre/the race course.
It was a great pleasure meeting your colleagues/meeting everyone/getting to know everyone.
Please thank (name) for all her/his help.
Please say 'hello' to (name) for me.
Thanks again for everything.
I hope very much that you'll be able to visit us here one day/that I'll be able to repay your kindness soon.

2 **Write a letter.**

After his visit to Southern Power, Werner wrote a letter to Bernard ('Bernie') Wright, the Contracts Manager and Werner's main contact at the company. Look back at the pictures and conversations on page 120 and the phrases in the box above and write his letter. Invent other names and details yourself. Then compare your letter with a partner's.

FOR TIPS ON WRITING LETTERS → PAGE 142

3 **Work in a small group (2–4 people).**

Next month you are expecting a visit from a British or American business partner. He or she will be with you in your company for five days. You will need four full days for meetings, but one day – and the evenings – will be free.

1 In your group, brainstorm a list of things to do socially with your visitor. (It's his or her first visit to your country.)
2 Now write a 'Visit Schedule' for the five days.
3 Tell the class about your plans.
On the first day we're going to ...

Grammar summary

The passive

USE

English **is spoken** in many countries around the world.
The company **was founded** in 1897.
Our products **are used by** people worldwide.

Das Passiv

VERWENDUNG

Das Passiv wird verwendet, wenn man auf eher unpersönliche Art und Weise über Fakten und Daten berichten möchte.

‚Von/Durch' wird in Passivsätzen durch das Wort *by* ausgedrückt.

FORM

simple present	it **is**	**made**
simple past	it **was**	
present perfect	it **has been**	
will future	it **will be**	

Our products **can be used** by everyone. (1)
The invoice **must be paid** in 30 days. (1)

Where **are** they **manufactured**? (2)
When **was** the company **founded**? (2)
How long **have** they **been made** here? (2)
When **will** the new factory **be opened**? (2)

Who **are** your products **used by**? (3)
Who **was** the company **founded by**? (3)

FORM

Das Passiv wird dem Verb *to be* und dem Partizip Perfekt gebildet. Die verschiedenen Zeitformen des Passivs werden gebildet, indem die Zeitform von *to be* entsprechend verändert wird.

Nach *can* und *must* wird der Infinitiv des Passivs verwendet (1).

Fragen werden im Passiv mit den normalen Frageformen von *to be* gebildet (2). Das Wort *by* steht normalerweise am Ende einer Frage (3).

Verb forms in English

Verbformen im Englischen

Zum Schluss ein Überblick über die wichtigsten Verbformen im Englischen, die Ihnen im Laufe des Kurses begegnet sind. Bitte beachten Sie: Die deutschen Übersetzungen sind lediglich Entsprechungen!

Tense	Example	German
simple present	I **work** for a German company. The company **manufactures** furniture.	*Ich arbeite bei einer deutschen Firma.* *Die Firma stellt Möbel her.*
present continuous	I'**m writing** an email at the moment. I'**m meeting** Mr Smith tomorrow morning at 9.00.	*Ich schreibe gerade eine E-Mail.* *Ich treffe Herrn Smith morgen früh um 9 Uhr.*
past continuous	I **was working** there when the stock market crashed.	*Ich arbeitete dort, als die Börse zusammenbrach.*
simple past	I **worked** in the USA five years ago.	*Ich arbeitete vor fünf Jahren in den USA.*
present perfect	**Have** you ever **been** to London? I'**ve lived** in Austria for two years.	*Waren Sie schon mal in London?* *Ich lebe seit zwei Jahren in Österreich.*
will future	If all goes well, our new product **will be** in the shops next month. The package? We'**ll send** it tomorrow.	*Wenn alles gut geht, wird unser neues Produkt nächsten Monat im Handel sein.* *Das Paket? Wir schicken es morgen.*
going to future	My company **is going to open** a new branch in Cologne.	*Meine Firma hat vor, eine neue Filiale in Köln zu eröffnen.*

Grammar

1 Which sentences are active and which are passive? Write A or P.

1 Amsel makes knives. ☐
2 The knives are made in their factory in Solingen. ☐
3 They're sold all over the world. ☐
4 People in England speak English. ☐
5 But English is also spoken by over six billion other people worldwide. ☐
6 The company was founded 20 years ago. ☐
7 Your package will be delivered tomorrow. ☐
8 I've finished the report. ☐
9 The hotel has been booked. ☐
10 You can find our products in all good shops. ☐

2 Active or passive? Choose the correct form.

1 Our sports products ~~*manufacture*~~*/are manufactured* in Taiwan.
2 They *use/are used* by professional tennis players.
3 Millions of people *use/are used* the Internet.
4 Our office *visited/was visited* yesterday by an important client.
5 Last week I *visited/was visited* one of our customers in Austria.
6 We *have developed/have been developed* this new model for the American market.
7 Our products *can find/can be found* in all good shops.

3 Make questions about the underlined words. Use the passive.

1 The company was founded in 1826. *When was the company founded?*
2 The first shop was opened in Dortmund. *Where …*
3 The telephone was invented in 1876.
4 These cars are manufactured in Detroit.
5 The personnel department is managed by Rebecca Langley.
6 New products are developed by the R&D department.

4 Complete the sentences using the correct tense of the verbs in brackets.

1 I ……… (not/wear) a tie today – it ……… (be) 'dress down Friday'.
2 ……… they ……… (deliver) the package yet? It ……… (not/arrive) yesterday.
– Yes, it ……… (come) this morning.
3 Normally she ……… (work) in the Purchasing Department, but today she ……… (work) in Marketing.
4 What ……… you ……… (do) tomorrow?
– I ……… (fly) to Milan. I ……… (not/be) back until Friday.
5 How long ……… you ……… (live) here?
– For five years. Before that we ……… (live) in Cologne.
6 Our company ……… (open) a new sales office next month. It ……… (be) in Warsaw.
7 My boss ……… (not/work) when I ……… (arrive) at work yesterday. He ……… (read) the newspaper!

Words and phrases

5 Can you identify the different departments?

1 The CGPURNHASI department buys raw materials and equipment.
2 The KEINRMATG department does market research and organizes advertising campaigns.
3 The ALSSE department sells the products.
4 The SOMSTTRECUOURPP department deals with customers' problems.
5 The CNTASOUC department oversees the company's finances.
6 The UACOLIYLNTQOTR department checks the products before they leave the factory.
7 The ODTIRNPUOC department makes the products.

6 Complete this food crossword with the English translations.

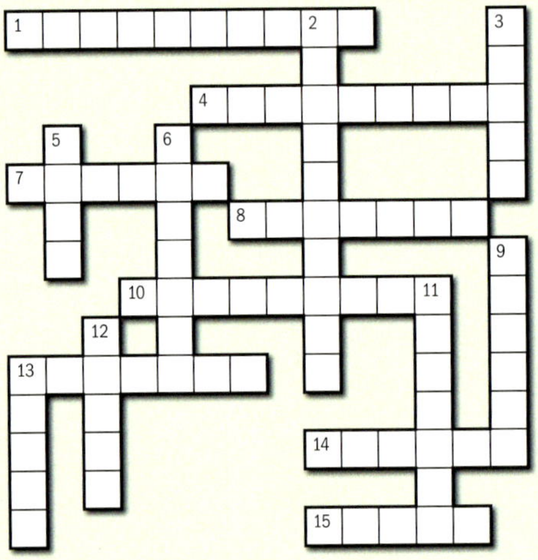

Across

1 Hauptgang
4 Gemüse
7 gekocht (im Wasser)
8 geröstet
10 lecker, köstlich
13 Vorspeise
14 sahnig
15 gebraten

Down

2 Spezialität
3 süß
5 Schweinefleisch
6 Nachtisch
9 Pute
11 Würstchen, Wurst
12 Soße
13 würzig

7 Rearrange the words to make 'small talk' questions. In each sentence there is one word that you don't need.

1 journey was how who your?
2 find OK do you did us?
3 offer can offering you drink I a?
4 visit your are first here is this?
5 long are how staying stay you?
6 think the what from do food you of?
7 German this eat is dish typical a?
8 live where you who do?

- **Now match these answers to the questions above.**

a In London. But I want to move to Brighton.
b A coffee would be nice, thanks.
c It was OK, thanks.
d Yes, no problem. Your map was very clear.
e More or less. It's a speciality of this region.
f Delicious!
g Actually no. I was here once in 1997.
h I'm going to be here until Friday.

8 Choose the correct word.

1 I'm feeling a bit tired – I got *up/down/on* at 5 this morning for the early flight.
2 Are we all here? Let's get *down/across/out* to business.
3 I don't get *on/down/up* with my colleagues – in fact, I hate them!
4 I had a cold last week, and I still haven't got *across/over/out* it.
5 I said I would do the presentation in English, and now I can't get *down/over/out* of it.
6 I think I got my ideas *across/down/up* well in the meeting.

Translating

9 Translate into English.

1 Die Produkte werden hier in dieser Fabrik von Facharbeitern hergestellt.
2 Unsere Firma wurde vor über 200 Jahren gegründet.
3 Wo arbeitet Robert?
– In der Personalabteilung, denke ich.
4 Die Nachspeisen hier sind sehr gut.
5 Ich liebe diese Art von Musik.
6 Ich besuche oft dieses Restaurant. Mir gefällt es sehr.
7 Es tut mir Leid, aber ich muss jetzt gehen. Morgen muss ich sehr früh aufstehen.

TYPICAL MISTAKES

1 Spanish is spoken in many countries.
NOT Spanish is *spoke* in many countries.
2 Acme Promotions was founded in 1993.
NOT Acme Promotions *is* founded in 1993.
3 Our products are used by people in the car industry.
NOT Our products are used *from* people in the car industry.
4 Would you like a dessert?
NOT Would you like a *desert*? (dessert = *Nachtisch*, desert = *Wüste*!)
5 Minestrone is a kind of soup.
NOT Minestrone is *an art from* soup. (kind = *Art*, art = *Kunst*)
6 Do you like this beer? Yes, very much.
NOT Do you like this beer? Yes, *very*.
7 I get up at 6 every morning.
NOT I *stand* up at 6 every morning.
8 She works in the personnel department.
NOT She works in the *personal* department. (= *persönlich*)

Wining and dining in the UK and USA

CULTURE SPOT

Going to the pub is an important part of social life in the UK. There is not normally table service in pubs. Instead, one person from your group goes to the bar and orders a round of drinks for everyone in the group. Ask people what they want to drink by saying 'It's my round – what will you have?'

Table service is common in American bars or you can sit at the bar. In either case, it's normal to leave a tip of between 15% to 20% of the total bill. Remember, in the USA, staff in cafés and restaurants are paid very little and rely on tips to earn a decent wage.

In the UK people don't normally tip in pubs, but they occasionally give the bar staff money to buy themselves a drink later. Say 'have one yourself' when you order if you want to do this. British people normally tip around 10% in restaurants and just leave the money on the table at the end of the meal.

Partner files

FILE 01

Unit 1, Business file 2

PARTNER A

FILE 02

Unit 2, Business file 2

PARTNER B

1 You are the telephone receptionist at ABC Ltd. Answer your partner's calls. Here's a list of people in your company and notes on whether they're available or not.
Mr Black is busy and doesn't want to take calls (except from Mr/Ms White).
Ms Brown is at her desk.
Mr Redman is on a business trip. Transfer calls to Ms Brown.
Mrs Plum is in a meeting until 3 pm.

2 Now make these calls to your partner. He/She is the telephone receptionist at XYZ Ltd.
a You're Mr/Ms Adams. You'd like to speak to Ms Baker.
b You're Mr/Ms Fairweather. You'd like to speak to Mr Goodwin.
c You're Mr/Ms Harris. You'd like to speak to Mr Ingram.
d You're Mr/Ms Davis. You'd like to speak to Mrs Edwards.
e You're Mr/Ms Botto. You'd like to speak to Ms Baker.

FILE 03

Unit 3, Business file 3

PARTNER B

PC Life

PC Life sells computers for home and business use. You have an excellent range of three workstation computers for the office: the D-100, the D-200 and the D-300Pro.

Your office workstation computers

D-100. Your basic model. It has a 2.67GHz processor and a 2GB memory. Full guarantee for 2 years.	D-200. Your middle-of-the-range model. Very popular! It has a 3GHz processor and 4GB of memory. Full guarantee for 3 years.	D-300 Pro. Your top-of-the-range model. It has a memory of up to 8GB and a 2.8GHz processor. Many extra features. Full guarantee for 3 years.
PRICE: €2,000	PRICE: €3,000	PRICE: €3,800

Special offers?
You have a special offer this week: 20% off all notebook (laptop) PCs.

Discounts?
You can give discounts of up to 10% on orders over €10,000.

Delivery?
You offer free, same-day delivery.

FILE 04

Unit 4, Business file 3

PARTNER A

Write the following email and send it to Partner B.

You work for a company in your country that designs and prints brochures. At the moment you are producing a German-language sales catalogue for your partner's company, Amco.com, an American company which exports to your country. Write an email to your partner in the USA. Attach a copy of the first page of the new brochure as a pdf file and ask if he/she is happy with it. Ask for the company's price list so that you can now print it in the brochure. Your partner is a regular contact so make your email personal and friendly.

Now reply to Partner B's email.

You work in the Canadian office of an international company, Interco.com, which is based in your country. Your partner works in the personnel department at head office.

FILE 05

Unit 5, B5

Company profiles

COMPANY 1
Your company is based in your country. It employs 20 people and makes children's toys.

COMPANY 2
Your company is based in your country and employs 30 people. You import flowers from Holland and distribute them to retailers (flower shops).

COMPANY 3
Your company is you and two business partners. You make and sell pottery.

Tips for designing a website

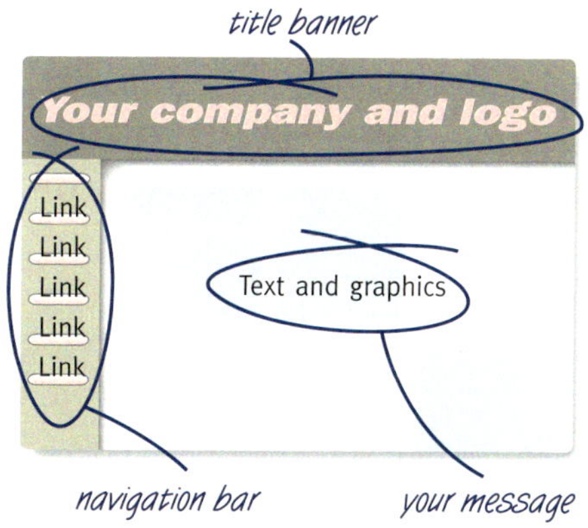

1 Here is a very simple home page for a small business website.

2 There are three basic types of sites:
- Very simple: just information about your company, products, etc.
- More complicated: company and product information + an online catalogue
- Most complicated: all the above + visitors can buy online (an e-commerce site)

3 Typical links are
- home
- about us/company/our company
- products/services
- dealers
- site map
- contact/contact us

4 Text
Remember that people don't read web pages as they read a book or a newspaper. They want short pieces of information. And do you want your website in more than one language?

5 Graphics
Websites often show pictures of the company's offices, or give an idea of the company 'at work'. You can also show pictures of your latest products (perhaps with a link): this is very useful for advertising them.

FILE 06

Unit 1, Business file 2

PARTNER B

FILE 07

Unit 5, Business file 3

The trade fair is a Leisure Show. All the companies below are based in your country (they can be as big or small as you like). Choose one of the companies and fill in the 'Company Form'. Decide your prices and terms with your partner.

Albatross engineering

You build and sell small motor boats for water sport enthusiasts. You have a range of boats from relatively cheap to one luxury model.

Pro-Tennis

You manufacture and sell tennis equipment: racquets, balls, clothing, tennis shoes. Your products are top-of-the-range and many professionals buy them.

COMPANY FORM

Company name

Products

Prices by specific product

Commercial Trading Terms (for trade customers)

- Delivery costs
- Terms of payment
- Delivery times
- Discounts

Fitness unlimited

You manufacture and sell fitness equipment (home gyms, exercise cycles, etc.).

AVC electronics

You make and sell consumer electronic equipment. At the trade fair you're showing your latest Home Movie Theatre – a complete package of widescreen TV, DVD player and sound system.

Galaxy guides

You write and sell travel guides, illustrated books in a country by country series. You began only two years ago but already your guides are in every good bookshop.

FILE 08

Unit 6, Business file 3

PARTNER A

You represent the marketing department on the project team.

Your diary

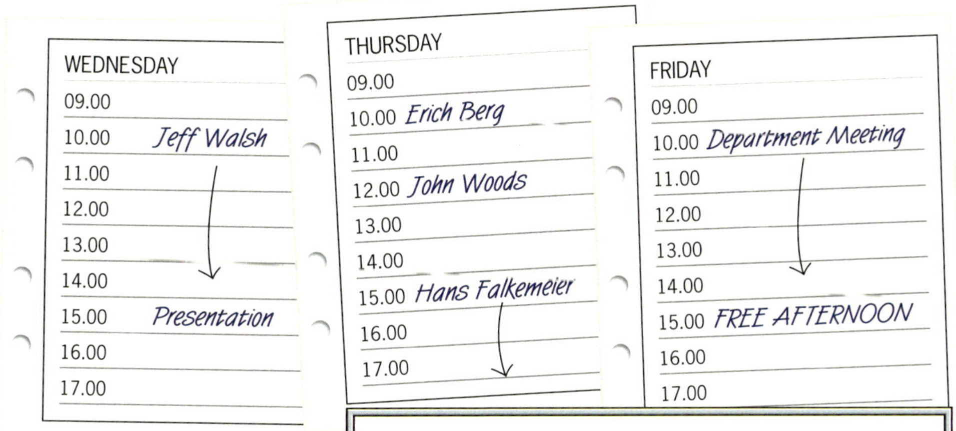

You have this email from one of the British colleagues, the architect James Gold.

Hi
Thanks for your phone call about the meeting next week. I'm free at the following times:
- Wednesday: 14.00-18.00
- Thursday: 09.00-13.00
- Friday: all day.
Good luck!
Very best wishes
James

FILE 09

Unit 8, B5

PARTNER A

Situation 1

You are the hotel receptionist.
It's evening and a guest (your partner) phones you from her/his room.
You are fully booked this evening – there aren't any free rooms.
You have the following available at the desk: aspirin, a hair dryer, extra toothbrushes and ear plugs (*Ohrenstöpsel*).

Situation 2

You are the guest.
You left home yesterday evening and drove overnight to the hotel. You arrived five minutes ago. It's 10 o'clock in the morning: you're tired, hungry and thirsty! You are standing at the reception desk of the hotel with a very large suitcase.

Situation 3

You are the hotel receptionist.
Catastrophe! Your hotel computer crashed half an hour ago and you've lost all the information about guests, bills, bookings, etc. A guest comes to the reception desk ...

FILE 10

Unit 7, B5

PARTNER B

You are Derek. You and Kathy both work for BlueSky. First answer Kathy's questions. Then interview 'Kathy' and complete the form. Where does Kathy work? What's her job? How long has she been with the company? And what are her ideas and plans for the future?

Name	Derek Carter
Job	Receptionist
Place of work	BlueSky's London office
How long with company?	6 months
Good thing(s) about job?	First job, so interesting to be in an office; meet a lot of people
Bad thing(s)?	No responsibility; job the same every day; not challenging
Ideas about future?	To study at college and to get a qualification (perhaps in personnel work?)
Plans?	Get information about colleges and courses; visit local colleges on open days

Name	Kathy Fischer
Job	
Place of work	
How long with company?	
Good thing(s) about job?	
Bad thing(s)?	
Ideas about future?	
Plans?	

FILE 11

Unit 7, B6

THE HOLLAND PERSONALITY TEST

According to the American psychologist John Holland, most people are one of six personality types: Realistic, Investigative, Artistic, Social, Enterprising or Conventional. For each personality type there is also a 'work environment' with the same categories. The list of jobs in the test includes typical jobs from the six environments (five for each, 30 in all). The jobs are:

- **Realistic**: bus driver, farmer, mechanic, pilot, police officer
- **Investigative**: chemist, electrical technician, pharmacist, surveyor, vet
- **Artistic**: actor, book editor, clothes designer, graphic artist, musician
- **Social**: counsellor, librarian, nurse, social worker, teacher
- **Enterprising**: auctioneer, estate agent, lawyer, sales person, travel agent
- **Conventional**: bank clerk, bookkeeper, postman/postwoman, secretary, typist

How to score your personality test:

Look at the jobs you ticked and give yourself 1 point for each. Put the points in the table below: You're perhaps in more than one personality type – but where do you have *the most* points? Do you agree with the result of the test?

EXAMPLE:

Realistic	Investigative	Artistic	Social	Enterprising	Conventional
1 1 1 1	1 1 1		1	1 1 1	

FILE 12

Unit 6, Business file 3

PARTNER B

You represent the finance department on the project team.

Your diary

You have this email from one of the British colleagues, the project manager Vanessa Hutchinson.

> Hello
> Thanks for your email about the meeting next week. I could make the following:
> Thursday: all day
> Friday: 14.00-18.00
> I'm afraid Wednesday isn't possible at all.
> Kind regards
> Vanessa

FILE 13

Unit 8, B5

PARTNER B

Situation 1

You are the guest.
It's your first evening in the hotel. You are staying for four nights from today. Your room is directly above the hotel bar and is very noisy. Phone the reception desk and ask for a different room. You won't be able to sleep tonight!

Situation 2

You are the hotel receptionist.
It's 10 o'clock in the morning. In your hotel, guests can stay in their rooms until noon and nobody has left their room yet. The hotel is fully booked.

Situation 3

You are the guest.
You have stayed at the hotel for four days and now it's time to leave. You are at the reception desk. Ask for your bill.

FILE 14

Unit 8, A7

Your company, PAPERWORLD, manufactures and sells office paper – mainly for photocopying and laser printing. You employ around 3,000 people in your factories and offices and produce around a million tonnes of paper a year. You're one of the global market leaders in your sector.

Company turnover (€ million)

4 years ago	3 years ago	2 years ago	last year	this year
251.4	284.5	284.2	290.0	356.3

FILE 15

Unit 7, Business file 1

PARTNER B

Here is an excerpt from the 'Logos-To-Go' price list. Answer your partner's questions about the prices and product codes for the first items on the list. Then ask questions and find out your missing prices and product codes. If you have a problem understanding, use the phrases in the box below.

LOGOS-TO-GO
CORPORATE GIFTS

Item	Product code	Price $
Men's polo shirt	JGTM9090	15.00
Women's polo shirt	JGTW9091	
Baseball cap	ZSRA8854	1.50
Umbrella	IYYI0007B	7.50
Travel bag	DTPL75	10.00
Travel alarm clock	UHOH9752	8.00
PDA case		8.50
Business card holder		
Key ring		
Mousepad with calculator		
Pen		
Mug		

How can I be clear about names, numbers, prices, etc.?

INFO

Sorry. I didn't catch that. Could you say it again/repeat it, please?
Was that ... ? (or ... ?)
So that was ... . Is that right?
Have I got that right?
I'll just read that back to you. B for bravo, A–2–5 ...

The international spelling alphabet

A	Alpha	H	Hotel	O	Oscar	V	Victor
B	Bravo	I	India	P	Papa	W	Whisky
C	Charlie	J	Juliet	Q	Quebec	X	X-ray
D	Delta	K	Kilo	R	Romeo	Y	Yankee
E	Echo	L	Lima	S	Sierra	Z	Zulu
F	Foxtrot	M	Mike	T	Tango		
G	Golf	N	November	U	Uniform		

FILE 16

Unit 8, A7

Your company, TOM AND TOBY'S HOMEMADE ICE CREAM, began only ten years ago with two friends and €12,000 capital. Today it is one of the world's top producers of quality ice cream.

Company turnover (€ million)

10 years ago	8 years ago	6 years ago	4 years ago	2 years ago	this year
0.1	1.7	23.4	45.9	188.6	304.8

FILE 17

Unit 6, Business file 3

PARTNER C

You represent the production department on the project team.

Your diary

WEDNESDAY	
09.00	
10.00	
11.00	
12.00	*Henni Kipper*
13.00	
14.00	*Rainer*
15.00	
16.00	
17.00	

THURSDAY	
09.00	
10.00	*Interview assistant*
11.00	
12.00	*Michael Jones*
13.00	
14.00	
15.00	
16.00	*Department Meeting*
17.00	

FRIDAY	
09.00	*Install new machinery*
10.00	
11.00	
12.00	
13.00	
14.00	
15.00	
16.00	
17.00	

You have this email from one of the British colleagues, the project engineer Steven Bates.

Hi
I'm free:
Wednesday from 09.00-13.00.
All day on Thursday.
Friday p.m. from lunchtime until about 18.00.
Hope this helps!
Steven

FILE 18

Unit 8, Business file 3

PARTNER B

outbound flight: Wed, 23 March		
flight BU3381	06.55	leave Dusseldorf (DUS)
	07.15	arrive London Stansted (STN)
flight BU3389	07.55	leave Dusseldorf (DUS)
	08.15	arrive London Stansted (STN)
flight BU3385	09.55	leave Dusseldorf (DUS)
	10.15	arrive London Stansted (STN)
flight BU3387	18.15	leave Dusseldorf (DUS)
	18.40	arrive London Stansted (STN)
flight BU3383	21.25	leave Dusseldorf (DUS)
	21.50	arrive London Stansted (STN)

inbound flight:		Fri, 25 March
flight BU3382	09.15	leave London Stansted (STN)
	11.40	arrive Dusseldorf (DUS)
flight BU3386	13.00	leave London Stansted (STN)
	15.25	arrive Dusseldorf (DUS)
flight BU3384	18.40	leave London Stansted (STN)
	21.00	arrive Dusseldorf (DUS)

FILE 19

Unit 8, Business file 4

PARTNER B

Fairway Hotel***

Colchester

Single Room: £44.95 per night. Includes full English breakfast	
Location: Located in a quiet area on the outskirts of Colchester but only 15 minutes by taxi from town centre and railway station.	
Style and no. of rooms: Modern business hotel with full business facilities. 65.	
Restaurant	Yes
Fitness centre	Yes
Non-smoking rooms	Yes (whole of first floor)
Free parking	Yes
Facilities for disabled	Yes

Dedham Valley Hotel****

Dedham (near Colchester)

Single Room: £115.00 per night. Breakfast £12.00	
Location: Located in the beautiful, small village of Dedham about 25 minutes by taxi from Colchester town centre.	
Style and no. of rooms: Superb, quiet 18th century house in extensive gardens near the River Stour. 14.	
Restaurant	No
Fitness centre	No
Non-smoking rooms	Yes (whole of first floor)
Free parking	Yes
Facilities for disabled	Yes

George and Dragon Hotel***

Colchester

Single Room: £60.00 per night. Includes full English breakfast.	
Location: Located in Colchester High Street right in the town centre.	
Style and no. of rooms: 17th century inn with character (one of the oldest hotels in Britain). Popular restaurant with local people. 8 quiet bedrooms (at back of hotel).	
Restaurant	Yes
Fitness centre	No
Non-smoking rooms	No
Free parking	No (nearby car park £2.50 per day)
Facilities for disabled	Two special rooms

FILE 20

Unit 8, Business file 4

PARTNER B

Your partner will phone to make a booking. Get all the necessary information and complete the booking form below.

Full name: ....

Company name: ....

Type of room: *single/double/twin* ....

Date of arrival *(with approximate time)*: ....

Date of departure *(with approximate time)*: ....

Method of payment: *Visa/American Express/company invoice* ....

Card number: ....

Expiry date: ....

Contact telephone number: ....

FILE 21

Unit 9, B3

PARTNER B

Price list

3038 **Tourniermesser** Peeling knife
€31.00 7cm

3109 **Gemüsemesser** Paring knife
€35.00 7cm

3527 **Tomatenmesser** Tomato knife
€39.00 14cm

3157 **Brotmesser** Bread knife **NEW**
€60.00 20cm

3259 **Brotmesser** Bread knife
€65.00 23cm

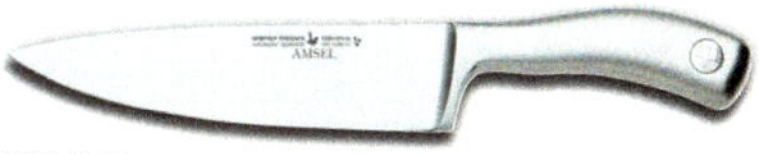

3819 **Kochmesser** Chef's knife
€75.00 20cm

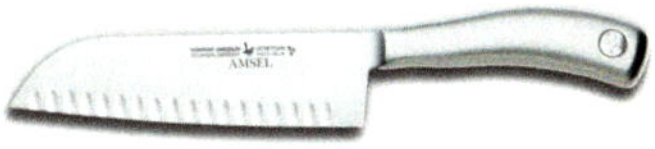

3063 **Japanisches Kochmesser**
Oriental chef's knife €75.00 17cm

Knife sets

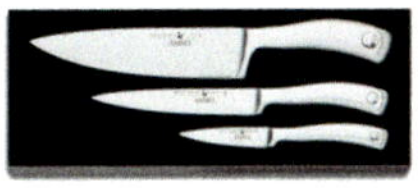

9338	5-piece	€320.00
9448	6-piece	€350.00
9558	7-piece	€400.00
9668	9-piece	€450.00
9778	12-piece	€720.00

NOTES

There is a special deal on Oriental Chef's knives until the end of June. Normal list price €75.00. Special offer price €70.00.

A new, smaller bread knife (20cm) is now available.

Discounts on orders:

€5,000–€10,000	5%
€10,000–€20,000	10%
Over €20,000	15%

Invoice

Cat. No.	Quantity	Description	Unit price €	Amount €
3038	5	Peeling knife 7cm	31.00	155.00
3527	5	Tomato knife 14cm	39.00	195.00
3529	10	Bread knife 23cm	65.00	650.00
3819	20	Chef's knife 20cm	75.00	1,500.00
9338	10	5-piece knife set	320.00	3,200.00
9558	10	7-piece knife set	400.00	4,000.00
9668	10	9-piece knife set	450.00	4,500.00
			SUBTOTAL	14,200.00
			With 10% DISCOUNT	12,780.00
			SHIPPING	00.00
			Please Pay This Amount:	€12,780.00

FILE 22

Unit 9, A7

Elexis e-Book
- Price: $299
- Size: about the same as a hardback book
- Stores 20 books + magazines and newspapers
- 1000s of books available: just download what you want when you want via a telephone. You pay as little as $5.00 per book
- You can be a member of an e-book library
- Battery lasts 20 hours

Pronto office-size espresso machine
- Normal price: $1,000, special price at the moment (!) $799.99
- Very simple to use: just put in whole coffee beans and water, the machine does EVERYTHING in 50 seconds (grinds the beans, etc.)
- Makes 40 cups
- *Cook's Magazine* describes the Pronto as 'the best espresso machine on the market today'

Arnie the walking-talking robot
- 1.2 metres high
- Walks naturally (can go up and down stairs)
- Understands the human voice and can answer with phrases
- A number of the world's biggest companies have an Arnie. He works as a receptionist for important visitors
- You can lease Arnie (not buy him) for 20 million yen ($166,200) a year

INTERLANG International Translating and Interpreting Service
- Has experts in 20 languages
- No job is too small or too big!
- Next-day translations by email
- Can translate brochures, websites, catalogues, letters ...
- Immediate quotation per page of text
- Typical price: $10 per page for a letter
- No permanent contract or long-term costs

FILE 23

Unit 9, Business file 2

PARTNER B

Here is the basic information for your report. Complete the chart. Ask your partner for the missing information and answer your partner's questions.

MODEL	Units sold last year (000s)	Customer rating last year*	Units sold this year (000s)	Customer rating this year*
T-10	....	....	12	●●●●○
T-20	9	●●●●○	....	●●●○○
T-150	18	....	22	....
T-250	....	●●○○○	....	●○○○○
V-80	11	●●●○○	....	●●●○○
V-90	....	....	9	●●○○○

* in terms of reliability and price

Customer ratings:

very poor	●○○○○
poor	●●○○○
average	●●●○○
good	●●●●○
very good	●●●●●

*in terms of reliability and price

How many did we sell last year?

How many have we sold this year?

What was the customer rating last year?

What's the customer rating been this year?

FILE 24

Unit 4, Business file 3

PARTNER B

Write this email and send it to Partner A.

You work in your country in the personnel department of an international company (Interco.com). Your project at the moment is to put photos of all the company employees around the world onto the company intranet. Write an email to your partner, who is in the company's Canadian office, and ask her/him to send you photos of the ten Canadian employees. You need them in the next three weeks if possible. Thank your partner for the reports that he/she sent last week and say they were very helpful. Your partner is a regular contact so make your email personal and friendly.

Now reply to Partner A's email.

You work for an American company (Amco.com) and at the moment your partner's company is producing a German-language sales catalogue for you.

FILE 25

Unit 7, Business file 3

PARTNER B

Logos-To-Go
601 Poydras Street,
New Orleans, LA 70130-4114

Invoice No. 1001999
Invoice Date: August 20, 20..

INVOICE

To:
Rick Simonette
WAFB-TV
844 Government Street
Baton Rouge, LA 70802-6030

Ship to (if different address)

Qty.	Cat. no.	Description	Unit price	Amount
20	JGTM1919	men's polo shirt, navy blue M	15.00	300.00
20	JGTW9091	women's polo shirt, light blue M	15.00	300.00
20	YIIY0007B	umbrella, blue	7.50	150.00
10	DTPL74	travel bag	10.00	100.00

Terms 3 days

SUBTOTAL	$850.00
SHIPPING AND HANDLING	$85.00
ONE-TIME LOGO DEVELOPMENT CHARGE	
AMOUNT DUE	$935.00

Signature *(if required)*

Thank you for your business

Numbers, dates, years and times

Numbers

Cardinal numbers		Ordinal numbers		Cardinal numbers		Ordinal numbers	
1	one	1st	first	21	twenty-one	21st	twenty-first
2	two	2nd	second	22	twenty-two	22nd	twenty-second
3	three	3rd	third	23	twenty-three	23rd	twenty-third
4	four	4th	fourth	30	thirty	30th	thirtieth
5	five	5th	fifth	31	thirty-one	31st	thirty-first
6	six	6th	sixth	40	forty	40th	fortieth
7	seven	7th	seventh	50	fifty	50th	fiftieth
8	eight	8th	eighth	60	sixty	60th	sixtieth
9	nine	9th	ninth	70	seventy	70th	seventieth
10	ten	10th	tenth	80	eighty	80th	eightieth
11	eleven	11th	eleventh	90	ninety	90th	ninetieth
12	twelve	12th	twelfth	100	one/a hundred	100th	hundredth
13	thirteen	13th	thirteenth				
14	fourteen	14th	fourteenth	110	one hundred **and** ten		
15	fifteen	15th	fifteenth	1000	one/a thousand		
16	sixteen	16th	sixteenth	6,496	six thousand four hundred **and** ninety-six		
17	seventeen	17th	seventeenth	100,000	one/a hundred thousand		
18	eighteen	18th	eighteenth	1,000,000	one/a million (1m)		
19	nineteen	19th	nineteenth	1,000,000,000	one/a billion (1bn)		
20	twenty	20th	twentieth				

Dates

Dates are said and written differently in Britain and the USA.

Britain

Dates are normally written with a cardinal number followed by the month:
23 March

When only numbers are used, the order is day, month, year:
12/09/06 12 September 2004

Dates are said using ordinal numbers:
23 March "the twenty-third of March"
12/09/06 "the twelfth of September, two thousand and six"

USA

In the USA, the day is usually written *after* the month:
March 23

When only numbers are used, the order is month, day, year:
09/12/06 September 12, 2006

Ordinal *or* cardinal numbers can be used to say the date:
March 23 "March twenty-third/March twenty-three"
09/12/06 "September twelfth/twelve, two thousand and six"

Years

1900	nineteen hundred	2000	two thousand
1905	nineteen oh five	2008	two thousand and eight
1910	nineteen ten	2010	two thousand and ten/twenty ten
1998	nineteen ninety-eight	2020	two thousand and twenty/twenty twenty

Times

The 12-hour clock

The 12-hour clock is used in everyday conversation. Remember that *half past ten* in English is 10.30, not 9.30!

ten o'clock

five *past* ten

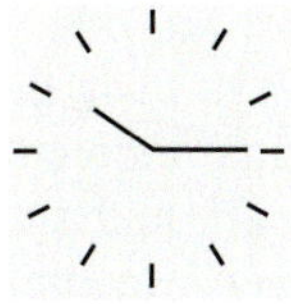
(a) quarter past ten

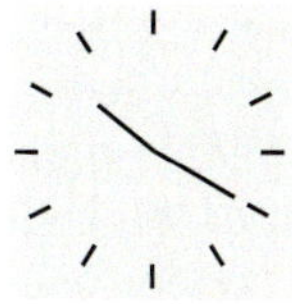
twenty past ten

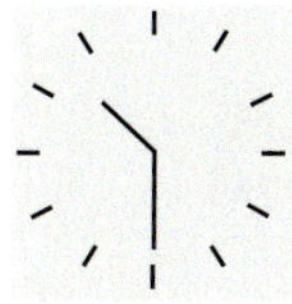
half past ten

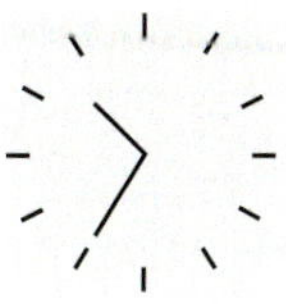
twenty-five *to* eleven

(a) quarter to eleven

ten to eleven

twelve *minutes* to eleven

midnight or *noon/midday*

In American English *after* is sometimes used instead of *past*, and *of* instead of *to*:

10.15: a quarter *after* 10
10.40: twenty *of* eleven

The 24-hour clock

TRAVEL TIMES

In everyday situations, the 24-hour clock is used in Britain only when talking about travel timetables (flight times for example). It is almost never used in the USA.

0000	zero hundred	1100	eleven hundred
0015	zero zero (oh oh) fifteen	1103	eleven oh three
0950	zero (oh) nine fifty	1430	fourteen thirty
0955	zero (oh) nine fifty-five	2250	twenty-two fifty

APPOINTMENTS, ETC.

In many everyday business situations in Britain, the 24-hour clock is used to *write* times (for example in a diary, or to confirm the time of a meeting in an email), but when speaking we use the 12-hour clock. It is not normal in Britain – as it is in German-speaking countries – to talk of a meeting beginning at *sixteen hundred* ('sechzehn Uhr'). Instead, we can use the 12-hour clock (above) but very often we just say figures (five, six, etc.) and *a.m.* and *p.m.* (or *am* and *pm*) for morning or afternoon/evening. Sometimes we write these times with a colon:

09:00	nine a.m.	13:00	one p.m.
09:05	nine oh five	13:47	one forty-seven p.m.
09:15	nine fifteen	12:00	twelve a.m.
09:30	nine thirty	00:00	twelve p.m.

Prepositions in time expressions

in + years, months, parts of the day	**on + days, dates**	**at + times**
in 2001	*on* Monday	*at* ten o'clock
in May	*on* Friday morning	*at* noon
in the morning (afternoon, evening)	*on* 23 June	

Telephone numbers and addresses

Telephone numbers

The important thing to remember is that in English we say the individual numbers of telephone numbers one after the other. If you give your telephone number as some people do in German (eg, if you say the number 416723 as 'forty-one sixty-seven twenty-three'), people probably won't understand you. When saying a phone number, make a pause after the code (*Vorwahl*) and also in the middle of longer numbers.

416723 four one six, seven two three

962 1397 nine six two, one three nine seven

- In the USA, all phone numbers are made up of seven digits plus the 3-digit area code (*Vorwahl*). Americans often give their phone numbers like this:
  (313) 845-3912 Area code three one three, eight four five, three nine one two
- '0' is usually said as the letter 'O' (also sometimes as *zero* in the USA):
  (01206) 451879 *oh* one two *oh* six, four five one, eight seven nine
- In British English double numbers (eg 22, 33) are said as *double-two*, *double-three*, etc.
  744311 seven *double-four*, three *double-one* (US: seven *four four*, three *one one*)
- Three identical numbers (eg 555) can be said as *treble five, five double-five* or *double-five five* (US: *five five five*).
- A few numbers, usually of larger companies, can end in 000. These are usually said as *thousand*:
  020 785 8000 oh two oh, seven eight five, eight thousand

Postal addresses

British and American postal addresses each follow a standard format: (company) name, street, town or city and in the UK a 'postcode', in the USA a five (or sometimes a nine) digit 'zip code'. Remember that in the UK and the USA the street number is placed *before* the street name.

Britain	USA
Sigma Consulting Ltd.	DataCorp, Inc.
4 Mosspark Road	1037 Richmond Avenue
Glasgow	Houston, TX 77042-1810
G62 8NL	USA
UK	

Email and website addresses (URLs)

.	**dot**	_	**underscore**
-	**hyphen, dash**	@	**at**
/	**(forward) slash**	:	**colon**

peter.morris@aol.com	Peter *dot* Morris at A-O-L *dot* com
d_klein@t-online.de	D *underscore* Klein at T *dash* online *dot* D-E
john.smith@citybank.co.uk	John *dot* Smith *at* City Bank *dot* co *dot* U-K
http://www.kulinar.at/sales	H-T-T-P *colon forward slash forward slash* W-W-W- *dot* Kulinar *dot* A-T *slash* sales

Business correspondence

A Letters

1 The layout of a business letter

Pauline Harris's company, Matrix Software, is based in Liverpool in the north of England. At the moment it is updating its sales literature and its website, and it wants to translate these into four languages. Last week Pauline phoned around a number of translation agencies.

This is a reply from one of the agencies. It is an example of a typical British business letter.

Scott-Hendrick Translation Services

1 → 115 Summertown Road
OXFORD
OX2 3QT
UK

Telephone: (+44) 01865 444317
Fax: (+44) 01865 444100
Email: sh@translate.co.uk

Your Reference:
Our Reference: LS/oo3 ← 2
Date: 12 April 2004 ← 3

4 → Ms P Harris
Matrix Software Ltd
120 Penny Lane
Liverpool
L33 7SW

5 → Dear Ms Harris

6 → **<u>Translation services and fees</u>**

7 → Thank you for your telephone call today and your interest in our translation services.

As I said in our conversation, we can offer you all the services that you need to help with the development of your website and sales literature.

Please find enclosed our current brochure. In it you will find a description of our full range of services and also details of our fees, which I think you will find extremely competitive.

I look forward to hearing from you again very soon.

Yours sincerely ← 8

Lawrence Scott

9 → Lawrence Scott
Scott-Hendrick Translation Services
New Business Manager

10 → Encl. Company brochure

The parts of a business letter

INFO

1 **The letterhead** *(Briefkopf)*
2 **The reference** *(Bezugszeichen) Oft abgekürzt: 'Your Ref./Our Ref'.*
3 **The date** *(Datum) Beachten Sie, dass die Reihenfolge in Großbritannien Tag/Monat, aber in den USA Monat/Tag ist. Vermeiden Sie Monatsangaben als Ziffer (03/09/2004), da dies verwirrend sein kann.*
4 **The inside address** *(Empfängeranschrift) Wenn bekannt, wird der Name der Person, an die Sie schreiben, gewöhnlich auch angegeben.*
5 **The salutation** *(Anrede) Die folgenden Formen der Anrede sind alle üblich in Großbritannien:*
Dear Sir or Madam *Wenn Sie an eine Firma oder Person schreiben, aber weder Name noch Geschlecht kennen. Diese Anrede kommt der deutschen Form ‚Sehr geehrte Damen und Herren' am nächsten.*
Dear Mr Jones *Wenn Ihnen die Person namentlich bekannt ist. Wenn Sie an eine Frau schreiben, sollten Sie die neutrale Form der Anrede ‚Ms' verwenden, sofern nicht ausdrücklich eine andere Form der Anrede gewünscht ist.*
Dear Sarah *Bei einem/einer Geschäftspartner/in, wenn Sie sich mit dem Vornamen ansprechen. Dieselben Formen der Anrede werden in den USA verwendet, aber die Formel:* To whom it may concern *(etwa, an die zuständige Abteilung') ist auch bei Schreiben an Firmen üblich. Beachten Sie, dass auf* Mr/Mrs/Ms/Dr *in den USA ein Punkt folgt* (Mr./Mrs./Ms./Dr.). *Darüber hinaus wird in amerikanischen Geschäftsbriefen ein Doppelpunkt hinter die Anrede gesetzt* (Dear Mr. Jones:).
6 **The subject line** *(Betreffzeile) Sowohl in britischen als auch in amerikanischen Briefen steht die Betreffzeile **hinter** (!) der Anrede.*
7 **The body of the letter** *(Brieftext) Dies ist der eigentliche Text des Briefes. In Großbritannien wie auch in den USA beginnt der erste Satz mit einem **Großbuchstaben** (!).*
8 **The complimentary close** *(Schlussformel) In Großbritannien ist die Schlussformel abhängig von der zu Beginn des Briefes gewählten Anrede.*

Dear Sir or Madam	**Yours faithfully**
Dear Mr Jones or Dear John	**Yours sincerely**
Ein freundlicher und nicht förmlicher Schluss ist	**With best wishes/Kind regards** *bei einer Anrede mit dem Vornamen*

In den USA werden alle Geschäftsbriefe bevorzugt mit Sincerely *geschlossen, aber* Yours truly *oder* Sincerely yours *werden auch verwendet.*
9 **The signature block** *(Unterschriften)*
10 **Enclosure(s)** *(Anlage(n)) Die Abkürzung* Enc. *(manchmal* Encl.*) weist darauf hin, dass dem Brief ewas beigefügt* (enclosed) *wurde – in diesem Fall eine Broschüre.*

Now you ...

1 Look at the letter on page 142 (but don't look above) and find:

a the salutation
b the reference
c the subject line

2 How is the position of the *subject line* different in English and German letters?

3 What is the English for 'Anlagen'?

4 What are the best complimentary closes for the following salutations?

a Dear Sir or Madam
b Dear Mr Williams (Britain)
c Dear Ms. Morgan (USA)
d Dear Jack

2 A first contact with a company

Companies can find new business partners from:

- advertisements in magazines and trade journals
- trade fairs
- the Internet
- chambers of commerce
- mutual customers

1 Look at the letter below. How did this British company learn about the German company? What does the writer of the letter request?

FISHER AEROSPACE LTD
3 AIRPORT WAY • CAMBRIDGE • CB5 8RX • ENGLAND
Telephone: +44 (01223) 773774 • Fax:+44 (01223) 323200
Email: info@fisheraero.co.uk • Web: http://www.fisheraerospace.co.uk

Your Ref:
Our Ref: DS/mh
Date: 15 September 20..

ENGAM Prüfgeräte GmbH
Max-Stromeyer-Straße 100
D-78467 Konstanz
Germany

Dear Sir or Madam

Request for sales catalogue and price lists

We were interested in the test equipment on display on your stand at the recent trade fair in Düsseldorf.

We are a UK-based engineering company and a major supplier to the aerospace industry worldwide.

Could you please send us your current sales catalogue and price lists? We would also appreciate details of your delivery times and trade discounts that you offer.

Thank you in advance for your help. We look forward to hearing from you soon.

Yours faithfully

D. Sandford

Dennis Sandford
Research and Development Manager
Fisher Aerospace Ltd

Now you ...

2 Here are some useful phrases for contacting a company. Use the phrases to write the letters below.

We understand from	your	advertisement		in this month's ... in the May edition of ...
	your	website ...		
We obtained	your	name address	from	the chamber of commerce in ... a mutual customer. an online trade directory.
We were interested in the products on display on your stand at the recent trade fair in ...				
We are a an	German/Swiss Austrian	company/importer/manufacturer ... retailer/wholesaler ...		
Please Could you please	send us your current catalogue and price lists (?) arrange a visit by your sales representative (?) arrange a product presentation for us (?)			
We would also	like be grateful for appreciate	details of information about samples of your products.	delivery times. trade discounts.	
Thank you in advance for your help. We look forward to hearing from you	soon. shortly.			

LETTER 1
Sie sind als Einkäufer/in für eine Hotelkette in Ihrem Land tätig. Sie sehen in der aktuellen Ausgabe des International Hotel Trade Magazine die Anzeige eines englischen Unternehmens, das Seifen (soaps) *vertreibt. Verfassen Sie einen Brief an das Unternehmen Wildflower Soaps Ltd, 17–20 Old Farm Road, Kirkby, CA17 3AP, in dem Sie um einen Katalog, Preislisten und Muster der Produkte des Unternehmens bitten. Denken Sie sich die Einzelheiten (wie den Namen Ihres Unternehmens etc.) selbst aus.*

LETTER 2
Sie sind Geschäftsführer/in der Fabrik (factory manager) *einer Herstellerfirma in Ihrem Land. Sie müssen Luftfilter* (air cleaners) *für Ihre Fabrik kaufen und ein gemeinsamer Kunde empfiehlt Ihnen ein französisches Unternehmen: Mécanélec, 43 rue du Chemin des Vignes, 93012 Bobigny, Frankreich. Verfassen Sie einen Brief, in dem Sie um einen Katalog und eine Produktpräsentation bitten. Denken Sie sich weitere Einzelheiten (wie den Namen Ihres Unternehmens etc.) selbst aus.*

Writing tip
Die goldene Regel für das Verfassen von Geschäftsbriefen lautet: KISS
Keep
It
Short and
Simple
Versuchen Sie, den Leser nicht mit langen Sätzen und wichtig klingenden Wörtern zu beeindrucken – die Wahrscheinlichkeit, dass Sie Fehler machen, ist größer.

3 A reply to a first contact

Susanne Klein's German electronics company is looking for a new storage system *(Lagerungssystem)* for its warehouse. Susanne works in her company's purchasing department. A customer recommends an English manufacturer, Alite. Susanne visits their website, fills in a contact form and requests a catalogue. This is Alite's reply.

1 Look at the letter. Write down four things that you learn in the letter about the English company.

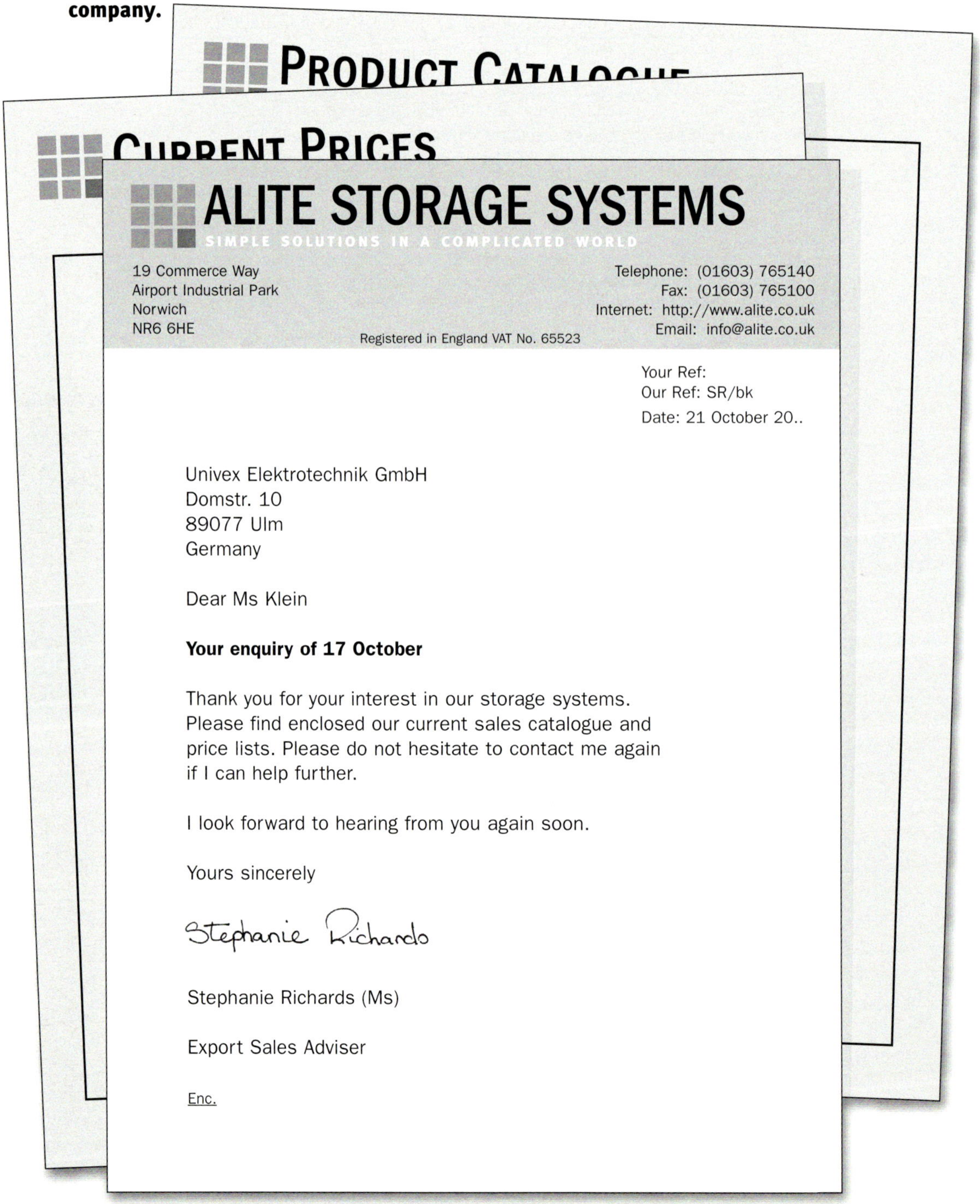

CURRENT PRICES

ALITE STORAGE SYSTEMS
SIMPLE SOLUTIONS IN A COMPLICATED WORLD

19 Commerce Way
Airport Industrial Park
Norwich
NR6 6HE

Registered in England VAT No. 65523

Telephone: (01603) 765140
Fax: (01603) 765100
Internet: http://www.alite.co.uk
Email: info@alite.co.uk

Your Ref:
Our Ref: SR/bk
Date: 21 October 20..

Univex Elektrotechnik GmbH
Domstr. 10
89077 Ulm
Germany

Dear Ms Klein

Your enquiry of 17 October

Thank you for your interest in our storage systems. Please find enclosed our current sales catalogue and price lists. Please do not hesitate to contact me again if I can help further.

I look forward to hearing from you again soon.

Yours sincerely

Stephanie Richards

Stephanie Richards (Ms)

Export Sales Adviser

Enc.

Now you ...

2 Here are some useful phrases for replying to a first contact. Use the phrases to write the letters below.

Thank you for	your letter your telephone call your email	of 3 March today	in which you enquired about ... in which you requested ...
Thank you for	your request for your enquiry about	our latest sales catalogue. our products and prices. our services and fees.	
Thank you for	your interest in	our products/services.	

Please find enclosed I am enclosing I have pleasure in sending you	our latest brochure. our sales catalogue and current price lists. samples of our products.
Our representative Ms Webster will contact you in the next few days to arrange an appointment.	

I am sure that	you will find	our products/services of the highest standard. our prices extremely competitive.
Please do not hesitate	to contact us again to phone me	if I can help further. if you have any questions.

I look forward	to hearing from you to receiving your order to calling you	very soon. in due course. in the next few days.

LETTERS

Sie arbeiten in Ihrem Land für ein Unternehmen, dass Ferngläser (binoculars) *und andere optische Geräte herstellt. Sie haben heute auf Ihrer Website zwei Anfragen bekommen. Die erste ist von einem Herrn Kees Heijn von Calmar BV, Oldenzaalsestraat 125, 7514 DP Enschede, Niederlande, der um einen Produktkatalog bittet. Die zweite ist von einer Ms Judy Lake von Outdoor Sports Ltd, 11 King Street, Peterborough, PE3 8DZ, die um einen Besuch Ihres Repräsentanten bittet. Schreiben Sie entsprechende Antworten auf beide Anfragen. Denken Sie sich die Einzelheiten (wie den Namen Ihres Unternehmens etc.) selbst aus.*

Writing tip

Verwenden Sie keine Kurzformen (I'm, we're, they don't, it hasn't, I'd *usw.*) *in förmlichen Briefen. Verwenden Sie nur die Langformen:* I am, we are, they do not, it has not, I would *usw.*

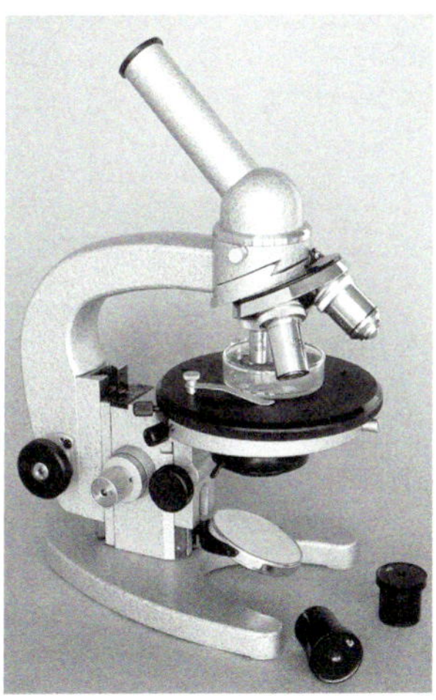

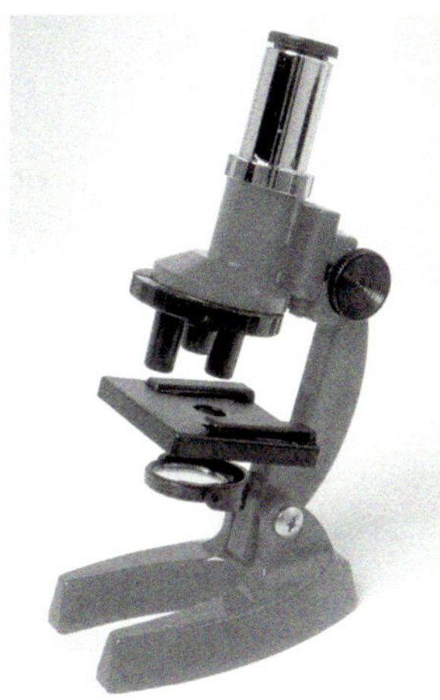

4 Asking for a quotation

Maximilian Scheling Weinimport is a wine wholesaler in Cologne. Wolfgang Müller is one of the company's buyers. Last week Wolfgang was at a trade fair and became interested in the products of a Californian wine producer, Golden Valley Vineyards in the Napa Valley. Now he is writing for a quotation for a number of cases *(Kisten)* of wine.

1 Read the letter and write a list of all the information that Wolfgang asks for.

MAXIMILAN SCHELING

Weinimport GmbH
Hansaring 20
D-50670 Köln
Germany

Ihr Zeichen/Your ref	Unser Zeichen/Our ref	Datum/Date
	WM/gf	August 29, 20..

Ms. Nina da Silva
Golden Valley Vinyards Inc.
2545 Las Amigas Road
Napa, CA 94559-2130
USA

Dear Ms. da Silva:

Quotation

I very much enjoyed meeting you at the trade fair last week here in Cologne and was impressed with your wines. If your prices and terms are right, we may want to place substantial orders with you.

Would you please send us a quotation DEQ Hamburg for the following:

10 cases of Golden Valley Chardonnay 2003
10 cases of Golden Valley Cabernet Sauvignon 2003
10 cases of Golden Valley Merlot 2003
10 cases of Golden Valley Zinfandel Reserve 2002

We would also be grateful for details of discounts that you can offer us, delivery times and your terms of payment.

We look forward to receiving your quotation shortly.

Sincerely

Wolfgang Müller

Wolfgang Müller
Buyer

Telefon: (+49) (0) 221 139 72 58 • Fax: (+49) (0) 221 139 72 59 • Internet: www.maxwein.de

Incoterms

Wolfgang asks for a price for the wines 'DEQ Hamburg'. In international commerce, companies often use Incoterms (International Commercial Terms) like these to show what a price includes. Here are six common Incoterms.

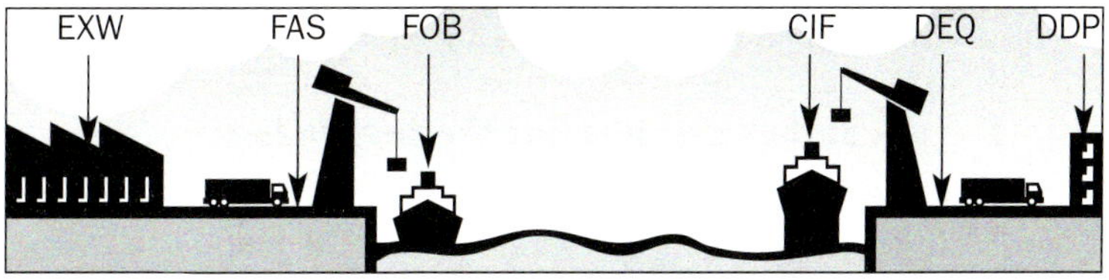

Seller → **Buyer**
Verkäufer → *Käufer*

EXW Ex-works *(ab Werk)* The basic price.
FAS (San Francisco) Free alongside ship *(frei Längsseite Schiff)*. The seller pays the costs until the goods are at the port (e.g. San Francisco).
FOB (San Francisco) Free on board *(frei an Bord)*. The seller pays the costs until the goods are on the ship.
CIF (Hamburg) Cost, insurance and freight *(Kosten, Versicherung, Fracht)*. The seller pays the costs (including insurance) until the goods are at the port in the buyer's country.
DEQ (Hamburg) Delivered ex quay *(geliefert ab Kai)*. The seller pays the costs until the goods are on the quay.
DDP (Buyer's works) Delivered duty paid *(geliefert verzollt)*. The seller pays all the costs until the goods are at the buyer's works.

Now you ...

2 Use these phrases and Wolfgang's letter to write the letter below.

Thank you for	your sales catalogue. the samples/the information that you sent us.		
We find your products		(very) satisfactory.	
We are impressed by We are particularly interested in		your products.	
Could you Would you	please	send us a quotation quote us ...	for the following ...
We would also	like be grateful for appreciate	details of information about	discounts. delivery times. your terms of payment.
If your prices and terms are right, we may want to place substantial orders with you. We look forward to receiving your quotation shortly.			

LETTER

Sie arbeiten für ein Bauunternehmen (construction company) *in Ihrem Land. Sie haben Interesse am Kauf von schwedischem Bauholz* (timber) *von Scanwood Timber AB, Axel Enströms väg 10, SE-913 31 Holmsund, Schweden. Sie haben Muster des Produkts erhalten und möchten nun ein Preisangebot für 20 Tonnen 10 Meter langer Kiefernbretter* (10-metre pine planks) *DDP (Ihr Betrieb) sowie Einzelheiten über Rabatte, Lieferzeiten und Zahlungsbedingungen. Schreiben Sie an Ihre Kontaktperson in dem Unternehmen, Herrn Olof Alm. Denken Sie sich Einzelheiten (wie den Namen Ihres Unternehmens etc.) selbst aus.*

5 An offer

This is Nina da Silva's reply to Wolfgang Müller's letter on page 148.

1 Look at the letter and find the English for:

a *Menge*
b *Beschreibung*
c *Gesamtbetrag*
d *Einführungsrabatt*
e *Skonto bei Barzahlung innerhalb von 10 Tagen*
f *Lieferung*
g *gültig*
h *Bezahlung in voller Höhe innerhalb von 30 Tagen nach Lieferung*
i *Warensendungen*
j *höchst zufrieden*

GOLDEN VALLEY
2545 Las Amigas Road, Napa, CA 94559-2130 *Vineyard*

Mr. Wolfgang Muller
Maximilian Scheling Weinimport
Hansaring 20
50670 Cologne
Germany

September 5, 20..

Dear Mr. Muller:

Your request for a quotation of August 29, 20..

I also enjoyed our meeting at the trade fair. Thank you for your interest in our excellent wines and your request for a quotation. I am pleased to send you the following offer:

Quantity	Description	€ Price/case	Total
10	12 bottle case Chardonnay 2003	99.50	995.00
10	12 bottle case Cab. Sauvignon 2003	125.00	1250.00
10	12 bottle case Merlot 2003	99.00	990.00
10	12 bottle case Zinfandel Reserve 2002	476.00	4760.00
GRAND TOTAL			7995.00

These prices are DEQ Hamburg. I will be very pleased to offer you an introductory discount of 10% on this order and a further generous 5% cash discount for payment within 10 days of delivery. This offer is valid for three months.

Our terms are payment in full within 30 days of delivery.

You can normally expect to receive consignments from us around three weeks after we receive your order.

I am certain that you will be delighted with our product and I look forward to receiving your order in the near future. Please do not hesitate to get in touch with us immediately if you have any questions.

Sincerely yours,

Nina da Silva

Nina da Silva
GOLDEN VALLEY VINEYARDS INC.

Encls: Terms and Conditions of Business

Now you ...

2 Use these phrases and Nina's letter to write the letter below.

Thank you for your request for a quotation of August 29.						
We are pleased to		send you		the following offer:		
		quote you		as follows:		
We have pleasure in sending you				the following quotation:		
These prices		are	DDP your works/store/offices in ...			
All prices			EXW.			
The above prices			DEQ Liverpool.			
We are pleased	to offer	you	a	trade		discount of ...%.
We are willing	to give			volume		
				cash		
			an	introductory		
Our terms of payment		are	payment in advance.			
			COD.			
			payment within 30 days (of delivery).			
			by letter of credit.			
We will dispatch		the	goods		immediately on receipt of your order.	
deliver			consignment		within ... days of receipt of your order.	
send			order			
You can normally expect to receive your goods/consignment ...						
... within three weeks/around a week/5 days after we receive your order.						
This offer		is valid	for ... months/weeks.			
quotation			until ... (date).			
We look forward to		receiving your order soon.				
		doing business with you in the future.				

LETTER

Sie arbeiten für ein Unternehmen in Ihrem Land, das Edel-Schokoladenkekse (luxury chocolate biscuits) *herstellt. Ihr Chef hat eine Anfrage aus den USA erhalten und bittet Sie, das Antwortschreiben zu verfassen. Schreiben Sie diesen Brief unter Verwendung der Notizen Ihres Chefs.*

Herr Peterson von Peterson's World Foods, 17 Quincy Market, Boston, MA 02122 schrieb uns am 4. November bezüglich eines Angebots für 50 Kisten Chocolate Heaven Kekse, versandt per Luftfracht CIF New York. Teilen Sie ihm mit: Gesamtbetrag $ 2100. Bedingungen: 30 Tage (2% Skonto, wenn er innerhalb von 15 Tagen zahlt). Lieferzeit: ca. 1 Woche.

Writing tip

In den unten stehenden Sätzen ist ein Wort falsch. Es ist entweder falsch geschrieben oder es ist das falsche Wort oder die falsche Form. Können Sie die Fehler finden und korrigieren?

- Our adress is 14 Richmond Street, London.
- Thank you for your letter from 3 March.
- I look forward to hear from you soon.

6 A job application

Peter Scheibl works in Vienna as a translator for an online Austrian newspaper. He sees this advertisement in a magazine and writes a letter of application.

1 Look at the ad. What (and where) is the job? What qualifications and experience are necessary for it?

2 Now look at Peter's covering letter. Do you think that he is a good candidate for the job? Why (not)?

> **TEXT EXPRESS**
>
> **We are looking for an experienced**
>
> **GERMAN TRANSLATOR**
>
> **(mother tongue)**
>
> You will write the subtitles for films for international distribution. We offer full training in writing subtitles, plus a friendly environment and an attractive salary.
>
> The successful candidate will be a fully qualified translator and have at least 2 years' experience of translation work. Good computer skills are also essential.
>
> **If you are interested, please send your CV with a covering letter to:** Caroline Tucker, HR Department, Text Express Media, 8 Charlotte Street, London W1T 2NS.

Donauergasse 14A
A-1060 Vienna
Austria

12 October 20..

Ms Caroline Tucker
HR Department
Text Express Media
8 Charlotte Street
London W1T 2NS

Dear Ms Tucker

I am writing to apply for the position of German translator which you advertised in the European Media Magazine of 11 October.

As you will see from my CV, I have a degree in English translation from the Business University of Vienna. For the last three years I have worked as a translator with *This Is Austria*, an online English language daily newspaper. My work involves translation from and into English in a wide range of fields including sport, culture, current affairs, business and technology. As we are an online newspaper I have advanced computer skills.

I have a deep interest in creative media. I would welcome the opportunity to develop my career in your company and believe that I could make a valuable contribution to Text Express Media.

I look forward to hearing from you in due course.

Yours sincerely

Peter Scheibl.

Peter Scheibl

Encl.

Now you ...

3 Use these phrases and Peter's letter to write a letter of application for one of the job advertisements below.

I am writing I would like	to apply for the position of ...		which you advertised in the ... of ...
I am writing	in response to		your advertisement in the ... of ...
Please find enclosed my CV (UK)/resumé (USA).			
As you will see	from	my the	CV/resumé, ... enclosed CV/resumé, ...
I am I have I have I have worked	a qualified accountant/engineer/... a qualification/degree in business from *(school/university)* in ... 3 years' experience in advertising/marketing/sales. for three years in ...		
In my present/current job		I am responsible for ... my duties include ...	
My current/present job involves ... I have (also) worked in/been responsible for/been involved in ...			
I would welcome the opportunity		to work for your company. to develop my career with your company.	
I believe that I could I feel that with my background and experience I could		make a valuable contribution be a valuable asset	to your company.
I would be available for an interview at any time. Please contact me at the above address if you require any further information.			
I look forward to hearing from you		in the near future. in due course.	

CONFERENCE MANAGER

We are an international conference centre and are looking for a CONFERENCE MANAGER. The successful candidate will be responsible for an enthusiastic team of 10 people. You will have excellent communication skills, and at least five years' experience in the conference industry. Knowledge of at least two languages is an advantage. If you are interested, please write with CV to Caroline Goldie, Central Conference Centre, London, W2A 4RT, UK

LONDON

General MANUFACTURING

MARKETING ASSISTANT

We are a leading international manufacturing company based in the USA. We are looking for a marketing assistant for our office in *(your country)*. You will have an excellent knowledge of English and be a good 'team player'. We offer full training in marketing.

If you would like to apply, please write with your resumé to:
David Wozynski,
General Manufacturing, Inc.,
1079 Webster Boulevard,
Chicago, Illinois 60607-5432

www.general-manufacturing.com

Writing tip

Schreiben Sie Ihre Adresse in privaten Briefen oben rechts. Schreiben Sie Ihren Namen nicht über die Adresse, wie Sie das in Deutschland tun würden!

B Emails

1 Formal and informal emails

There aren't many clear rules for writing emails. Emails (sometimes written 'e-mails') vary from 'formal' (like a business letter) to very 'informal' ('a telephone conversation in writing').

1 Look at the two emails below. Which is 'formal' and which is 'informal'? What differences can you find between the two emails?

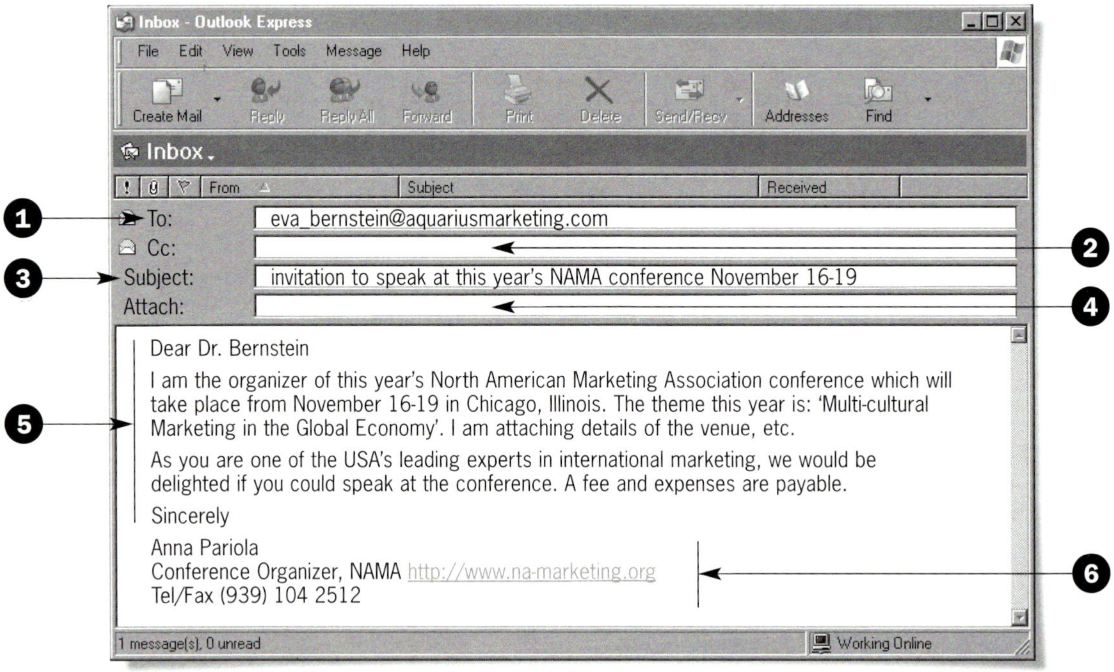

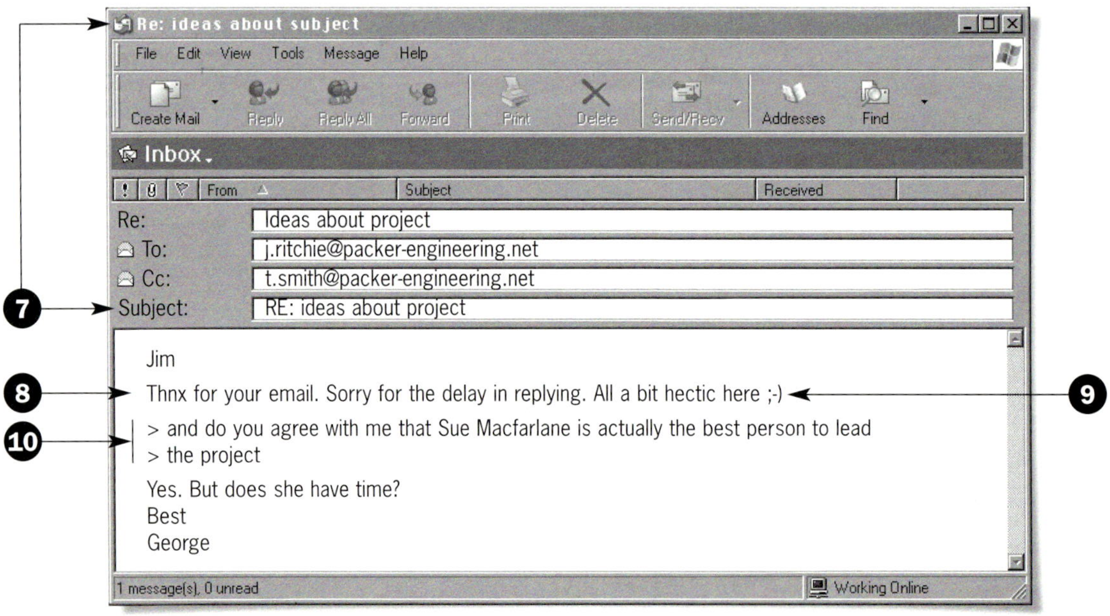

The parts of an email

INFO

1 **The recipient** *(Empfänger)*
2 **Copies** *(Kopien)* (Cc = carbon copy: *Durchschlag)*
3 **The subject line** *(Betreffzeile)* Vergessen Sie nie die Betreffzeile! Viel Beschäftigte müssen sich schnell eine Vorstellung vom Inhalt der E-Mail machen können und wollen sie vielleicht später noch einmal lokalisieren.
4 **Attachment(s)** *(Anhang)* Entspricht der Anlage eines Briefes.
5 **The message** *(Nachricht) In förmlichen E-Mails entsprechen Anrede und Schlussformel denen eines Geschäftsbriefes (siehe Seite 143). In nicht förmlichen E-Mails sind die folgenden üblich:*

Jim *(d.h. nur der Vorname)*	**Kind regards/Regards/Best wishes**
Hi/Hello Jim	**All the best/Very best/Best/Yours**

6 **The signature** *(Signatur) E-Mail-Programme erlauben es dem Verfasser, automatisch eine elektronische Signatur hinzuzufügen. Verschiedene Möglichkeiten, mit dem Verfasser Kontakt aufzunehmen, können für den Empfänger hilfreich sein.*
7 **Re (With reference to)** *(Betreff) Meistens beantwortet man eine E-Mail, indem man auf* Reply *(Antworten) klickt. Eine Folge von E-Mails, bei der zwei Personen immer wieder auf die eine eingehende E-Mail geantwortet haben, heißt* a thread.
8 **Abbreviations** *(Abkürzungen) Abkürzungen wie* thnx *für* thanks *sind üblich in nicht förmlichen E-Mails zwischen Muttersprachlern. Siehe unten. Unvollständige Sätze wie die in Georges E-Mail sind unter Muttersprachlern ebenfalls üblich.*
9 **An emoticon or smiley** *Siehe unten.*
10 **A quotation/quote** *(Zitat) Der Verfasser hat einen Abschnitt aus der E-Mail des Senders in seine eigene E-Mail eingefügt: So lässt sich schnell und eindeutig darstellen, worauf man sich bezieht.*

Abbreviations and 'Smileys'

Neue Abkürzungen und Smileys werden tagtäglich erfunden. Unten sind nur einige Beispiele dafür aufgeführt. Eine Warnung! Die erste Regel, die für eine E-Mail gilt, ist, dass ihr Sinn vollkommen klar sein muss – Abkürzungen können verwirren. Am besten bleibt man bei den bekanntesten wie ASAP, BTW *und* FYI.

Some abbreviations in emails			
ASAP	as soon as possible	:-)	*glücklich oder freundlich*
B4	before	:D	*sehr glücklich*
BTW	by the way	;-)	*ironisch oder wissend*
FYI	for your information	:-o	*überrascht*
HAND	have a nice day	:-\	*perplex*
IMHO	in my humble opinion	:-(	*enttäuscht oder unglücklich*
PLS	please		
THNX/THX	thanks		

Now you ...

2 Find suitable closes for these salutations:

a (US) Dear Mr. Friedman
b (UK) Dear Ms Walters
c Hi Lucy
d Mike

3 Write in more formal language:

a Pls send me the info asap. Thx.
b FYI: The payment is in the post. Will be with you asap.
c Btw, sorry for the delay. Was on holiday. :-)

2 An invitation

Public relations (PR) are an important part of business. Rebecca Perry is the HR manager with a logistics company in the east of England. In the first email below she receives an invitation to dinner from a recruitment agency that she often works with.

1 Look at the two emails. Why is the Five Star Recruitment Agency organizing the dinner? Does Rebecca accept or refuse (*ablehnen*) the invitation?

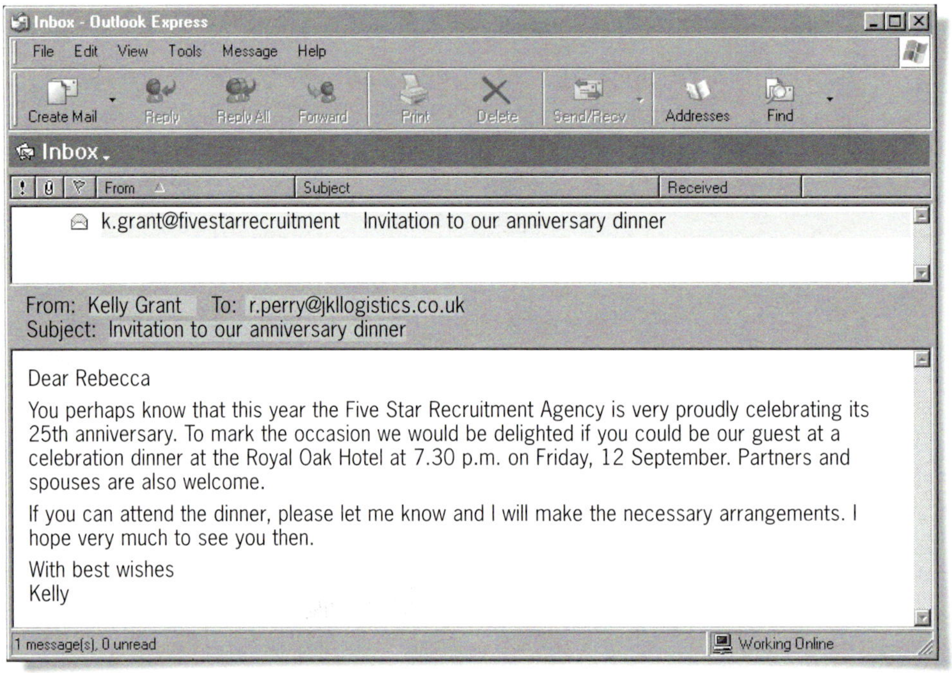

From: Kelly Grant To: r.perry@jkllogistics.co.uk
Subject: Invitation to our anniversary dinner

Dear Rebecca

You perhaps know that this year the Five Star Recruitment Agency is very proudly celebrating its 25th anniversary. To mark the occasion we would be delighted if you could be our guest at a celebration dinner at the Royal Oak Hotel at 7.30 p.m. on Friday, 12 September. Partners and spouses are also welcome.

If you can attend the dinner, please let me know and I will make the necessary arrangements. I hope very much to see you then.

With best wishes
Kelly

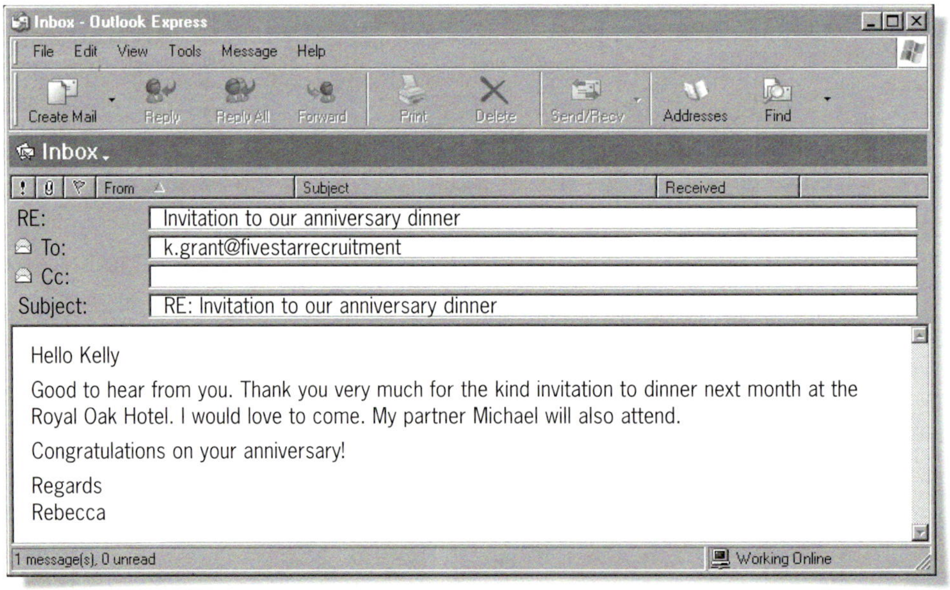

RE: Invitation to our anniversary dinner
To: k.grant@fivestarrecruitment
Cc:
Subject: RE: Invitation to our anniversary dinner

Hello Kelly

Good to hear from you. Thank you very much for the kind invitation to dinner next month at the Royal Oak Hotel. I would love to come. My partner Michael will also attend.

Congratulations on your anniversary!

Regards
Rebecca

Now you ...

2 Look at the phrases below and the emails on page 156 to write the emails below.

SENDING AN INVITATION

This year we are celebrating our ... anniversary.		
We are currently organizing	a meeting of local businesses. a farewell dinner for Mrs Harrison. a Christmas dinner for our most valued customers.	
The meeting/dinner will take place at	the Royal Hotel ... the British Chamber of Commerce ... our offices ...	
... on Saturday 29 April at 7.30 p.m.		
We would be delighted if you could	attend the meeting. be a guest at the dinner.	
Spouses and partners are welcome. Unfortunately we cannot invite spouses and partners.		
Please	let me know ring me on (01206) 449300 write to me at the above address	as soon as possible if you can attend.
I look forward very much to seeing you then/at the dinner/at the meeting.		

REPLYING TO AN INVITATION

(Friendly/informal)		
Thank you very much for your kind invitation to dinner on ... at ...		
I would very much like love *(very informal!)*	to attend/to come.	
I'm very sorry but I'm afraid	I can't/won't be able to come I'll be away on business I have another commitment	then/that day/that evening.
(Formal)		
I have (great) pleasure in accepting	your invitation to dinner on ... at ...	
I regret that Unfortunately	I will not be able to accept your kind invitation ... I have a prior commitment/will be away on business.	
I wish you a pleasant evening.		

EMAILS

Sie haben zwei Einladungen bekommen: (1) von der örtlichen Handelskammer zu einem Abendessen, das von ortsansässigen Firmen organisiert wird, die Handelsverbindungen in der USA haben; (2) von einer Kontaktperson in einem ortsansässigen britischen Unternehmen, mit dem Sie geschäftliche Beziehungen pflegen, zu dessen alljährlichem Weihnachtslunch.

Writing tip

Wie bei jedem geschäftlichen Umgang müssen Sie beim Erfassen von E-Mails sorgfältig abschätzen, welchen Eindruck ein Geschäftspartner von Ihnen bekommt. Seien Sie in der Regel förmlich (verwenden Sie Mr/Ms usw.), bis die Umstände eine andere Verhaltensweise nahe legen.

C Faxes

A confirmation of a hotel reservation

Jamie Rybacker, a VP with an American publishing company, is going on a business trip to London in two weeks. His assistant Paul Zydel phones a hotel to make a reservation and then sends the fax below to confirm it.

1 Look at the fax. How long is Jamie staying in London? Is he going alone? Will he pay the bill himself when he leaves?

Lane & Murray Publishing Inc.
456 Broadway
New York, NY 10012
Fax: (212) 941-7482

FAX

To:	Reservations, Metro Hotel, London UK
Fax Number:	0044 20 888 4444
Date:	2005-February-18
Subject:	Confirmation of telephone reservation
No. of pages incl. this one:	1
From:	Paul Zydel, Lane & Murray Publishing Inc.

This is to confirm the room reservation made today by telephone for Mr. J. Rybacker from our company:

Dates: Four nights, March 27-30 inclusive
Room: Single room with shower

Note that Lane & Murray Publishing Inc. will pay the bill directly and in full. Please send an invoice to us at the above address on Mr. Rybacker's departure.

Paul Zydel

Notes on faxes INFO

- *Statt des Wortes* Fax *im Briefkopf eines Dokuments kann dort auch stehen:* Facsimile, Fax/Facsimile Transmission *oder* Fax/Facsimile Transmittal *(USA).*
- *Die Angaben am Anfang eines Faxes sind unterschiedlich. Die hier aufgeführten* (To, Fax number; Date, Subject, *usw.) sind die am häufigsten verwendeten. Ebenfalls üblich ist die Formel:* For the attention of (name) *oder einfach:* Attention/Attn. (name).
- *Normalerweise wird auf einem Fax die Anzahl der Seiten angegeben, wobei als Standardaussage oft erscheint:* Number of pages including this one, *oder:* Number of pages including cover page/cover sheet *(die erste Seite des Faxes).*
- *Da verschiedenste Dokumente (Bestellungen, Rechnungen, technische Angaben und selbst Geschäftsbriefe) regelmäßig gefaxt werden, gibt es nur wenige Regeln zu dem, was ‚normal' ist. Wenn die Nachricht unkompliziert ist, wie hier, fassen Sie sie kurz und einfach ab. Eine förmliche Anrede und Schlussformel sind nicht notwendig.*
- *Faxe werden oft mit einer handschriftlichen Unterschrift versehen, um ihnen eine persönliche Note zu geben.*

Now you ...

2 Here are some useful phrases for confirming a hotel reservation. Use the phrases and the fax on page 158 to write the faxes below.

This is I am writing	to confirm the room reservation(s) made earlier today by telephone.		
Please reserve	a single room two single rooms a double room a twin room	for one/two/three nights ... ... from (date) – (date) inclusive	for (name). in the name of (name).
We would	be grateful appreciate it	if you could ensure that the room	is quiet. on the ground/first floor.
Please ensure that the room		is non-smoking. is suitable for a disabled person.	
Our company	will pay the bill in full. will be responsible for	payment. payment for the room and meals.	
Please send an invoice to us on (name's) departure.			
(Name)	will pay will settle	the bill personally on departure. the bill by credit card on departure.	

FAXES

Das Unternehmen, für das Sie in Ihrem Land arbeiten, bucht das Metro Hotel in London für Mitarbeiter auf Geschäftsreise in Großbritannien. Hier sind zwei für Sie bestimmte Notizen mit der Bitte, Buchungen (für zwei getrennte Reisen) im Metro vorzunehmen. Sie haben die Zimmer telefonisch reserviert. Schreiben Sie die Faxe.

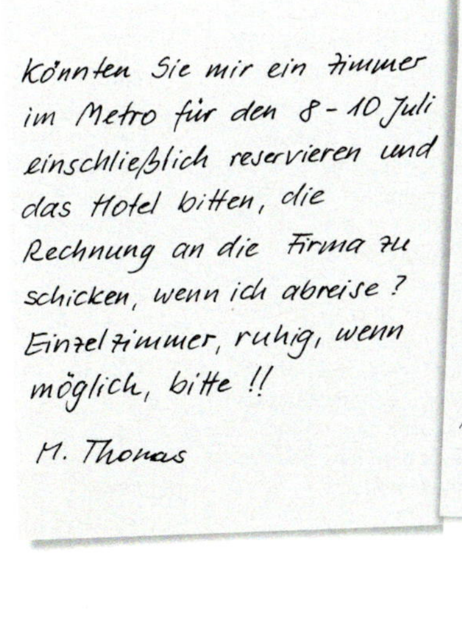
Könnten Sie mir ein Zimmer im Metro für den 8-10 Juli einschließlich reservieren und das Hotel bitten, die Rechnung an die Firma zu schicken, wenn ich abreise? Einzelzimmer, ruhig, wenn möglich, bitte!!

M. Thomas

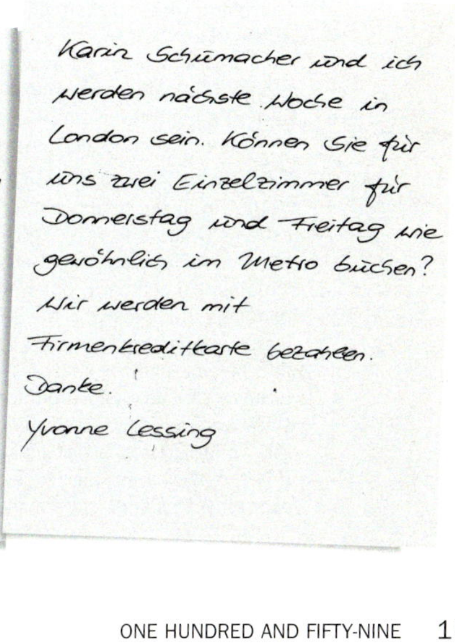
Karin Schumacher und ich werden nächste Woche in London sein. Können Sie für uns zwei Einzelzimmer für Donnerstag und Freitag wie gewöhnlich im Metro buchen? Wir werden mit Firmenkreditkarte bezahlen.
Danke.
Yvonne Lessing

Transcripts

UNIT 1 A4

1/03

1 Hello. My name's Andrea Graf and I come from Germany. I work for a company called Amsel. We make knives and I sell them. Well, not exactly. I'm the sales manager there. Amsel has its head office and factory in Solingen, and that's where I work. But I live in Düsseldorf, about 10 kilometres away.

2 Hi. I'm Eckhard Kellermann and I'm an account manager with a big German logistics company called Helle Logistics. I live and work in Hamburg. How can I explain 'account manager'? Well, my company has a lot of big clients. When a client is very big it has a permanent 'account' with us and one person from Helle works with that one company all the time. I'm the account manager for a big American company called Nimbus. It makes sportswear – trainers and T-shirts and so on.

3 I'm Lee Mazry and, as you can hear, I'm from the United States. I'm the CEO, the chief executive officer – the boss if you like – of a big international software company. We develop and sell business software. We're called BlueSky and we're based in Portland, Oregon.

UNIT 1 BUSINESS FILE 3

1/07

Harry I'm Harry Parker. I'm the export manager for Woodman Cards. We're based in London and we make handmade greeting cards. The company began ten years ago with just two people: Michael and Linda Woodman. Today we employ 25 people, 16 of them sales representatives. So we're not a big company, but it's a nice place to work with a very friendly atmosphere. Surprisingly, we export about 50% of our production. Our cards are popular in the Netherlands, for example. In total, our turnover last year was just over €2.5m.

Nina The Napa Valley is only a part of the wine industry here in California but it produces the best wines, in fact, some of the best wines in the world. There are 232 wineries in the valley and I'm the export sales manager with one of them. I'm Nina da Silva and I'm with the Golden Valley Vineyard. We're 20 years old, and we specialize in Chardonnay and Cabernet Sauvignon wines in the medium price range. So our wines aren't too expensive. We produce about a million cases a year. 100% of our production is for export. The market for California wine is just so big now all around the world. Our biggest market is the UK, but we sell all over Europe.

Chantal I work in Paris, France, and my name is Chantal Millot. I'm in the public relations department of Parfums Odile, a French perfume manufacturer. Our company office is in Paris because we're an international company, but we produce our perfumes in Provence in the south of France. Parfums Odile began in 1904 and today we're the fifth biggest perfume manufacturer in France. Our turnover last year was around €450m. 20% of the sales were in France itself, but we export all around the world. Japan is a big market for us, and the USA too. We have a big range of perfumes from very expensive to simple supermarket products.

UNIT 2 A7

1/09

Manfred Gerber is the production manager of a German company in Dresden. It makes components for the automobile industry. Manfred is 41 years old, married, and has two children. He lives in Dresden. At the moment, Manfred's company (it's called Kiewitz, K-I-E-W-I-T-Z) is expanding and Manfred is always busy. Kiewitz is developing three new products and it's Manfred's job to adapt the production process. In fact, Manfred is *very* busy. He's also moving to a new flat at the moment, from the city centre to a nice suburb.

UNIT 2 BUSINESS FILE 1

1/10

CALL 1

Receptionist LCD Electronics.
Sheila Could I speak to John Gardner, please?
Receptionist Thank you. It's ringing for you now.
Tony Research and Development. Tony speaking.
Sheila Good morning. Could I speak to John Gardner, please?
Tony I'm sorry, John isn't here this morning. Can I help at all?
Sheila Thanks, but I think I need to talk to John personally. Do you know when he'll be in?
Tony No, I don't, I'm afraid. Can he perhaps call you back?
Sheila Yes, thanks very much.
Tony Just a minute. I'll get a pen. OK. Who's calling please?
Sheila It's Sheila Murray from Microdot Computers. John's got my telephone number.
Tony Great. I'll tell him.
Sheila Thanks very much. Bye.
Tony Bye.

CALL 2

Receptionist A&M Chemicals Ltd.
Jack Good afternoon. Could I have the sales department, please?
Receptionist One moment, please.
Woman Sales.
Jack Good afternoon. Could I speak to Bill Nicholson, please? This is Jack Rogers from British Gas.
Woman I'm afraid Bill's in a meeting at the moment, Mr Rogers. Would you like to leave a message?
Jack No, it's OK, thanks. I'll call back later. Do you know when he'll be free?
Woman It's hard to say, I'm afraid. Try again at about 4 o'clock. The meeting should be finished then.
Jack OK. Thanks very much. Bye now.
Woman Goodbye.

CALL 3

You're through to Delta Services. We're sorry that there's no one here to take your call at the moment, but if you leave your name and number, we'll get back to you as soon as possible. Please speak after the tone.

Man This is Michael Roder, R-O-D-E-R, from Elbe AG in Germany. I'd like to speak to Mrs Lucas as soon as possible, please. My telephone number is 040 6544 8765.

CALL 4

Sarah Claire Stone's office. Sarah speaking.
Ian Good morning, Sarah. It's Ian Roberts from Atlas Lasers here. Is Claire available at the moment?
Sarah Oh, hello Ian. I'll check. ... She's on the other line at the moment. Can she call you back?

Ian Yes, OK. Fine.

Sarah Ah. Just a minute. It's OK, she's free now. I'll put you through.

UNIT 2 BUSINESS FILE 4

1/11

MESSAGE 1 *Message timed at oh seven forty-seven today.*
My name is Peter Hobday, that's H-O-B-D-A-Y. I'm calling about your advertisement in today's newspaper for a part-time sales assistant. My number is 01925 713 335.

MESSAGE 2 *Message timed at oh seven fifty-three today.*
Hi, it's Susan. I'm sorry, my daughter is very ill and I can't come in today. If you need to speak to me, you can get me on my mobile. The number is 07786-732 563.

MESSAGE 3 *Message timed at oh seven fifty-six today.*
This is a message for Mr March. Could he call me as soon as possible, please? I have a meeting with him at 10 o'clock this morning and I'm in terrible traffic on the motorway. My name is James Glennie, that's G-L-E-N-N-I-E and my mobile number is 07805 747 770. Thanks.

UNIT 3 B4

1/14

Kay So what do you guys do for fun?

Sam Eckhard goes skiing a lot, don't you Eckhard?

Eckhard Very funny, Sam.

Kay Excuse me?

Sam Sorry, Kay, it's a joke. Northern Germany is, well, flat. Hamburg isn't exactly the ski capital of the world.

Kay Oh, I see. So what do you like doing, Eckhard?

Eckhard Me? I love sailing. You could say I'm a sailing fanatic.

Kay Do you have a boat?

Eckhard I bought one together with a friend last year, yes. We go out in it every weekend when we can in the summer.

Kay It sounds great.

Eckhard It is. Hamburg's a nice place to live, but I work in an office all day and when I'm not working I hate being indoors.

Kay And what about you, Sam? Are you a sporty person?

Sam Well, yes, I go to the gym a couple of times a week and I like cycling, but that's not my main interest. Actually, I play in an orchestra.

Eckhard In an orchestra? I didn't know that, Sam. What do you play?

Sam The violin.

Kay Wow, I'm impressed. Is it a big orchestra?

Sam Well, it's a symphony orchestra, but we aren't famous or anything. Just amateurs. But last year we went on a tour of Europe, so that was good.

Kay How long was the tour?

Sam Well, that was the only problem. I love travelling but I hate staying in hotels and we were away for nearly three weeks. It was a bit long for me ...

UNIT 3 BUSINESS FILE 1

1/15

Receptionist Martin's Office Supplies.

Jill Good morning. Could I speak to someone about your advertisement in this morning's newspaper, please? It's about the office chairs.

Receptionist I'll put you through to the sales department. It's ringing for you now.

...

Karen Sales department. Karen speaking.

Jill Yes, hello, good morning. This is Jill Parsons from Royal Oak Insurance. I'm ringing about your advertisement in this morning's newspaper. I understand that you have a special offer on office chairs at the moment.

Karen Yes, that's right. We're offering £40 off our standard chairs this week. The normal price is £180, but we're offering the chairs at £140.

Jill I see. What colours do you have?

Karen Blue or red.

Jill Can you supply ten blue chairs?

Karen Let me check. Yes, that's fine.

Jill And when can you deliver them?

Karen Today's Monday. We could deliver on Wednesday. That's the, er, 15th of April.

Jill OK. Can that be before 10 o'clock?

Karen Yes, fine. No problem.

Jill Is there a charge for delivery?

Karen Is your office in town?

Jill Yes.

Karen Delivery in town is free.

Jill Yes, well, that all sounds OK. I'd like to place an order then.

Karen Good, thank you. Can I just take your details? Just a minute, I'll get an order form. Right. So that's ten blue office chairs, price £140 each. What's the address for delivery?

Jill Royal Oak Insurance, Royal Oak House, Bristol BS1 4WG.

Karen BS1 ...

Jill 4WG

Karen And how would you like to pay?

Jill I'd like to pay by credit card. Is that OK?

Karen Yes, fine.

Jill It's a VISA card, number 1977 4888 7162 0664. The expiry date is 05/13.

Karen I'll just repeat that: 1977 4888 7162 0664. Expiry date 05/13.

Jill That's right.

Karen OK. We'll deliver the chairs on Wednesday before 10 o'clock.

Jill Great. Bye now.

Karen Thanks very much for your call. Goodbye.

UNIT 4 A2

1/17

... Right. First then, how do we organize our company? Helle operates in three regions. You can see them here on this map. Our world headquarters are in Hamburg, here, and our first region is this one, Europe and South Africa. It's the smallest region in size, but actually the most important for sales. It accounts for around sixty-two per cent of our total turnover. Last year our total turnover was one point nine five billion euros. Of that one point two billion were in the Europe and South Africa region. OK. The second biggest region for us is this one, the Middle East, Asia and the Pacific. That includes Australia and Japan, of course. This region accounts for about twenty per cent of our turnover. And the third biggest region is the Americas, that's to say Canada, the USA and Latin America. If my mathematics are right, then that's the other eighteen per cent of our turnover. Just a word about offices and employees. Helle has around fifteen thousand employees worldwide, with two thousand of those in Germany itself. We have forty offices in Germany and three hundred in other countries, so three hundred and forty offices in all.

OK. Those are our regions. We also divide our business into these four divisions: overland freight, sea freight, air freight and other, that's mainly our courier service. As you can see on this pie chart, the most profitable of the four divisions is air freight. It accounts for thirty-four per cent of our total turnover – last year that was six hundred and sixty-one million euros. The next most important division is sea freight, about thirty-two per cent of our turnover, five hundred and seventy-five million euros. Then overland transport, twenty-five per cent, five hundred and seven million euros. And then last other, nine per cent, two hundred million – so still very important to us, then. Right, let me stop there for a moment. Any questions? Yes ...

UNIT 4 BUSINESS FILE 1

1/20

1 Hello Julie, it's Su Lim in Beijing. I hope you can help me. I have to speak to Annie and it's very urgent. I know she's on vacation this week, but she said I could call her at home in an emergency. Do you have her home number, please, and can you give it to me? Thanks very much.

2 Hi Julie. How are you today? This is Fernando Gonzales in Madrid. I'm ringing about Bob Baker's report on the investment market in Spain. I'm sorry, I know I should have it but I can't find it. Could you send the report to me again, please? Thanks.

3 Julie, hi, it's Sean O'Mally in Dublin here. Thanks for the information you sent yesterday but I'm afraid I can't open the file. Could you send it again in a different format? Sorry to give you extra work. I hope you get this message OK. Thanks very much. Bye now.

4 Hi there Julie, it's Mary in New York. How's life with you this morning? I'm just ringing to say I got the leaflets that you mailed me a couple of days ago. They arrived this morning. Thanks a lot. I think they'll be enough for what we need. Have a nice one.

UNIT 5 A1

1/21

Helle Logistics is based in Hamburg in northern Germany. It transports goods all over the world by truck, air and sea. Eckhard Kellermann is an account manager, that is to say he works with one big client, Nimbus, an American sportswear manufacturer. Eckhard's regular contact person there is Sam Engels. It's 6 o'clock on a Monday evening ...

UNIT 5 A6

1/22

CONVERSATION 1

Jayanne So that's possible is it?

Amber Oh yes, sure. No problem. ... Excuse me a minute, Jayanne. I have another call. ... Amber Lee.

Joe Amber? Hi, it's Joe Petronelli here. Amber, do you know Phil Weslake's email address?

Amber Hi, Joe. Phil Weslake? No, I don't I'm afraid, but it'll be here in the office somewhere. Look, sorry, but I'm on the other line at the moment. Just give me a couple of minutes, OK? ...

CONVERSATION 2

Amber It's open.

Jody Amber, hi, sorry to disturb you.

Amber That's OK, Jody. Come on in. What can I do for you?

Jody I just had Lilian Catanze on the phone ...

Amber From GoldSaxburg?

Jody Right. There's a big panic over there. She says she needs all the documents for the Allen Hanssen merger today.

Amber I thought ...

Jody Yes, I know.

Amber OK. I have to go to lunch with a client right now but ...

CONVERSATION 3

Amber Hi Jerry.

Jerry Oh, hi Amber. How're things this morning?

Amber Fine, thanks.

Jerry Oh, by the way, I still need that list of investors in the Calcom project. Do you have it?

Amber Sorry, Jerry. I still have three or four names that I have to add.

Jerry OK, but asap, yes?

Amber Sure. ...

CONVERSATION 4

Amber Amber Lee.

Man This is the front desk, Ms Lee. Your eleven-thirty is here. ...

CONVERSATION 5

Amber Let me just look at my planner. No, this afternoon I'm totally busy, Megan. And tomorrow afternoon isn't much better. I have a window tomorrow morning around ten. Could you come here then?

Megan Yes, that's fine.

Amber I'll just write that down. ...

UNIT 5 B3

1/23

Hi. My name's Jo MacKenzie and I work for Helle in Canada. The company has five offices here. The head office is in Toronto, and there are branches in Montreal, Edmonton, Vancouver and Calgary. That's where I work. If you don't know Canada well, then Calgary is in the province of Alberta in western Canada. I'm the manager of the Calgary office.

OK, so, our website. What do we use it for? Well, I'd say there were three reasons, one fairly standard reason and two that are, well, perhaps a bit special to Helle and logistics companies generally.

First, like all companies, we use our website for promoting our business. It's our 'Internet presence'. Maybe people find us on the Internet when they're just browsing. Or they visit us when they're looking for a logistics company. Potential customers certainly use our website for getting more information about Helle. Investors use our website for getting financial information.

OK, that's one thing. The second, and this is a bit special, our website is also our company intranet. With around three hundred or more offices worldwide, the website connects us all the time. I use the website every day for sending emails to colleagues and for contacting the head office in Hamburg. We sometimes also have web conferences on our intranet and that's great for solving problems and making decisions.

Third, our website is extremely useful for our customers. Without doubt the most important feature for them is the tracking and tracing page. What's tracking and tracing? Well, for example, a customer is sending goods from Canada to, say, South America. It's day five. Where are the goods now? When will they arrive? Is everything OK? You can look at the tracking and tracing page and check the status. Tracking means following your order from A to B, tracing means finding where it is now. And, of course, you can do this 24 hours a day and from the computer in your office. Like I said, it's the most useful thing on the website for our customers.

UNIT 5 BUSINESS FILE 1

1/24

Brian You've got some great cars here, Willi.

Willi Thank you.

Brian	So how did you find the paint samples that I sent you?
Willi	Yes, I liked the paints very much. The quality is good and the colours are authentic.
Brian	Do you think you'd like to place an order with us?
Willi	I have some questions first.
Brian	Fine. Go ahead.
Willi	About the prices on your price list. Are they ex-works or do they include delivery?
Brian	They're the basic, ex-works prices. The delivery costs depend on the size of your order. Just a minute. Yes, here. This is the scale of delivery charges.
Willi	Scale?
Brian	Skala.
Willi	You speak German!
Brian	No, not really. Just some words.
Willi	Thanks. Yes, that's clear. Yes, that's OK, quite normal, I think. And that includes insurance, does it?
Brian	Everything. That's the total cost of the paints to your door.
Willi	Yes, OK. About payment. What are your terms?
Brian	We normally say 30 days. If it's a first order and if it's very big, we sometimes ask for payment in advance or COD, but for you, payment in full within thirty days will be fine.
Willi	Good, thanks. And I can pay by cheque?
Brian	Well, our preferred method of payment is a bank transfer. It's quicker and easier. But basically it's not a problem. You can pay by cheque, bank transfer or credit card. They're all acceptable.
Willi	So long as you get your money.
Brian	That's right.
Willi	OK. What happens if there's a problem with the paints when I get them?
Brian	Well, obviously that depends on the reason. If it's a question that you just, well if you change your mind when you see the paints ...
Willi	I don't understand.
Brian	OK. If you order red then decide that you really wanted green ...
Willi	OK.
Brian	Then you have to pay to send the red paint back.
Willi	Of course.
Brian	But if it's the quality of the paint, basically if it's our fault, then we'll refund – give back – your money immediately and pay the transport costs.
Willi	Yes, that's clear. Fine. Now, what discounts can you offer me?
Brian	We have a very clear company policy about that, Willi. We never give discounts on a first order.
Willi	But if I order more paints, if I place more orders later ... ?
Brian	Then of course we can talk about discounts then. What I can say, is that with our good customers we normally give a rebate after six months. So, six months after your first order, if you place more orders with us, we can give you a discount that goes back to the beginning on all your orders.
Willi	How much?
Brian	Four, maybe five per cent.
Willi	Can we agree that now? Say, a five per cent rebate after six months?
Brian	OK, agreed.
Willi	Can you let me have that in writing?
Brian	Of course. Fine. So, Willi. Would you like to place an order today? I have an order form here.
Willi	Yes. Let's go and have a cup of coffee.
Brian	And fill out the order form.

UNIT 6 B2

2/03

Tony	So what are you two doing this week?
Martin	We're giving a lot of demonstrations, basically. We're flying to Berlin this afternoon and giving a demonstration tomorrow morning at the German Chamber of Commerce.
Tony	When are you coming back?
Holly	Tomorrow evening.
Tony	So, Martin, are you taking Wednesday off? Did that work out?
Martin	Well, yes, but only in the morning. Unfortunately, we're designing a new demo in the afternoon.
Tony	What about Thursday and Friday?
Martin	Let's see. I think we're going to Fuyi Film here in Munich on Thursday ...
Holly	... and on Friday we're flying to the trade fair in Cologne for the day.
Tony	Sounds like a busy week! Glad it's you and not me. Well, good luck with your demos ...

UNIT 6 B4

2/04

Holly	So, Martin, have you booked the flights to Cologne yet?
Martin	Yes, I have. I booked them two weeks ago so we got a good price. Mmm. Taxis. Has someone ordered them for Friday morning yet?
Holly	No, not yet. I'll do that tomorrow.
Martin	OK. What about the equipment? Have you reserved a projector yet?
Holly	Yes, I did that last week. OK. Oh, have you phoned Gerhard in the Cologne office yet to arrange things there?
Martin	Oh, no, I haven't done that yet. I'll phone him now.

UNIT 6 BUSINESS FILE 2

2/05

CONVERSATION 1

Tom	Tom Reynolds.
Joscelyn	Hi Tom. It's Joscelyn Taylor.
Tom	Oh, good day, Joscelyn. How are you?
Joscelyn	Fine, thanks. Tom, look, I'm sorry but I have a problem with our meeting on Thursday morning. I can't make it.
Tom	That's OK. Do you want to find another time?
Joscelyn	Well, I can see from my diary that we have a second meeting next week anyway, on Tuesday morning. It would be best for me if we can just cancel this one. Would that be OK with you?
Tom	Yes, sure, fine. So I'll see you a week tomorrow then at nine o'clock. Is that right?
Joscelyn	That's absolutely right. Thanks a lot, Tom.
Tom	No problem, Joscelyn. I'll look forward to that. Bye now.
Joscelyn	Great, Tom. Bye.

CONVERSATION 2

Jean	Jean Yates.
Joscelyn	Good morning, Mrs Yates. This is Joscelyn Taylor from your law firm.
Jean	Good morning, Ms Taylor. How can I help you?
Joscelyn	It's about our meeting on Thursday.
Jean	Yes, is there a problem?
Joscelyn	Yes, I'm afraid something unexpected has come up and I can't keep our appointment.
Jean	Oh well, never mind. These things happen. I would still like to see you, though, if it's possible.

Joscelyn	Of course. I'm busy all day on Wednesday, but at the moment I'm free tomorrow at the same time or on Friday.
Jean	Let me just look at my diary. Well, how about tomorrow? I'm free then, too.
Joscelyn	Fine. So that's tomorrow morning at nine thirty. Thank you very much indeed, Mrs Yates.
Jean	You're very welcome, Ms Taylor. I look forward to seeing you then.

CONVERSATION 3

Woman	Paul Barry's office.
Joscelyn	Good morning. Could I speak to Paul Barry, please? It's Joscelyn Taylor.
Woman	Hold the line, please.
Paul	Joscelyn. Hi. How are you this morning?
Joscelyn	Morning Paul. I'm just fine, thanks. And you?
Paul	Yes, I'm fine, thanks. As a matter of fact, I wanted to phone you this morning. Look, I'm really sorry, Joscelyn, but I can't make our appointment on Thursday.
Joscelyn	Please don't worry. That's why I'm phoning you. I can't make it either.
Paul	Oh, well, that's OK then. Can we find another time?
Joscelyn	Sure. This week is a bit hectic, but I have some time next week. Would Wednesday next week suit you?
Paul	Just a minute. Wednesday next week would be just fine. How about ten o'clock again?
Joscelyn	Great. Can you still make lunch again afterwards?
Paul	Yes, that's fine, too. OK, Joscelyn, see you then.
Joscelyn	I'll look forward to it. Bye now.
Paul	Bye.

CONVERSATION

Woman	Pamela Eby.
Joscelyn	Good morning. It's Joscelyn Taylor here from the law firm. I got your voicemail message this morning. I'm terribly sorry to hear what's happened. Would you like to come into the office and see me this morning?
Woman	Oh, yes. Thank you very much. Is that possible?
Joscelyn	How about ten o'clock? Is that too soon for you?
Woman	No, ten o'clock is great.
Joscelyn	Good. Can I just ask you, how do you spell your name?
Woman	It's Pamela Eby. E-B-Y.
Joscelyn	OK. And don't worry too much.
Woman	Thank you. See you then.
Joscelyn	Fine. Ten o'clock. Bye.
Woman	Bye.

UNIT 7 B2

2/07

Hi. I'm Martin Schiller and I work for BlueSky Software in Germany. I guess I'm one of the 'old hands' there now. I joined the company ten years ago. My first job was in technical support – I answered people's questions about their software on the hotline. But then, I think it was in 1999, I got a job in the sales department and that's where I still work now. Do I like the job? Well, the good things about it are that I meet a lot of interesting people, I work with a really nice colleague, Holly, and our software is good, so it's not hard to sell. But the bad thing is that I travel a lot. My wife and I had a baby last year and I'd like to have a job now where I can be at home more. In this job I often spend half my life in hotels and I don't want to do that from now on. BlueSky Software is a good company, but early next year I'm going to look for a new job.

UNIT 7 BUSINESS FILE 2

2/08

Recording	Welcome to Logos-To-Go. To place an order, press one. If you have a query about an existing order, press two. If you want to order a catalogue, press three. To hear this menu again, press four. For all other queries, please stay on the line.
Rick	God, I hate these things. OK, one.
Nancy	Good morning. You're talking with Nancy. How may I help you today?
Rick	Hi, I have your catalogue from a business partner but I have a couple of questions for you before I place an order.
Nancy	Sure. What do you want to know?
Rick	OK. You can print my company logo on your range of products, is that right?
Nancy	That's right.
Rick	So how do I send you the logo?
Nancy	Well, you can send it to us by email ...
Rick	As a jpg file for example?
Nancy	Yes, that would be fine. Or if you prefer you can just mail us a page of your company notepaper or whatever, something that has your logo on it.
Rick	And you can take the logo from that?
Nancy	That's correct. It's all very simple.
Rick	So do the prices in the catalogue include printing the logo or is that extra?
Nancy	No, the prices include the printing costs. But when you place your first order, there's a one-time charge for producing your logo. We call it a one-time logo development charge.
Rick	How much is that?
Nancy	Eight-five dollars.
Rick	But I only pay that the first time, right?
Nancy	Right. After your first order, we keep your logo here and we just use it again when you order more goods from us.
Rick	OK. And what are your terms of payment?
Nancy	Thirty days after you get the goods and you're satisfied with them.
Rick	And shipping and handling costs?
Nancy	Twenty dollars if your order is under five hundred dollars. If you place an order for five hundred dollars or more, then shipping and handling is free.
Rick	OK, well, that sounds good. I'd like to place an order with you then.
Nancy	OK, first I'll need your name and the name of your company.
Rick	That's Rick Simonette – S-I-M-O-N-E-T-T-E. And the company is WAFB-TV.
Nancy	One moment. OK, Rick. I'm ready for your order.
Rick	So, first, men's polo shirts. I'd like to order twenty. Women's polo shirts. Also twenty.
Nancy	And the colours and sizes?
Rick	All light blue and all medium.
Nancy	OK.
Rick	Next, twenty blue umbrellas.
Nancy	Twenty blue umbrellas.
Rick	And then ten of the travel bags.
Nancy	They're really nice. You'll love them. Is that it, Rick?
Rick	Yes, that's all.
Nancy	I'll just read that back to you. Twenty men's polo shirts, light blue, medium. Twenty women's polo shirts, light blue, medium. Twenty blue umbrellas. Ten travel bags. And when can you let us have your logo?
Rick	I'll email it to you now with my address, OK?
Nancy	Great. I'll hold your order until I hear from you.

Rick Oh, one more thing. When can I expect to get the goods?

Nancy We normally ship in about two weeks.

Rick Fine. OK, well thanks, Nancy.

Nancy You're welcome, Rick. Thanks very much for calling Logos-To-Go. Have a nice one now.

Rick You too. Bye.

UNIT 8 A5

2/10

Steve And now the good news, guys. First quarter sales were back on target, around €750,000 again, the same as the first quarter last year. But this quarter has been, how can I put this, dramatic. It hasn't finished yet, and so far sales have already reached almost a million euros. I think they'll go over the million by the end of the month.

Klaus Wow!

Rosa So why ...

Steve It's the 'Delila Effect'. Delila Smith is a TV chef. Extremely popular in the UK. She has a weekly show and a couple of months ago she started using our knives on her programme. What Delila uses today, the world buys tomorrow morning. Since then, sales of our knives have increased by over a hundred per cent.

Klaus Do you think this Delila Smith would like a job with Amsel?

Steve Unfortunately, I don't think so!

UNIT 8 B1

2/11

AT THE RECEPTION DESK

Receptionist Good afternoon.

Andrea Good afternoon. You have a room reserved for me. My name's Graf, G-R-A-F.

Receptionist Just a moment. Yes, a single room for two nights, Mrs Graf. Is that right?

Andrea Yes, that's right.

Receptionist OK, would you just fill in the registration form, please?

Andrea Here you are.

Receptionist Here's you room key. It's room 10 on the first floor. The lift and the stairs are just over there.

Andrea Thank you. Oh, are there any messages for me?

Receptionist I'll just look. Er, yes, a Mr Steve Knight phoned about an hour ago. Here you are.

Andrea Thanks very much.

Receptionist You're welcome. Enjoy your stay with us.

IN THE HOTEL ROOM

Receptionist Reception.

Andrea Oh hello. This is Andrea Graf in room 10. I wonder if you could help me, please? I'm afraid I don't have any towels in my room.

Receptionist Oh dear. I'm sorry about that. I'll send some up straight away. Is everything else okay, Mrs Graf?

Andrea Yes, everything else is fine, thanks.

Receptionist Good. You'll have the towels in a couple of minutes.

Andrea Thanks very much.

IN THE HOTEL LOBBY

Waiter Good afternoon, madam. Would you like some tea or coffee?

Andrea Some tea would be nice, please.

Waiter A pot of assam?

Andrea Fine. And could I have some biscuits or cake with that?

Waiter I'll bring you our afternoon tea selection. There's a bit of everything in that. (...) So, here we are. There's some hot water in this pot if the tea's too strong.

Andrea Thanks very much.

UNIT 8 B4

2/12

CONVERSATION 1

Receptionist Reception.

Mr Black Yes, good evening. This is Derek Black in room three one four. I'm afraid my television isn't working.

Receptionist Oh, I'm sorry about that Mr Black. I'll send someone up straight away to see what the problem is.

Mr Black Great. Thanks a lot.

Receptionist You're welcome, sir.

CONVERSATION 2

Receptionist Reception. Mark speaking.

Mrs White This is Helen White in room 12. I wonder if you could help me? I rang room service about half an hour ago and ordered a snack and a drink. I'm afraid it hasn't arrived yet.

Receptionist I'm terribly sorry, Mrs White. The kitchen's exceptionally busy this evening, but I'll bring your order up myself straight away. What was it exactly that you ordered?

Mrs White A chicken sandwich with a small salad and a bottle of still mineral water.

Receptionist OK. I'll be with you in about five minutes. Again, I'm sorry about this. There won't be a charge for your order.

Mrs White Oh, fine, thanks very much.

Receptionist You're welcome, madam.

CONVERSATION 3

Receptionist Good morning, Mr Green. Are you checking out?

Mr Green Yes, time to go!

Receptionist I've got your bill ready. Here we are. That comes to a total of €357.76 all together.

Mr Green Erm, I'm sorry, but I don't think this is right. Could you check it again?

Receptionist A single room for two nights?

Mr Green Yes, that's right.

Receptionist And then you made three phone calls and these items here are drinks from the minibar.

Mr Green I didn't make any phone calls. I had a bottle of fruit juice from the minibar, but that doesn't cost €20, does it?

Receptionist Just a moment, Mr Green. I'll check this on the computer again. It seems right, I'm afraid. Oh, just a minute. You were in room 14, is that right?

Mr Green No, room 37.

Receptionist Mr Green, I'm terribly sorry. I've made a mistake. You're Mr Kevin Green. I've given you the bill for Mr William Green in room 14. I'll write out a new bill for you straight away.

Mr Green OK, good. Never mind. We all make mistakes ...

UNIT 8 BUSINESS FILE 2

2/13

Right, this business trip next week, then. Let me just get my diary. Yes. I need to be in Colchester on Wednesday and Thursday. I'll fly over on Wednesday morning, it'll have to be very early – I need to be in the meeting at 11 o'clock – but I'll stay over after the meeting on Thursday night. We'll probably go to dinner or something. OK, so that's, let me see, departing from here early Wednesday morning the 23rd of March and returning on Friday morning – not too early this time, sort of mid-morning if possible – what's Friday? yes, the 25th of March.

Airport. Hmm. Well, the best airport for Colchester is Stansted, it's only about half an hour away by taxi and there are some very good cheap flights from Düsseldorf to Stansted. It's only a short flight, it seems stupid to spend money when it's not necessary. So get me a return flight from Düsseldorf to Stansted with one of the budget airlines if you can. OK? There are some very nice hotels in or near Colchester. The main thing is that the hotel is quiet. Can you ask about that when you phone them? Otherwise, you decide. I need to contact Frank Harris in London before I go, but, no, I'll do that myself. Right. I think that's it. Thanks very much.

UNIT 9 A2

2/14

Andrea Good morning. Can I help at all?
Paul Oh, hello. I'm just looking at your knives.
Andrea Are you interested in knives for professional use or for yourself?
Paul Well, for professional use actually. My name's Paul Hornby, I'm a buyer for a hotel chain here in the UK.
Andrea I'm Andrea Graf. Amsel's European sales manager.
Paul Nice to meet you.
Andrea Nice to meet you, too. Do you have a couple of minutes now? We can look at the knives together and I can tell you a bit about them.
Paul Yes, that's fine. I'd like that.
Andrea Good. Let's sit over here. It's a bit quieter ... OK, well. Can I assume that you're looking for knives for your hotel kitchens?
Paul Yes, that's right.
Andrea What kind of quantities did you have in mind?
Paul Well, that depends, of course. But our chain owns 24 major hotels in the UK and three in Ireland.
Andrea I see. Do you use any Amsel knives at all at the moment?
Paul No.
Andrea Is there a reason why you haven't bought our knives before?
Paul Yes, it's just a question of price, basically. We normally buy from another manufacturer because its products are cheaper.
Andrea And are you happy with what you're getting from them?
Paul Hm, their knives are OK, yes.
Andrea Well, I don't know the manufacturer, naturally, but I can promise you that our knives are better.
Paul Well, maybe, but I really don't think I can justify the extra expense. Your prices are, well, around 20% above what I'm paying at the moment. That's a big difference.
Andrea Obviously I can see that and I think a problem we have at Amsel is that it isn't always easy to see straight away the difference between what I'll call an 'ordinary' kitchen knife and a really high quality knife, like an Amsel knife. They look the same and of course the ordinary knife does its job and it's often, you know, perfectly OK. But in fact there are very real differences between the two and over a longer period of time these differences become more and more important.
Paul Yes, I can see that your knives will last longer, of course, but ...
Andrea Sorry to interrupt, but it isn't just that they'll last *longer*, they'll actually last a lifetime. I mean, once you buy an Amsel knife, that's it. You'll never need to change it. You have to look at this as an investment. You pay a bit more at the beginning, but in the long run you actually save money.
Paul So what happens if we break a knife, or something goes wrong?
Andrea We replace it. It's easy. Every knife comes with a lifetime guarantee and if something goes wrong you'll get a new knife. Free. No questions.
Paul I see.

UNIT 9 A3

2/15

Andrea There are other differences, too. These knives are really popular with chefs. I'll show you why. Here, would you like to just hold a knife for a moment? How does it feel?
Paul Very solid.
Andrea Comfortable to hold?
Paul Hmm, yes. Actually, very comfortable to hold in fact.
Andrea Well, comfort's important if you use a knife every day and chefs do that, of course. You just don't become as tired. The reason is that the knife's perfectly balanced. We've made knives for a very long time now, and, well, this is what you learn to do. Cheaper knives look OK, but they'll never feel like this. And there's another thing, too. Because the handle is ergonomically designed, it's a lot safer. This knife won't slip out of your hand. I mean, you'll get a lot fewer accidents with a good knife like this.
Paul What about the blade? Is the blade sharper than on other knives?
Andrea It's *extremely* sharp, yes, but that isn't actually the main thing. The main thing with our blades is that they'll *stay* sharp much longer than with an ordinary knife. If your chefs sharpen their knives at the moment, I don't know, what, two or three times a week, then they'll only need to sharpen this at most once a month. You see, it's made of a very special steel and we have some special production processes. It's a question of experience again.
Paul Hmm.
Andrea Look, it's nearly lunchtime. Do you have any plans for lunch?
Paul No, not at the moment.
Andrea How about some lunch together and we can talk a bit more?
Paul Yes, OK. Fine. That sounds good ...

UNIT 9 B1

2/16

MESSAGE 1
Hello Jan. It's Paula Morris from Cookshops Ltd. in England. I've got a couple of queries about your last invoice. I've just faxed a copy to you with my comments. Could you check it for me and either phone me back or email me as soon as you can? Thanks.

MESSAGE 2
Jan, hi, it's Lucia in Rome. I need some more company brochures, the Italian versions obviously. Could you send me two thousand? I've just opened the last box of a hundred and I'm going to the Milan trade fair the week after next, so could you send them as soon as possible? Thanks. Ciao.

MESSAGE 3
Hello. I hope I'm ringing the right number. It's the one on the guarantee for my knives. I've had a set of Amsel knives for five years now and I've just broken the blade of one of them. The problem is that the shop where I bought the knives has closed down. My name's David Roberts, that's R-O-B-E-R-T-S, and I live in Durham in the north of England. If this message reaches you,

could you phone me on 0191 374 3018, or my email address is d.roberts@aol.com. Thanks.

MESSAGE 4

My name's Claude Lebon and I'm a chef at a restaurant in Amsterdam. I've just seen your website on the Internet and I'd like to talk to someone about buying knives for our kitchen. Do you have a representative in the Netherlands and, if so, how can I contact him or her? My phone number is 0031 20 6229044.

UNIT 10 A1

2/17

Andrea Paul, hi. Good to see you again.
Paul Hello Andrea. It's good to be here.
Andrea How was your journey?
Paul Oh, fine, thanks. No problems.
Andrea And did you find us OK?
Paul Yes, I just took a taxi straight from the airport. The traffic was bad, but I'm here now. I hope I'm not late?
Andrea Oh no, not at all. OK, look, you can leave your suitcase here at the reception desk. Can I offer you a cup of tea or coffee?
Paul I'm fine, thanks. I'd just like to wash my hands quickly, if that's OK.
Andrea Sure. There's a toilet just along the corridor here. ...
Andrea OK, here we are. This is our conference room. The others should be here already. Please come in. So, Paul, can I introduce our marketing manager, Gerd Haase? Gerd, this is Paul Hornby from Fairway Hotels in the UK.
Gerd How do you do?
Paul How do you do.
Andrea And this is Karin Josef. Karin is from our finance department.
Karin Pleased to meet you.
Paul Nice to meet you, too.
Gerd Welcome to Solingen, Mr Hornby. Is this your first visit here?
Paul Yes, it is. In fact, it's my first visit to Germany.
Andrea Oh, that's great. If you have time, perhaps we can show you around Düsseldorf. How long are you here for?
Paul I've got a hotel here for this evening, then tomorrow I'm travelling down to Nuremberg. An old school friend works there now and I've arranged to visit him for a couple of days.
Karin That's really nice. You'll like Nuremberg. It's a beautiful city.
Andrea OK, everybody. If you're all ready, we'll get down to business ...

UNIT 10 BUSINESS FILE 1

2/19

CONVERSATION 1

Driver Mr Held?
Werner Yes.
Driver Good morning. I'm from Southern Power. Welcome to Heathrow.
Werner Oh, hello. Thank you.
Driver The car's just outside, sir. Here, let me take your suitcase.
Werner Thanks.
Driver Would you like to follow me? So, how was your flight? ...

CONVERSATION 2

Bernie This is Judy Masterson, our financial director.
Judy How do you do, Mr Held?
Werner How do you do.
Bernie Colin Gregory from operations.
Colin How do you do?
Werner How do you do.
Bernie And Davina Shaw, from our purchasing department.
Davina Very pleased to meet you, Mr Held.
Werner You, too, Ms Shaw.
Bernie So, there's some coffee and biscuits over there. Just help yourselves, please. What time did you have to leave home to go to the airport this morning, Mr Held ...

CONVERSATION 3

Judy Are you going to have a bet, then, Werner?
Werner Yes, I like number 15, German Boy. I think that's a good name today.
Bernie You realize it's thirty-five to one, don't you?
Werner Of course. But I have a good feeling about it. I think it'll win.
Judy I like your optimism, Werner.

CONVERSATION 4

Davina How old were you?
Werner Thirteen, fourteen, maybe. It was a class trip from my school.
Davina So what happened?
Werner Well, I was completely lost. I didn't have any idea where I was, I didn't have any money. Then this very nice English couple, a man and woman, helped me. They telephoned the number I had on my piece of paper and they took me in their car to the address. They were very nice people. They were the first English people that I met.
Bernie What a nice story. Some more water, Werner?
Werner Hmm, thanks. This salad is delicious, by the way.
Bernie Good. I'm glad you like it. So that was your first visit here. I hope your next visit to England went better. ...

CONVERSATION 5

Werner The British Standard specification is three millimetres, but we offer four millimetres, that means the insulation is 25 per cent thicker than absolutely necessary. Our tests have shown that this increases the life of the cable by maybe five years and the power loss is much smaller over long distances.
Bernie Judy.
Judy But is that reflected in the cost of the cable?
Werner Yes, initially, but you have to look at the long-term ...

Unit word list

Hier finden Sie die Wörter in der Reihenfolge ihres Vorkommens im Text. Nicht aufgeführt sind ungefähr 400 elementare Wörter, die vorausgesetzt sind, Wörter mit der gleichen Bedeutung im Deutschen (*computer, bank*), Zahlwörter (*four, twenty*) sowie grammatische Bezeichnung (*singular*).

Die Zahl am linken Rand gibt die Seitenzahl an.
p = das Wort befindet sich im Partner file
t = das Wort befindet sich im Transcript
AE = Amerikanisches Englisch

UNIT 1 WHAT WE DO

6	**Pleased to meet you** [ˌpliːzd tə 'miːt ju]	Es freut mich, Sie kennen zu lernen
	company ['kʌmpəni]	Unternehmen, Firma
	called [kɔːld]	namens
	business agency ['bɪznəs eɪdʒənsi]	Geschäftsagentur
	foreign ['fɒrən]	ausländisch
	start-up ['stɑːt ʌp]	Start-up(-Unternehmen)
	business partner ['bɪznəs pɑːtnə]	Geschäftspartner/in
	joint venture [ˌdʒɔɪnt 'ventʃə]	Gemeinschaftsunternehmen
	exactly [ɪg'zæktli]	exakt, genau
	consultant [kən'sʌltənt]	Berater/in
	contact ['kɒntækt]	Kontakt, Verbindung
	interesting ['ɪntrəstɪŋ]	interessant
	to **travel** ['trævl]	reisen
	around [ə'raʊnd]	herum
	to **complete** [kəm'pliːt]	ergänzen, vervollständigen
	phrase [freɪz]	(Rede-)Wendung, Ausdruck
7	to **remember** [rɪ'membə]	sich erinnern, daran denken
	business activity [ˌbɪznəs æk'tɪvəti]	Geschäftstätigkeit
7t	**sales manager** ['seɪlz mænɪdʒə]	Verkaufsleiter/in
	head office [ˌhed 'ɒfɪs]	Zentrale
	factory ['fæktəri]	Fabrik
	account manager [ə'kaʊnt mænɪdʒə]	Kundenbetreuer/in
	to **explain** [ɪk'spleɪn]	erklären, erläutern
	client ['klaɪənt]	Kunde/Kundin
	permanent ['pɜːmənənt]	ständig, Dauer-
	account [ə'kaʊnt]	(Stamm)Kunde
	sportswear ['spɔːtsweə]	Sportkleidung
	trainers ['treɪnəz]	Turn-, Tennisschuhe
	CEO (chief executive officer) [ˌtʃiːf ɪg'zekjətɪv ɒfɪsə]	(Haupt)Geschäftsführer/in
	to **develop** [dɪ'veləp]	entwickeln
	to **sell** [sel]	verkaufen
	to **be based in** [bi 'beɪst ɪn]	den Firmensitz haben in
8	**expression** [ɪk'spreʃn]	Ausdruck
	to **compare** [kəm'peə]	vergleichen
	service company ['sɜːvɪs kʌmpəni]	Dienstleistungsunternehmen
	manufacturing company [ˌmænjʊ'fæktʃərɪŋ]	Herstellerfirma
	retailer ['riːteɪlə]	Einzelhändler/in
	insurance company [ɪn'ʃʊərəns kʌmpəni]	Versicherungsgesellschaft
	to **manufacture** [ˌmænju'fæktʃə]	herstellen
	to **produce** [prə'djuːs]	produzieren
	to **provide** (a service) [prə'vaɪd]	(eine Leistung) anbieten, erbringen
	high quality [haɪ 'kwɒləti]	von hoher Qualität
	kitchen ['kɪtʃɪn]	Küche
	knife [naɪf]	Messer
	package ['pækɪdʒ]	Paket, Bündel
	goods [gʊdz]	Ware(n), Güter
	worldwide ['wɜːldwaɪd]	weltweit
	customer ['kʌstəmə]	Kunde/Kundin
	to **correct** [kə'rekt]	korrigieren
	note [nəʊt]	Notiz
	approximately [ə'prɒksɪmətli]	ungefähr, zirka
	to **introduce** [ˌɪntrə'djuːs]	vorstellen
9	**Nice to meet you** [ˌnaɪs tə 'miːt ju]	Freut mich, Sie kennen zu lernen
	again [ə'gen]	wieder
	Nice to see you again [naɪs tə 'siː ju əgen]	Schön, Sie wieder zu sehen
	How are you? [haʊ ə 'juː]	Wie geht es dir/Ihnen?
	I'm fine, thanks [aɪm 'faɪn, θæŋks]	Danke, gut
	Good to see you [ˌgʊd tə 'siː ju, tuː]	Freut mich, Sie zu sehen
	face-to-face meeting [ˌfeɪs tə 'feɪs miːtɪŋ]	persönliche Begegnung
	to **know** [nəʊ]	wissen
	mobile phone [ˌməʊbaɪl 'fəʊn]	Mobiltelefon, Handy
	How do you do? [ˌhaʊ dju 'duː]	Es freut mich, sie kennen zu lernen
	on the phone [ɒn ðə 'fəʊn]	am Telefon
	at last [ət 'lɑːst]	endlich
	to **welcome** ['welkəm]	begrüßen
	flight [flaɪt]	Flug
	to **ring** [rɪŋ]	klingeln, läuten
	to **excuse** [ɪk'skjuːz]	entschuldigen
	important [ɪm'pɔːtnt]	wichtig
10	**rhyme** [raɪm]	Reim
	double ['dʌbl]	doppelt, Doppel-
	capital ['kæpɪtl]	groß
	to **spell** [spel]	buchstabieren, schreiben
	to **unscramble** [ˌʌn'skræmbl]	entschlüsseln, in die richtige Reihenfolge bringen
	map [mæp]	(Land-)Karte
11	**conversation** [ˌkɒnvə'seɪʃn]	Gespräch, Unterhaltung
	Please, call me ... [pliːz, 'kɔːl mi]	Nennen Sie mich bitte ...
	Great to see you [ˌgreɪt tə 'siː ju]	Ich freue mich sehr, Sie zu sehen
	I didn't catch your name [aɪ dɪdnt ˌkætʃ jɔː 'neɪm]	Ich habe Ihren Namen nicht verstanden
	to **catch** (a name) [kætʃ]	(einen Namen) verstehen
	Come and join us [ˌkʌm ən 'dʒɔɪn ʌs]	Kommen Sie zu uns
	to **practise** ['præktɪs]	(ein)üben
	each [iːtʃ]	jede/r/s
	to **invent** [ɪn'vent]	erfinden
	name badge ['neɪm bædʒ]	Namensschild
	conference ['kɒnfərəns]	Konferenz, Besprechung, Tagung
12	**card** [kɑːd]	Visitenkarte
	to **try** [traɪ]	probieren, versuchen
	to **write down** [raɪt 'daʊn]	aufschreiben

b **bad** | d **did** | f **five** | g **got** | h **how** | j **yes** | k **cat** | l **leg** | m **man** | n **no** | p **pen** | r **red**

	web address [ˌweb əˈdres]	Internet-Adresse
	postal address [ˌpəʊstl əˈdres]	Briefanschrift
	to **check** [tʃek]	(über)prüfen
	code [kəʊd]	Vorwahl, Code
	area code (AE) [ˈeəriə kəʊd]	Vorwahl
	post code [ˈpəʊst kəʊd]	Postleitzahl
	to **exchange** [ɪksˈtʃeɪndʒ]	(aus)tauschen
13	**chain** [tʃeɪn]	Kette
	department store [dɪˈpɑːtmənt stɔː]	Kauf-, Warenhaus
	trade fair [ˈtreɪd feə]	Handelsmesse
	to **collect** [kəˈlekt]	sammeln
	details [ˈdiːteɪl]	Einzelheiten, Details
	address book [əˈdres bʊk]	Adressbuch
	job title [ˈdʒɒb taɪtl]	Berufsbezeichnung
13p	**export sales manager** [ˌekspɔːt ˈseɪlz mænɪdʒə]	Exportleiter/in
	public relations [ˌpʌblɪk rɪˈleɪʃnz]	Öffentlichkeitsarbeit
	officer [ˈɒfɪsə]	hier: Mitarbeiter/in
13	**memo** [ˈmeməʊ]	(Akten-)Notiz, Kurzmitteilung
	main point [meɪn ˈpɔɪnt]	Hauptpunkt
13t	**south** [saʊθ]	Süden
	handmade [ˌhændˈmeɪd]	handgemacht
	greeting card [ˈgriːtɪŋ kɑːd]	Glückwunschkarte
	ago [əˈgəʊ]	vor
	just [dʒʌst]	nur, gerade
	to **employ** [ɪmˈplɔɪ]	beschäftigen
	sales representative [ˈseɪlz reprɪzentətɪv]	(Handels-)Vertreter/in
	friendly [ˈfrendli]	freundlich, informell
	atmosphere [ˈætməsfɪə]	Atmosphäre, Betriebsklima
	surprisingly [səˈpraɪzɪŋli]	überraschenderweise
	popular [ˈpɒpjələ]	beliebt, populär
	for example [fər ɪgˈzɑːmpl]	zum Beispiel
	in total [ɪn ˈtəʊtl]	insgesamt
	turnover [ˈtɜːnəʊvə]	Umsatz
	just over [dʒʌst ˈəʊvə]	etwas über
	in fact [ɪn ˈfækt]	tatsächlich
	winery [ˈwaɪnəri]	Weinkellerei
	years old [ˈjɪəz əʊld]	... Jahre alt
	medium [ˈmiːdiəm]	mittlere
	price range [ˈpraɪs reɪndʒ]	Preisgruppe, -segment
	expensive [ɪkˈspensɪv]	teuer
	case [keɪs]	Kiste
	market [ˈmɑːkɪt]	(Absatz-)Markt
	all over [ɔːl ˈəʊvə]	überall (in)
	department [dɪˈpɑːtmənt]	Abteilung
	perfume [ˈpɜːfjuːm]	Parfüm
	sales [seɪlz]	Umsatz, Verkäufe
	range [reɪndʒ]	Sortiment, Palette, Auswahl
	simple [ˈsɪmpl]	einfach
14	**summary** [ˈsʌməri]	Zusammenfassung
15	to **fill in** [ˌfɪl ˈɪn]	eintragen, -setzen
	gap [gæp]	Lücke
	possible [ˈpɒsəbl]	möglich
	to **choose** [tʃuːz]	(aus)wählen
	to **match** [mætʃ]	zuordnen
	to **rearrange** [ˌriːəˈreɪndʒ]	umstellen
16	to **use** [juːz]	benutzen, verwenden
	hidden [ˈhɪdn]	verborgen
	square [skweə]	Quadrat
	either [ˈaɪðə]	entweder
	horizontal [ˌhɒrɪˈzɒntl]	horizontal, waagerecht
	vertical [ˈvɜːtɪkl]	senkrecht, vertikal
	from top to bottom [frəm ˌtɒp tə ˈbɒtəm]	von oben nach unten
	reply [rɪˈplaɪ]	Antwort
	to **identify** [aɪˈdentɪfaɪ]	erkennen, identifizieren
17	**typical** [ˈtɪpɪkl]	typisch
	common [ˈkɒmən]	normal, üblich
	first name [ˈfɜːst neɪm]	Vorname
	family name [ˈfæməli neɪm]	Nach-, Familienname
	normally [ˈnɔːməli]	normalerweise
	difference [ˈdɪfrəns]	Unterschied
	between [bɪˈtwiːn]	zwischen
	unmarried [ˌʌnˈmærid]	unverheiratet

UNIT 2 PROJECTS

18	**at the moment** [ət ðə ˈməʊmənt]	im Augenblick
	clothes [kləʊðz]	Kleidung
	to **wear** [weə]	tragen, anhaben
	usually [ˈjuːʒuəli]	normalerweise, meistens
	skirt [skɜːt]	Rock
	trousers [ˈtraʊzəz]	Hose(n)
	often [ˈɒfn]	oft, häufig
	tie [taɪ]	Krawatte
	dictionary [ˈdɪkʃənri]	Wörterbuch
	picture [ˈpɪktʃə]	Bild
	shirt [ʃɜːt]	Hemd
	phone call [ˈfəʊn kɔːl]	Anruf, Telefongespräch
	to **arrange** [əˈreɪndʒ]	vereinbaren, verabreden
	to **attend** [əˈtend]	teilnehmen (an), besuchen
	to **book** [bʊk]	buchen, bestellen
	trip [trɪp]	Reise
	to **drink** [drɪŋk]	trinken
	suit [suːt]	Anzug
19	to **sit** [sɪt]	sitzen
	to **describe** [dɪˈskraɪb]	beschreiben
	to **expand** [ɪkˈspænd]	sich ausdehnen, expandieren
	site [saɪt]	(Stand-)Ort
	to **discuss** [dɪˈskʌs]	besprechen, erörtern
	pros and cons [ˌprəʊz ənd ˈkɒnz]	Für und Wider
	to **open** [ˈəʊpən]	eröffnen
20	**group** [gruːp]	Gruppe
	meaning [ˈmiːnɪŋ]	Bedeutung
	pattern [ˈpætn]	Muster
	word order [ˈwɜːd ɔːdə]	Wort-, Satzstellung
	to **tell** [tel]	sagen, erzählen
	something [ˈsʌmθɪŋ]	etwas
	always [ˈɔːlweɪz]	immer
	frequently [ˈfriːkwəntli]	oft, häufig
	sometimes [ˈsʌmtaɪmz]	manchmal
	occasionally [əˈkeɪʒənəli]	gelegentlich
	never [ˈnevə]	nie(mals)
	by bike [baɪ ˈbaɪk]	mit dem Rad
	morning [ˈmɔːnɪŋ]	Morgen, Vormittag
	punctual [ˈpʌŋktʃuəl]	pünktlich
	to **visit** [ˈvɪzɪt]	besuchen
	true [truː]	richtig, zutreffend
	to **take notes** [teɪk ˈnəʊts]	(sich) Notizen machen
20t	**component** [kəmˈpəʊnənt]	Bauteil
	child [tʃaɪld]	Kind
	busy [ˈbɪzi]	beschäftigt
	to **adapt** [əˈdæpt]	anpassen

s **so** | t **tea** | v **van** | w **wet** | z **his** | ʃ **she** | ʒ **vision** | tʃ **chin** | dʒ **June** | θ **three** | ð **the** | ŋ **ring**

	process ['prəʊses]	Prozess, Ablauf
	also ['ɔ:lsəʊ]	auch, außerdem
	to **move** [mu:v]	umziehen
	flat [flæt]	Wohnung
	city centre [ˌsɪti 'sentə]	(Stadt-)Zentrum
	suburb ['sʌbɜ:b]	Vorort, Außenbezirk
20	**personal** ['pɜ:sənl]	persönlich, privat
	to **install** [ɪn'stɔ:l]	installieren, einrichten, anschließen
	to **reorganize** [ri'ɔ:gənaɪz]	umorganisieren
	to **launch** [lɔ:ntʃ]	einführen, auf den Markt bringen
	to **downsize** ['daʊnsaɪz]	abbauen
	course [kɔ:s]	Kurs, Lehrgang
21	**room** [ru:m]	Zimmer, Raum
	window ['wɪndəʊ]	Fenster
	notice board ['nəʊtɪsbɔ:d]	schwarzes Brett
	safe [seɪf]	Tresor
	briefcase ['bri:fkeɪs]	Aktentasche
	desk [desk]	(Schreib-)Tisch
	letter rack ['letə ræk]	Sortierbox
	curtain ['kɜ:tn]	Vorhang, Gardine
	pen [pen]	Kugelschreiber
	pencil ['pensl]	Bleistift
	chair [tʃeə]	Stuhl
	plant [plɑ:nt]	Pflanze
	waste-bin ['weɪst bɪn]	Papierkorb
	printer ['prɪntə]	Drucker
	cupboard ['kʌbəd]	Schrank
	file [faɪl]	(Akten-)Ordner
22	**provincial** [prə'vɪnʃl]	Provinz-
	brochure ['brəʊʃə]	Broschüre, Prospekt
	not yet [nɒt 'jet]	noch nicht
	to **be situated** [bi 'sɪtʃueɪtɪd]	liegen
	famous ['feɪməs]	berühmt
	river ['rɪvə]	Fluss
	composer [kəm'pəʊzə]	Komponist/in
	food [fu:d]	Essen, Nahrung(smittel)
	third largest [ˌθɜ:d 'lɑ:dʒɪst]	drittgrößte
	northern ['nɔ:ðən]	nordlich, Nord-
	federal province [ˌfedərəl 'prɒvɪns]	Bundesstaat
	population [ˌpɒpju'leɪʃn]	Einwohner(zahl)
	commercial [kə'mɜ:ʃl]	Handels-, Geschäfts-
	industrial [ɪn'dʌstriəl]	Industrie-, industriell
	thriving ['θraɪvɪŋ]	aufstrebend
	centre ['sentə]	Zentrum
	world-class [ˌwɜ:ld'klɑ:s]	Weltklasse-
	exhibition [ˌeksɪ'bɪʃn]	Ausstellung
	historic [hɪ'stɒrɪk]	historisch
	sight [saɪt]	Sehenswürdigkeit
	castle ['kɑ:sl]	Schloss
	town hall [ˌtaʊn 'hɔ:l]	Rathaus
	both ... and [bəʊθ, ənd]	sowohl ... als auch
	cathedral [kə'θi:drəl]	Dom
	cultural ['kʌltʃərəl]	kulturell, Kultur-
	autumn ['ɔ:təm]	Herbst
	superb [su:'pɜ:b]	hervorragend
	concert hall ['kɒnsət hɔ:l]	Konzerthalle, -saal
	without [wɪ'ðaʊt]	ohne
	piece [pi:s]	Stück
23	**lake** [leɪk]	(Binnen-)See
	visitor ['vɪzɪtə]	Besucher/in, Gast

	to **be located** [bi ləʊ'keɪtɪd]	sich befinden
	idea [aɪ'dɪə]	Idee, Anregung
	useful ['ju:sfl]	nützlich
	southern ['sʌðən]	südlich, Süd-
	eastern ['i:stən]	östlich, Ost-
	western ['westən]	westlich, West-
	north [nɔ:θ]	Norden
	east [i:st]	Osten
	medium-sized ['mi:diəmsaɪzd]	mittelgroß
	building ['bɪldɪŋ]	Gebäude
	art gallery ['ɑ:t gæləri]	Kunstgalerie
	harbour ['hɑ:bə]	Hafen
24	to **telephone** ['telɪfəʊn]	anrufen, telefonieren (mit)
	to **happen** ['hæpən]	passieren, geschehen
	caller ['kɔ:lə]	Anrufer/in
	to **get through** [!get 'θru:]	durchkommen
	available [ə'veɪləbl]	anwesend
	leave [li:v]	hinterlassen
	message ['mesɪdʒ]	Nachricht
	voicemail ['vɔɪsmeɪl]	Mailbox
	receptionist [rɪ'sepʃənɪst]	Empfang(smitarbeiter/in)
24t	**research and development** [rɪˌsɜ:tʃ ən dɪ'veləpmənt]	Forschung und Entwicklung
	Good morning [ˌgʊd 'mɔ:nɪŋ]	Guten Morgen
	personally ['pɜ:sənəli]	persönlich
	to **be in** [bi 'ɪn]	im Büro sein
	I'm afraid ... [aɪm ə'freɪd]	leider
	perhaps [pə'hæps]	vielleicht, eventuell
	to **call someone back** [ˌkɔ:l 'bæk]	jdn. zurückrufen
	Just a minute [dʒʌst ə 'mɪnɪt]	einen Moment, bitte
	great [greɪt]	groß(artig), gut
	Good afternoon [gʊd ˌɑ:ftə'nu:n]	Guten Tag (nachmittags)
	later ['leɪtə]	später
	to **be free** [bi 'fri:]	frei sein
	hard [hɑ:d]	schwer, schwierig
	at ... o'clock [ə'klɒk]	um ... Uhr
	to **be finished** ['fɪnɪʃt]	zu Ende sein
	to **be through** [bi 'θru:]	sprechen mit
	to **take a call** [ˌteɪk ə 'kɔ:l]	einen Anruf entgegennehmen
	to **get back to someone** [ˌget 'bæk tə]	jdn. zurückrufen
	tone [təʊn]	(Signal-)Ton
	on the other line [ɒn ði ˌʌðə 'laɪn]	auf der anderen Leitung
	to **put someone through** [ˌpʊt 'θru:]	jdn. verbinden, durchstellen
24	**necessary** ['nesəsəri]	nötig, notwendig, erforderlich
25	**Hold the line** [həʊld ðə 'laɪn]	Bleiben Sie dran
	noon [nu:n]	Mittag
	Good evening [ˌgʊd 'i:vnɪŋ]	Guten Abend
	another time [ə'nʌðə taɪm]	(später) noch einmal
	to **reach** (sb) [ri:tʃ]	(jdn.) erreichen
	whether ['weðə]	ob
	ill [ɪl]	krank
	holiday ['hɒlədeɪ]	Ferien, Urlaub
	next [nekst]	nächste
	to **note** [nəʊt]	notieren

æ hat | ɑ: arm | e pen | ɜ: her | ə ago | ɪ sit | i: see | i many | ɒ got | ɔ: saw | ʌ cup | ʊ put

	subject ['sʌbdʒɪkt]	Thema, Grund
25p	**except** [ɪk'sept]	außer
	to **transfer** [træns'fɜ:]	durchstellen
	until [ən'tɪl]	bis
25t	to **be timed** [bi 'taɪmd]	mit der Zeitangabe versehen
	advertisement [əd'vɜ:tɪsmənt]	Anzeige
	part-time [,pɑ:t'taɪm]	Teilzeit-, Halbtags-
	daughter ['dɔ:tə]	Tochter
	to **get** [get]	jdn. (telefonisch) erreichen
	terrible ['terəbl]	fürchterlich, furchtbar
	traffic ['træfɪk]	(Straßen-)Verkehr
	motorway ['məʊtəweɪ]	Autobahn
26	**tea** [ti:]	Tee
	lunch [lʌntʃ]	Mittagessen
	dinner ['dɪnə]	Abendessen
	near [nɪə]	nahe, in der Nähe von
27	**personnel** [,pɜ:sə'nel]	Personal
	advert ['ædvɜ:t]	Inserat, Annonce, Anzeige
28	**crossword** ['krɒswɜ:d]	Kreuzworträtsel
	translation [træns'leɪʃn]	Übersetzung
	across [ə'krɒs]	waagerecht
	gallery ['gæləri]	Galerie
	such as ['sʌtʃ əz]	wie zum Beispiel
	early ['ɜ:li]	früh
29	**downtown** (AE) ['daʊntaʊn]	(im) Stadtzentrum
	apartment (AE) [ə'pɑ:tmənt]	Wohnung
	vacation (AE) [və'keɪʃn]	Urlaub, Ferien
	bathroom ['bɑ:θru:m]	Bad(ezimmer); auch AE: Toilette
	cell phone (AE) ['sel fəʊn]	Handy, Mobiltelefon
	underground ['ʌndəgraʊnd]	U-Bahn
	subway (AE) ['sʌbweɪ]	U-Bahn
	biscuit ['bɪskɪt]	Keks
	cookie (AE) ['kʊki]	Keks
	elevator (AE) ['elɪveɪtə]	Fahrstuhl
	let's [lets]	lass uns
	tonight [tə'naɪt]	heute Abend
	movie (AE) ['mu:vi]	(Spiel-)Film
	petrol ['petrəl]	Benzin
	gas (AE) [gæs]	Benzin
	ground floor [,graʊnd 'flɔ:]	Erdgeschoss
	spelling ['spelɪŋ]	Rechtschreibung, Schreibweise
	cheque [tʃek]	Scheck
	colour ['kʌlə]	Farbe
	licence ['laɪsns]	Lizenz

UNIT 3 WORK AND LEISURE

30	**leisure** ['leʒə]	Freizeit
	to **be born** [bɔ:n]	geboren sein
	career [kə'rɪə]	Karriere, Beruf
	originally [ə'rɪdʒənəli]	ursprünglich
	actually ['æktʃuəli]	eigentlich
	A-levels ['eɪ levl]	(*entspricht*) Abitur
	high school diploma (AE) [,haɪ sku:l dɪ'pləʊmə]	Abschlusszeugnis der Oberschule
	to **study** ['stʌdi]	studieren
	still [stɪl]	(immer) noch
	business diploma [,bɪznəs dɪ'pləʊmə]	Abschlusszeugnis als Diplomkaufmann/frau
	qualification [,kwɒlɪfɪ'keɪʃn]	Zeugnis
	same [seɪm]	gleich
	management trainee [,mænɪdʒmənt treɪ'ni:]	Praktikant/in in der Geschäftsleitung
	first hand [,fɜ:st 'hænd]	aus erster Hand
	to **become** [bɪ'kʌm]	werden
	to **join** [dʒɔɪn]	gehen zu, anfangen bei
31	**CV (curriculum vitae)** [kə,rɪkjələm 'vi:taɪ]	Lebenslauf
	missing ['mɪsɪŋ]	fehlend
	full name [,fʊl 'neɪm]	voller Name
	energetic [,enə'dʒetɪk]	energisch, tatkräftig
	effective [ɪ'fektɪv]	effektiv, wirkungsvoll
	leading ['li:dɪŋ]	führend
	complete [kəm'pli:t]	voll(ständig)
	responsibility [rɪ,spɒnsə'bɪləti]	Verantwortung
	distribution [,dɪstrɪ'bju:ʃn]	Vertrieb, Auslieferung
	education [,edʒu'keɪʃn]	Ausbildung
	experience [ɪk'spɪəriəns]	(Berufs-)Erfahrung
	mother tongue ['mʌðə tʌŋ]	Muttersprache
	fluent(ly) ['flu:ənt]	fließend
	fair [feə]	angemessen
	skill [skɪl]	Fertigkeit, Fähigkeit
	sailing ['seɪlɪŋ]	Segeln
	photography [fə'tɒgrəfi]	Fotografie
	keeping fit [,ki:pɪŋ 'fɪt]	Fitnesstraining
	college ['kɒlɪdʒ]	(Fach-)Hochschule, Universität
	to **close** [kləʊz]	schließen
32	**invoice** ['ɪnvɔɪs]	Rechnung
	yesterday ['jestədeɪ]	gestern
	to **arrive** [ə'raɪv]	ankommen
	to **laugh** [lɑ:f]	lachen
	paragraph ['pærəgrɑ:f]	Absatz
33	to **find out** [,faɪnd 'aʊt]	herausfinden
	to **look after** [lʊk 'ɑ:ftə]	betreuen
	corporation [,kɔ:pə'reɪʃn]	(Aktien-)Gesellschaft
	equipment [ɪ'kwɪpmənt]	Ausrüstung, Geräte
	reception area [rɪ'sepʃn eəriə]	Empfang(sbereich), Rezeption
	small talk ['smɔ:l tɔ:k]	(höfliche) Konversation
	crime [kraɪm]	Verbrechen, Kriminalität
	really ['rɪəli]	wirklich, tatsächlich
	to **boom** [bu:m]	(auf)blühen, boomen
	mountain ['maʊntən]	Berg
	mile [maɪl]	Meile
	high [haɪ]	hoch
	foot [fʊt]	Fuß
	up [ʌp]	oben
	hour ['aʊə]	Stunde
	to **love** [lʌv]	lieben, sehr gern mögen
	skiing ['ski:ɪŋ]	Skilaufen
34	**weather** ['weðə]	Wetter
	teacher ['ti:tʃə]	Lehrer/in
	neighbour ['neɪbə]	Nachbar/in
	mostly ['məʊstli]	hauptsächlich
	young [jʌŋ]	jung
	activity [æk'tɪvəti]	Aktivität, Beschäftigung
	favourite ['feɪvərɪt]	liebst, Lieblings-
	to **enjoy** [ɪn'dʒɔɪ]	genießen, gern haben/tun
	to **prefer** [prɪ'fɜ:]	lieber mögen, bevorzugen
	to **dislike** [dɪs'laɪk]	nicht mögen
	to **hate** [heɪt]	hassen, gar nicht mögen
	cycling ['saɪklɪŋ]	Radfahren
	swimming ['swɪmɪŋ]	Schwimmen
	shopping ['ʃɒpɪŋ]	Einkaufen

u: **too** | u **actual** | aɪ **my** | aʊ **now** | eɪ **pay** | əʊ **home** | ɔɪ **oil** | ɪə **beer** | eə **hair** | ʊə **pure**

	window shopping [wɪndəʊʃɒpɪŋ]	Schaufensterbummel
	watching TV [wɒtʃɪŋ ˌti:'vi:]	Fernsehen
	to **play** [pleɪ]	spielen
	instrument ['ɪnstrəmənt]	(Musik-)Instrument
	cooking ['kʊkɪŋ]	Kochen
	cinema ['sɪnəmə]	Kino
	gym [dʒɪm]	Sportstudio
	snooker ['snu:kə]	Billard
	day trip ['deɪ trɪp]	Tagesausflug
	DIY [ˌdi: aɪ 'waɪ]	Heimwerken
	absolutely ['æbsəlu:tli]	absolut
	nothing ['nʌθɪŋ]	nichts
	It depends [ɪt dɪ'pendz]	Es hängt davon ab
35	**together** [tə'geðə]	zusammen
35t	**funny** ['fʌni]	komisch, lustig
	joke [dʒəʊk]	Witz, Scherz
	weekend [ˌwi:k'end]	Wochenende
	summer ['sʌmə]	Sommer
	to **sound** [saʊnd]	sich anhören
	indoors ['ɪndɔ:z]	drinnen
	sporty ['spɔ:ti]	sportlich
	a couple of times [ə 'kʌpl əv]	ein paarmal
	orchestra ['ɔ:kɪstrə]	Orchester
	violin [ˌvaɪə'lɪn]	Geige
	impressed [ɪm'prest]	beeindruckt
	symphony ['sɪmfəni]	Sinfonie
	or anything [ɔ:r 'eniθɪŋ]	oder sowas
	tour [tʊə]	Tournee
	to **stay** [steɪ]	übernachten
	nearly ['nɪəli]	beinahe, fast
	a bit [ə 'bɪt]	ein bisschen, etwas
35	**opposite** ['ɒpəzɪt]	Gegenteil
	to **agree** [ə'gri:]	zustimmen
	dancing ['dɑ:nsɪŋ]	Tanzen
	presentation [ˌprezn'teɪʃn]	Vorstellung, Präsentation
	to **fall asleep** [ˌfɔ:l ə'sli:p]	einschlafen
	extreme(ly) [ɪk'stri:mli]	äußerst
	market survey [ˌmɑ:kɪt 'sɜ:veɪ]	Marktanalyse
	data ['deɪtə]	Daten
	top three [ˌtɒp 'θri:]	die ersten drei
	result [rɪ'zʌlt]	Ergebnis
	board [bɔ:d]	(Wand-)Tafel
	sociable ['səʊʃəbl]	gesellig
	different ['dɪfrənt]	unterschiedlich
	according to [ə'kɔ:dɪŋ tə]	nach, entsprechend
	age [eɪdʒ]	Alter
36	**special offer** [ˌspeʃl 'ɒfə]	Sonderangebot
	office manager [ˌɒfɪs 'mænɪdʒə]	Büroleiter/in
	office supplies ['ɒfɪs səplaɪz]	Büromaterial
	furniture ['fɜ:nɪtʃə]	Möbel(stücke), Einrichtung
	to **understand** [ˌʌndə'stænd]	verstehen
	to **deliver** [dɪ'lɪvə]	(aus)liefern
	discount ['dɪskaʊnt]	Rabatt, Skonto, Nachlass
	charge [tʃɑ:dʒ]	Kosten, Gebühr
	delivery [dɪ'lɪvəri]	Zustellung, Auslieferung
	to **place an order** [pleɪs ən 'ɔ:də]	eine Bestellung aufgeben
	to **send** [send]	senden, schicken
36t	to **offer** ['ɒfə]	anbieten
	(£60) **off** [ɒf]	Nachlass (von £60)
	to **supply** [sə'plaɪ]	liefern
	before [bɪ'fɔ:]	vor
	order ['ɔ:də]	Bestellung
	to **pay** [peɪ]	(be)zahlen
	expiry date [ɪk'spaɪəri deɪt]	Ablaufdatum
	to **repeat** [rɪ'pi:t]	wiederholen
36	**item** ['aɪtəm]	Artikel
	quantity ['kwɒntəti]	Menge, Quantität
	unit price [ˌju:nɪt 'praɪs]	Einzelpreis
	method of payment [ˌmeθəd əv 'peɪmənt]	Zahlungsweise
37	**deal** [di:l]	(günstiges) Angebot
	trade discount ['treɪd dɪskaʊnt]	Händlerrabatt
	bulk discount [bʌlk 'dɪskaʊnt]	Mengenrabatt
	pound [paʊnd]	Pfund (Sterling)
	to **come in** [ˌkʌm 'ɪn]	lieferbar sein
	certainly ['sɜ:tnli]	sicherlich, gewiss
	branch [brɑ:ntʃ]	Filiale, Niederlassung
	flow chart ['fləʊ tʃɑ:t]	Flussdiagramm
	own [əʊn]	eigen
	budget ['bʌdʒɪt]	Etat
	drive [draɪv]	Laufwerk
	flatscreen ['flætskri:n]	Flachbildschirm
	keyboard ['ki:bɔ:d]	Tastatur
	mouse [maʊs]	Maus
37p	**excellent** ['eksələnt]	ausgezeichnet
	workstation ['wɜ:k steɪʃn]	Arbeitsplatz
	memory ['meməri]	Speicher
	guarantee [ˌgærən'ti:]	Garantie
	middle-of-the-range [ˌmɪdl əv ðə 'reɪndʒ]	aus dem mittleren Bereich
	top [tɒp]	Spitzen-, oberst
	extra ['ekstrə]	zusätzlich
	feature ['fi:tʃə]	Merkmal, Eigenschaft
	same-day [ˌseɪm 'deɪ]	am selben Tag
38	**secretary** ['sekrətri]	Sekretär/in
	dentist ['dentɪst]	Zahnarzt/-ärztin
39	**human resources** [ˌhju:mən rɪ'sɔ:sɪz]	Personalabteilung
	exercise ['eksəsaɪz]	Übung
	dialogue ['daɪəlɒg]	Dialog
	wife [waɪf]	(Ehe-)Frau
40	**sunny** ['sʌni]	sonnig
	extract ['ekstrækt]	Auszug
	heading ['hedɪŋ]	Überschrift
	dynamic [daɪ'næmɪk]	dynamisch
	successful [sək'sesfl]	erfolgreich
	responsible [rɪ'spɒnsəbl]	verantwortlich
41	**difficult** ['dɪfɪkəlt]	schwierig
41t	**almost** ['ɔ:lməʊst]	fast, beinahe
	Bachelor of Arts [ˌbætʃələr əv 'ɑ:ts]	1. Staatsexamen in Geisteswissenschaften
	Bachelor of Science [ˌbætʃələr əv 'saɪəns]	1. Staatsexamen in Naturwissenschaften
	Master of Science [ˌmɑ:stər əv 'saɪəns]	2. Staatsexamen in Naturwissenschaften
	Master of Arts [ˌmɑ:stər əv 'ɑ:ts]	2. Staatsexamen in Geisteswissenschaften

UNIT 4 A GLOBAL BUSINESS

42	to **name** [neɪm]	nennen
	headquarters [ˌhed'kwɔ:təz]	Hauptquartier, Zentrale

b **bad** | d **did** | f **five** | g **got** | h **how** | j **yes** | k **cat** | l **leg** | m **man** | n **no** | p **pen** | r **red**

	ladies and gentlemen ['leɪdiz ən 'dʒentlmən]	meine Damen und Herren
	sure [ʃʊə]	sicher
	operations [ˌɒpə'reɪʃnz]	Geschäfte, Aktivitäten
	region ['ri:dʒən]	Gebiet, Region
	to **operate** ['ɒpəreɪt]	operieren
	division [dɪ'vɪʒn]	(Betriebs-)Sparte
	actual ['æktʃuəl]	konkret, wirklich
	case study ['keɪs stʌdi]	Fallstudie
	unusual [ʌn'ju:ʒʊəl]	ungewöhnlich
	complicated ['kɒmplɪkeɪtɪd]	kompliziert
43	**overland freight** ['əʊvəlænd freɪt]	Fracht über Land
	eg (or e.g.) [ˌi: 'dʒi:]	z.B.
	courier ['kʊriə]	Kurier
	air freight ['eə freɪt]	Luftfracht
	sea freight ['si: freɪt]	Seefracht
43t	**point** [pɔɪnt]	Komma
	to **include** [ɪn'klu:d]	einbeziehen, umfassen
	to **account for** (20%) [ə'kaʊnt]	(20%) ausmachen
	employee [ɪm'plɔɪi:]	Beschäftigte/r
	to **divide** [dɪ'vaɪd]	(unter)teilen
	mainly ['meɪnli]	hauptsächlich, vor allem
	pie chart ['paɪ tʃɑ:t]	Kreisdiagramm
	profitable ['prɒfɪtəbl]	gewinnbringend, rentabel
	to **stop** [stɒp]	anhalten, aufhören
43	**percentage** [pə'sentɪdʒ]	Prozentsatz
	income ['ɪnkʌm]	Einkommen
	to **earn** [ɜ:n]	verdienen
44	**profit** ['prɒfɪt]	Profit, Gewinn
	to **notice** ['nəʊtɪs]	(be)merken
	manufacturing [ˌmænju'fæktʃərɪŋ]	Produktion, Fertigung
	probably ['prɒbəbli]	wahrscheinlich
	complex ['kɒmpleks]	kompliziert, komplex
	advanced [əd'vɑ:nst]	fortgeschritten
	focus ['fəʊkəs]	Schwerpunkt
	transportation [ˌtrænspɔ:'teɪʃn]	Transport, Beförderung
	cargo ['kɑ:gəʊ]	Fracht, Ladung
	consignment [kən'saɪnmənt]	(Waren-)Sendung, Lieferung
	to **prepare** [prɪ'peə]	vorbereiten
45	to **do business** [du 'bɪznəs]	Geschäfte machen
	custom ['kʌstəm]	Sitte, Brauch
	wonderful ['wʌndəfl]	wunderbar, -voll
	audience ['ɔ:diəns]	Publikum, Zuhörer
	enthusiastic [ɪnˌθju:zi'æstɪk]	begeistert
	to **smile** [smaɪl]	lächeln
	to **nod** [nɒd]	nicken
	end [end]	Ende, Schluss
	to **applaud** [ə'plɔ:d]	applaudieren
	to **show** [ʃəʊ]	zeigen
	must [mʌst]	müssen
	to **save face** [seɪv 'feɪs]	das Gesicht wahren
46	**dress down day** ['dres daʊn deɪ]	Tag mit legerer Kleidung
	to **mean** [mi:n]	bedeuten, heißen
	formal ['fɔ:ml]	formell, förmlich
	polite [pə'laɪt]	höflich
	immediately [ɪ'mi:diətli]	sofort, umgehend
	to **stay** [steɪ]	bleiben
	death [deθ]	Tod
	to **print** [prɪnt]	drucken
	unclean [ˌʌn'kli:n]	unsauber
	to **accept** [ək'sept]	annehmen
	magazine [ˌmægə'zi:n]	Zeitschrift
	honest ['ɒnɪst]	ehrlich
	to **exaggerate** [ɪg'zædʒəreɪt]	übertreiben
47	**etiquette** ['etɪket]	Etikette
	series ['sɪəri:z]	Serie, Reihe
	generally ['dʒenrəli]	im Allgemeinen, normalerweise
	direct(ly) [də'rekt]	direkt
	honesty ['ɒnəsti]	Ehrlichkeit
	authority [ɔ:'θɒrəti]	Autorität
	handshake ['hændʃeɪk]	Händedruck
	to **suggest** [sə'dʒest]	vorschlagen
	surprised [sə'praɪzd]	überrascht, erstaunt
	to **invite** [ɪn'vaɪt]	einladen
	meal [mi:l]	Essen, Mahlzeit
	to **go Dutch** [gəʊ 'dʌtʃ]	getrennt zahlen
	barbecue ['bɑ:bɪkju:]	Grillparty
	necessary evil [ˌnesəsəri 'i:vl]	notwendiges Übel
	way of life [weɪ əv 'laɪf]	Lebensweise
	column ['kɒləm]	Spalte
48	**corporate** ['kɔ:pərət]	Firmen-
48t	**urgent** ['ɜ:dʒənt]	dringend, eilig
	emergency [ɪ'mɜ:dʒənsi]	Notfall
	report [rɪ'pɔ:t]	Bericht
	investment market [ɪn'vestmənt mɑ:kɪt]	Anlagemarkt
	leaflet ['li:flət]	Broschüre, Prospekt
	enough [ɪ'nʌf]	ausreichend
	Have a nice one [həv ə 'naɪs wʌn]	Schönen Tag noch
48	**in reply** [ɪn rɪ'plaɪ]	als Antwort
	Kind regards [kaɪnd rɪ'gɑ:dz]	viele Grüße
	Oh dear [əʊ 'dɪə]	Ach du liebe Zeit
	Best wishes [best 'wɪʃɪz]	Mit besten Grüßen
	usual ['ju:ʒuəl]	gewöhnlich, normal
	hectic ['hektɪk]	hektisch
	glad [glæd]	froh
	to **hope** [həʊp]	hoffen
	further ['fɜ:ðə]	weiter
49	to **confirm** [kən'fɜ:m]	bestätigen
	in advance [ɪn əd'vɑ:ns]	im Voraus
	to **reply** [rɪ'plaɪ]	antworten
	anything else [ˌeniθɪŋ 'els]	noch etwas
	attachment [ə'tætʃmənt]	Anlage
	to **attach** [ə'tætʃ]	beilegen, -fügen
	to **apologize** [ə'pɒlədʒaɪz]	sich entschuldigen
	delay [dɪ'leɪ]	Verspätung, Verzögerung
	to **work through** [ˌwɜ:k 'θru:]	durcharbeiten
	inbox ['ɪnbɒks]	Posteingang
	monthly ['mʌnθli]	monatlich
	etc [ˌet 'setərə]	usw.
	up-to-date [ˌʌp tə 'deɪt]	aktuell, modern
	extension number [ɪk'stenʃn nʌmbə]	Durchwahlnummer
49p	**following** ['fɒləʊɪŋ]	folgend
	design [dɪ'zaɪn]	entwerfen, konstruieren
	copy ['kɒpi]	Kopie
	price list ['praɪs lɪst]	Preisliste

s **so** \| t **tea** \| v **van** \| w **wet** \| z **his** \| ʃ **she** \| ʒ **vision** \| tʃ **chin** \| dʒ **June** \| θ **three** \| ð **the** \| ŋ **ring**

50	**illegal** [ɪ'li:gl]	verboten, illegal
51	**incorrect** [ˌɪnkə'rekt]	falsch
	side [saɪd]	Seite
52	**guideline** ['gaɪdlaɪn]	Richtlinie
	allowed [ə'laʊd]	erlaubt
	to **smoke** [sməʊk]	rauchen
	male [meɪl]	männlich
	maker ['meɪkə]	Hersteller
	truth [tru:θ]	Wahrheit
	to **shake** [ʃeɪk]	schütteln
	nationality [ˌnæʃə'næləti]	Staatsangehörigkeit
53	**flag** [flæg]	Flagge, Fahne
	circle ['sɜ:kl]	Kreis

UNIT 5 IT'S URGENT!

54	**suitable** ['su:təbl]	geeignet, passend
	time [taɪm]	Zeit
55	**once** [wʌns]	einmal
	to **catch** [kætʃ]	erreichen
	to **collect** [kə'lekt]	abholen
	to **fly** [flaɪ]	fliegen
	to **land** [lænd]	landen
	journey ['dʒɜ:ni]	Reise, Fahrt
56	**contract** ['kɒntrækt]	Vertrag
	figure ['fɪgə]	Zahl
56t	**somewhere** ['sʌmweə]	irgendwo
	to **disturb** [dɪ'stɜ:b]	stören
	merger ['mɜ:dʒə]	Fusion
	asap [ˌeɪ es eɪ 'pi:]	so schnell wie möglich
	planner ['plænə]	Terminplaner
	totally ['təʊtəli]	völlig, total
57	**stockbroker** ['stɒkbrəʊkə]	Börsenmakler/in
	to **run** [rʌn]	leiten, führen
	PA [ˌpi: 'eɪ]	persönliche/r Assistent/in
	share price ['ʃeə praɪs]	Aktienkurs
	research [rɪ'sɜ:tʃ]	Nachforschung(en)
	to **promote** [prə'məʊt]	anpreisen, Werbung machen für
58	to **select** [sɪ'lekt]	auswählen
	provider [prə'vaɪdə]	Anbieter, Versorger
	shipping ['ʃɪpɪŋ]	Verfrachtung, Versand
	warehousing ['weəhaʊzɪŋ]	Lagerung
	specialized ['speʃəlaɪzd]	spezialisiert
	advice [əd'vaɪs]	Beratung
	solution [sə'lu:ʃn]	Lösung
	keyword ['ki:wɜ:d]	Stichwort
	search [sɜ:tʃ]	Suche
	to **track** [træk]	verfolgen
	to **trace** [treɪs]	zurückverfolgen, finden
	to **locate** [ləʊ'keɪt]	orten
	shipment ['ʃɪpmənt]	Sendung
58t	**fairly** ['feəli]	ziemlich
	presence ['prezns]	Anwesenheit, Präsenz
	to **browse** [braʊz]	surfen, stöbern
	potential [pə'tenʃl]	möglich, potenziell
	financial [faɪ'nænʃl]	finanziell
	to **connect** [kə'nekt]	verbinden
	to **contact** ['kɒntækt]	sich wenden an, Kontakt aufnehmen zu
	to **solve** [sɒlv]	lösen
	decision [dɪ'sɪʒn]	Entscheidung
	without doubt [ˌwɪθaʊt 'daʊt]	ohne Zweifel
58	**careful** ['keəfl]	sorgfältig
	to **summarize** ['sʌməraɪz]	zusammenfassen
59	**button** ['bʌtn]	Taste, Knopf
	history ['hɪstri]	Geschichte
	introduction [ˌɪntrə'dʌkʃn]	Einführung
	vacancy ['veɪkənsi]	offene Stelle
	application [ˌæplɪ'keɪʃn]	Bewerbung
	news [nju:z]	Nachricht(en)
	to **download** ['daʊnləʊd]	herunterladen
	rail [reɪl]	(Eisen-)Bahn
59p	to **distribute** [dɪ'strɪbju:t]	vertreiben, (aus)liefern
	pottery ['pɒtəri]	Keramik, Töpferwaren
	navigation bar [ˌnævɪ'geʃn bɑ:]	Navigationsleiste
	graphics ['græfɪks]	Grafiken
	type [taɪp]	Art, Sorte, Typ
	e-commerce [ˌi: 'kɒmɜ:s]	elektronischer Handel
	dealer ['di:lə]	Händler/in
	to **advertise** ['ædvətaɪz]	inserieren, werben (für)
59	to **contain** [kən'teɪn]	enthalten
60	**term** [tɜ:m]	Bedingung
	to **build** [bɪld]	bauen
	supplier [sə'plaɪə]	Lieferant/in, Zulieferer
	automotive [ˌɔ:tə'məʊtɪv]	Auto-
	paint [peɪnt]	Farbe
	representative [ˌreprɪ'zentətɪv]	(Handels-)Vertreter/in
	ex-works [ˌeks'wɜ:ks]	ab Werk
	COD (cash on delivery) [ˌkæʃ ɒn dɪ'lɪvəri]	Nachnahme, Barzahlung bei Lieferung
	bank transfer ['bænk trænsfɜ:]	(Bank-)Überweisung
	to **return** [rɪ'tɜ:n]	zurückgeben, -schicken
	rebate ['ri:beɪt]	(Preis-)Nachlass, Rabatt
	straight away [streɪt ə'weɪ]	sofort, umgehend
	to **decide** [dɪ'saɪd]	(sich) entscheiden
60t	**authentic** [ɔ:'θentɪk]	authentisch, echt
	go ahead [ˌgəʊ ə'hed]	schießen Sie los
	cost [kɒst]	Kosten
	scale [skeɪl]	Skala
	clear [klɪə]	klar, deutlich
	in full [ɪn 'fʊl]	vollständig
	within [wɪ'ðɪn]	innerhalb (von), in
	basically ['beɪsɪkli]	im Grunde
	acceptable [ək'septəbl]	annehmbar, akzeptabel
	obviously ['ɒbviəsli]	offensichtlich, selbstverständlich
	to **change one's mind** [tʃeɪndʒ wʌns 'maɪnd]	seine Meinung ändern
	fault [fɔ:lt]	Fehler, Schuld
	to **refund** [rɪ'fʌnd]	erstatten, zurückzahlen
	policy ['pɒləsi]	(Firmen-)Politik
	cup [kʌp]	Tasse
60	**trading terms** ['treɪdɪŋ tɜ:mz]	Handelsbedingungen
61	**tax** [tæks]	Steuer
	to **quote** [kwəʊt]	ein Angebot abgeben
	volume ['vɒlju:m]	Menge
61p	**relatively** ['relətɪvli]	relativ, verhältnismäßig
	luxury ['lʌkʃəri]	Luxus
	consumer [kən'sju:mə]	Konsument/in
	widescreen ['waɪdskri:n]	Breitwandbildschirm
	player ['pleɪə]	Laufwerk
	sound system ['saʊnd sɪstəm]	Tonübertragungssystem
	racquet ['rækɪt]	(Tennis-)Schläger
	professional [prə'feʃənl]	Profi, Fachmann
	guide [gaɪd]	(Reise-)Führer/in, Handbuch

æ hat | ɑ: arm | e pen | ɜ: her | ə ago | ɪ sit | i: see | i many | ɒ got | ɔ: saw | ʌ cup | ʊ put

	illustrated ['ɪləstreɪtɪd]	illustriert
	bookshop ['bʊkʃɒp]	Buchhandlung
61	**classroom** ['klɑːsruːm]	Klassenzimmer, -raum
	round [raʊnd]	umher
63	**spare part** [ˌspeə 'pɑːt]	Ersatzteil
	early bird ['ɜːli bɜːd]	Frühaufsteher/in
	to **pick up** [ˌpɪk 'ʌp]	abholen

UNIT 6 A NEW BOSS

66	**excerpt** ['eksɜːpt]	Auszug
	specialist ['speʃəlɪst]	speziell
	application [ˌæplɪ'keɪʃn]	Anwendung, Verwendungszweck
	to **manage** ['mænɪdʒ]	leiten
	widely ['waɪdli]	weit
	amazing [ə'meɪzɪŋ]	erstaunlich
	even ['iːvn]	sogar (noch)
	bottom line [ˌbɒtəm 'laɪn]	Endergebnis, das Fazit
	headline ['hedlaɪn]	Schlagzeile
	false [fɔːls]	falsch
67	to **lose** [luːz]	verlieren
	ever ['evə]	je(mals), schon (ein)mal
	beach [biːtʃ]	Strand
68	**impressive** [ɪm'presɪv]	beeindruckend
	slip (of paper) [slɪp]	Zettel
	to **guess** [ges]	erraten
69	**diary** ['daɪəri]	Terminkalender
	overseas [ˌəʊvə'siːz]	ausländisch
	subsidiary [səb'sɪdiəri]	Tochtergesellschaft
	agenda [ə'dʒendə]	Tagesordnung
	chamber of commerce [ˌtʃeɪmbər əv 'kɒmɜːs]	Handelskammer
	task [tɑːsk]	Aufgabe
	appointment [ə'pɔɪntmənt]	Termin, Verabredung
	lunchtime ['lʌntʃtaɪm]	Mittagszeit
	unfortunately [ʌn'fɔːtʃənətli]	unglücklicherweise, leider
	Good luck [ˌgʊd 'lʌk]	Viel Glück
70	**arrangement** [ə'reɪndʒmənt]	Vereinbarung, Termin
	to **order** ['ɔːdə]	bestellen
	to **reserve** [rɪ'zɜːv]	reservieren (lassen)
72	**lawyer** ['lɔːjə]	(Rechts-)Anwalt/Anwältin
	law firm ['lɔː fɜːm]	Anwaltskanzlei
	to **cancel** ['kænsl]	streichen, absagen
	to **postpone** [pə'spəʊn]	verschieben
	to **bring forward** [ˌbrɪŋ 'fɔːwəd]	vorverlegen
72t	**anyway** ['eniweɪ]	jedenfalls, sowieso
	unexpected [ˌʌnɪk'spektɪd]	unerwartet
	though [ðəʊ]	dennoch
	indeed [ɪn'diːd]	wirklich
	as a matter of fact [əz ə ˌmætər əv 'fækt]	eigentlich, tatsächlich
	to **worry** ['wʌri]	sich Sorgen machen
	afterwards ['ɑːftəwədz]	danach, hinterher
	terribly ['terəbli]	fürchterlich, furchtbar
73	to **fix** [fɪks]	festlegen
	tied up [ˌtaɪd 'ʌp]	beschäftigt
	instead [ɪn'sted]	stattdessen
	construction [kən'strʌkʃn]	Bau
	member ['membə]	Mitglied
73p	to **represent** [ˌreprɪ'zent]	vertreten, repräsentieren
75	to **receive** [rɪ'siːv]	erhalten, bekommen
	while [waɪl]	während
	dream [driːm]	Traum
76	to **believe** [bɪ'liːv]	glauben
77	**parent company** [ˌpeərənt 'kʌmpəni]	Muttergesellschaft
	equivalent [ɪ'kwɪvələnt]	Entsprechung
	limited company [ˌlɪmɪtɪd 'kʌmpəni]	Kapitalgesellschaft
	similar ['sɪmələ]	ähnlich
	privately ['praɪvətli]	privat
	shareholder ['ʃeəhəʊldə]	Aktionär/in, Anteilseigner/in, Teilhaber/in
	public limited company [ˌpʌblɪk ˌlɪmɪtɪd 'kʌmpəni]	AG
	share [ʃeə]	(Geschäfts-)Anteil, Aktie
	incorporated [ɪn'kɔːpəreɪtɪd]	(als Kapitalgesellschaft) eingetragen
	closed corporation [ˌkləʊzd kɔːpə'reɪʃn]	GmbH
	open corporation [ˌəʊpən ˌkɔːpə'reɪʃn]	AG
	proprietary limited company [prəˌpraɪətri ˌlɪmɪtɪd 'kʌmpəni]	GmbH

UNIT 7 LOOKING AHEAD

78	**pharmaceuticals** [ˌfɑːmə'suːtɪklz]	Pharmazeutika
	to **spend** [spend]	ausgeben
	weight control ['weɪt kəntrəʊl]	Gewichtskontrolle
	to **hire** ['haɪə]	ein-, anstellen
79	**accounting** [ə'kaʊntɪŋ]	Rechnungswesen, (Bilanz-)Buchhaltung
	stock control ['stɒk kəntrəʊl]	Inventur, Lagerhaltung
	user ['juːzə]	Anwender/in, Benutzer/in
	retail ['riːteɪl]	Einzelhandel(sgeschäft)
	fantastically [fæn'tæstɪkli]	fantastisch
	excited [ɪk'saɪtɪd]	(freudig) erregt
80	**storefront** ['stɔːfrʌnt]	Ladenfront
	to **increase** [ɪn'kriːs]	steigern, erhöhen
	shopper ['ʃɒpə]	Käufer/in
	to **purchase** ['pɜːtʃəs]	(ein)kaufen
	press release ['pres rɪliːs]	Pressemitteilung
81	**accountant** [ə'kaʊntənt]	Buchhalter/in
	hint [hɪnt]	Hinweis
	old hand [ˌəʊld 'hænd]	alter Hase
	support [sə'pɔːt]	(technische) Hilfe
	arithmetic [ə'rɪθmətɪk]	Rechnen. Arithmetik
	since [sɪns]	seit
82	**salary** ['sæləri]	Gehalt
	challenging ['tʃælɪndʒɪŋ]	herausfordernd
83	**personality** [ˌpɜːsə'næləti]	Charakter
	unsure [ˌʌn'ʃʊə]	unsicher, ungewiss
	auctioneer [ˌɔːkʃə'nɪə]	Auktionator
	bank clerk ['bæŋk klɑːk]	Bankangestellte/r
	book editor ['bʊk edɪtə]	Redakteur/in
	bookkeeper ['bʊkkiːpə]	Buchhalter/in
	chemist ['kemɪst]	Chemiker/in
	counsellor ['kaʊnsələ]	Berater/in
	electrical technician [ɪˌlektrɪkl tek'nɪʃn]	Elektriker, Elektrotechniker
	estate agent [ɪ'steɪt eɪdʒənt]	Immobilienmakler/in
	librarian [laɪ'breəriən]	Bibliothekar/in
	mechanic [mɪ'kænɪk]	Mechaniker/in
	nurse [nɜːs]	Krankenschwester, -pfleger/in

	pharmacist ['fɑ:məsɪst]	Apotheker/in, Pharmazeut/in
	police officer [pə'li:s ɒfɪsə]	Polizeibeamter/beamtin
	salesperson ['seɪlzpɜ:sn]	Verkäufer/in
	social worker ['səʊʃl wɜ:kə]	Sozialarbeiter/in
	surveyor [sə'veɪə]	Gutachter/in, Landvermesser/in
	typist ['taɪpɪst]	Schreibkraft
	vet [vet]	Tierarzt/ -ärztin
83p	**investigative** [ɪn'vestɪgətɪv]	investigativ
	enterprising ['entəpraɪzɪŋ]	unternehmenslustig
	conventional [kən'venʃənl]	konventionell
	environment [ɪn'vaɪrənmənt]	Umwelt, Umfeld
	to **score** [skɔ:]	(Punkte) zählen
84	**promotional** [prə'məʊʃənl]	Werbe-
	case [keɪs]	Etui
	umbrella [ʌm'brelə]	(Regen-)Schirm
85t	**recording** [rɪ'kɔ:dɪŋ]	Aufnahme, Aufzeichnung
	query ['kwɪəri]	Frage
	notepaper ['nəʊtpeɪpə]	Briefpapier
	letterhead ['letəhed]	Briefkopf
	satisfied ['sætɪsfaɪd]	zufrieden
	to **hold** [həʊld]	warten
	to **expect** [ɪk'spekt]	erwarten
85	**qty. (quantity)** ['kwɒntəti]	Menge
	description [dɪ'skrɪpʃn]	Beschreibung
	amount [ə'maʊnt]	Summe, Betrag
	subtotal ['sʌbtəʊtl]	Zwischensumme
	handling ['hændlɪŋ]	Bearbeitung, Beförderung
	due [dju:]	fällig
	signature ['sɪgnətʃə]	Unterschrift
	if required [ɪf rɪ'kwaɪəd]	falls erforderlich
86	**staff** [stɑ:f]	Personal, Mitarbeiter/innen
88	**during** ['djʊərɪŋ]	während
	bankrupt ['bæŋkrʌpt]	bankrott, pleite
89	**employer** [ɪm'plɔɪə]	Arbeitgeber/in
	to **fire** ['faɪə]	entlassen
	security [sɪ'kjʊərəti]	Sicherheit
	benefits ['benɪfɪts]	Vergünstigungen
	company pension scheme [ˌkʌmpəni 'penʃn ski:m]	betriebliche Altersversorgung
	completely [kəm'pli:tli]	völlig

UNIT 8 SALES

90	to **found** [faʊnd]	gründen
	chef [ʃef]	Chefkoch, Küchenchef
	blade [bleɪd]	Klinge
	century ['sentʃəri]	Jahrhundert
	founder ['faʊndə]	Gründer/in
	trademark ['treɪdmɑ:k]	Warenzeichen
	to **register** ['redʒɪstə]	eintragen (lassen), anmelden
	concern [kən'sɜ:n]	Konzern
	facility [fə'sɪləti]	Einrichtung
	steel [sti:l]	Stahl
	to **recognize** ['rekəgnaɪz]	(an)erkennen
91	to **hold a meeting** [həʊld ə 'mi:tɪŋ]	eine Sitzung abhalten
	review [rɪ'vju:]	Rückblick
	so far [ˌsəʊ 'fɑ:]	bis jetzt
	quarterly ['kwɔ:təli]	vierteljährlich
	quarter ['kwɔ:tə]	Quartal
	sharply ['ʃɑ:pli]	rasch, schnell, stark
	slightly ['slaɪtli]	leicht, geringfügig
	disappointing [ˌdɪsə'pɔɪntɪŋ]	enttäuschend
	to **rise** [raɪz]	(an)steigen, anwachsen
	to **decrease** [dɪ'kri:s]	abnehmen
	to **remain** [rɪ'meɪn]	bleiben
	stable ['steɪbl]	stabil
	to **level off** [ˌlevl 'ɒf]	sich einpendeln
	to **draw** [drɔ:]	zeichnen
92t	**dramatic(ally)** [drə'mætɪk]	dramatisch
92	**effect** [ɪ'fekt]	(Aus-)Wirkung, Effekt
	finances ['faɪnænsɪz]	Finanzangelegenheiten
	other ['ʌðə]	andere/r/s
92p	**leader** ['li:də]	Führer/in
	sector ['sektə]	Sektor, Bereich
	homemade [ˌhəʊm'meɪd]	selbstgemacht
93	**reception desk** [rɪ'sepʃn desk]	Rezeption, Empfang
	to **pick up** [ˌpɪk 'ʌp]	abheben
	lobby ['lɒbi]	Foyer, Eingangshalle
93t	**single** ['sɪŋgl]	Einzel-
	registration form [ˌredʒɪ'streɪʃn fɔ:m]	Anmeldeformular
	stairs [steəz]	Treppe(n)
	to **wonder** ['wʌndə]	sich fragen
	towel ['taʊəl]	Handtuch
	selection [sɪ'lekʃn]	Auswahl, Angebot
93	**soap** [səʊp]	Seife
94	**non-smoking** [ˌnɒn'sməʊkɪŋ]	Nichtraucher-
	complaining [kəm'pleɪnɪŋ]	Reklamieren, Beschweren
94t	**exceptionally** [ɪk'sepʃənəli]	außergewöhnlich
	to **seem** [si:m]	(er)scheinen
94	**apology** [ə'pɒlədʒi]	Entschuldigung
	speaker ['spi:kə]	Sprecher/in
	to **refer to** [rɪ'fɜ: tə]	sich beziehen auf
94p	**hair dryer** ['heə draɪə]	Fön
	toothbrush ['tu:θbrʌʃ]	Zahnbürste
	tired ['taɪəd]	müde
	hungry ['hʌŋgri]	hungrig
	thirsty ['θɜ:sti]	durstig
	suitcase ['su:tkeɪs]	Koffer
	catastrophe [kə'tæstrəfi]	Katastrophe
	to **crash** [kræʃ]	abstürzen
	bill [bɪl]	Rechnung
	booking ['bʊkɪŋ]	Reservierung, Buchung
	noisy ['nɔɪzi]	laut
	nobody ['nəʊbədi]	niemand
	fully ['fʊli]	vollständig
94	**disadvantage** [ˌdɪsəd'vɑ:ntɪdʒ]	Nachteil
	flyer ['flaɪə]	Flieger/in
	rule [ru:l]	Regel
95	**traveler (AE)** ['trævələ]	Reisende/r
	tale [teɪl]	Geschichte, Erzählung
	troubleshooter ['trʌblʃu:tə]	Problemlöser/in, Troubleshooter
	oil [ɔɪl]	Öl
	frequent ['fri:kwənt]	häufig, oft
	on average [ɒn 'ævərɪdʒ]	im Durchschnitt, durchschnittlich
	inside [ɪn'saɪd]	Innere/s
	experience [ɪk'spɪəriəns]	Erlebnis
	to **grow up** [ˌgrəʊ 'ʌp]	aufwachsen
	regularly ['regjələli]	regelmäßig
	bedtime ['bedtaɪm]	Schlafenszeit
	scene [si:n]	Szene
	packing ['pækɪŋ]	(Koffer-)Packen

b **bad** | d **did** | f **five** | g **got** | h **how** | j **yes** | k **cat** | l **leg** | m **man** | n **no** | p **pen** | r **red**

	permanently ['pɜːmənəntli]	permanent, ständig
	raincoat ['reɪnkəʊt]	Regenmantel
	passport ['pɑːspɔːt]	Reisepass, Pass
96	**departure** [dɪ'pɑːtʃə]	Abfahrt, Abreise, Abflug
	request [rɪ'kwest]	Bitte, Wunsch
96t	to **depart** [dɪ'pɑːt]	abreisen, abfahren, abfliegen
	sort of ['sɔːt əv]	irgendwie
	mid-morning [ˌmɪd 'mɔːnɪŋ]	vormittags
	stupid ['stjuːpɪd]	dumm, blöde
	airline ['eəlaɪn]	Fluggesellschaft
	otherwise ['ʌðəwaɪz]	ansonsten
97	**screen** [skriːn]	Bildschirm
	availability [əˌveɪlə'bɪləti]	Verfügbarkeit
	round trip [ˌraʊnd 'trɪp]	Hin- und Rückflug
	one-way [ˌwʌn'weɪ]	nur Hinflug, einfach
	infant ['ɪnfənt]	Kleinkind
	condition [kən'dɪʃn]	Bedingung
	fare [feə]	Flugpreis
97p	**outbound** ['aʊtbaʊnd]	Hin-, Abflug
	inbound ['ɪnbaʊnd]	Ankunft
97	**convenient** [kən'viːniənt]	bequem, angenehm
97p	**location** [ləʊ'keɪʃn]	Lage
	outskirts ['aʊtskɜːts]	Außengebiete, Stadtrand
	railway station ['reɪlweɪ steɪʃn]	Bahnhof
	style [staɪl]	Stil
	parking ['pɑːkɪŋ]	Parkmöglichkeit(en)
	disabled [dɪs'eɪbld]	(körper)behindert
	village ['vɪlɪdʒ]	Dorf
	extensive [ɪk'stensɪv]	ausgedehnt
	whole ['həʊl]	ganz
	inn [ɪn]	(Land-)Gasthaus
	bedroom ['bedruːm]	Schlafzimmer
	nearby ['nɪəbaɪ]	nahe gelegen, in der Nähe
	twin (room) [twɪn]	Zimmer mit zwei getrennten Betten
	arrival [ə'raɪvl]	Ankunft
98	**competent(ly)** ['kɒmpɪtəntli]	kompetent
	steadily ['stedɪli]	stetig
	automatic(ally) [ˌɔːtə'mætɪkli]	automatisch
	angry ['æŋgri]	wütend, verärgert
	angrily ['æŋgrɪli]	ärgerlich, wütend
	timetable ['taɪmteɪbl]	Fahr-, Stundenplan
99	**possibly** ['pɒsəbli]	möglicherweise
	easily ['iːzəli]	leicht, einfach
	wide [waɪd]	weit
101	to **forget** [fə'get]	vergessen
	to **complain** [kəm'pleɪn]	(sich) beschweren
	to **state** [steɪt]	feststellen, angeben
	objectively [əb'dʒektɪvli]	objektiv
	to **blame** [bleɪm]	beschuldigen
	to **soften** ['sɒfn]	abschwächen
	complaint [kəm'pleɪnt]	Beschwerde, Beanstandung

UNIT 9 AT A TRADE FAIR

102	**plastic** ['plæstɪk]	Kunststoff
103	**buyer** ['baɪə]	Einkäufer/in
	ordinary ['ɔːdnri]	gewöhnlich, normal
103t	to **assume** [ə'sjuːm]	annehmen
	major ['meɪdʒə]	groß, größer
	naturally ['nætʃrəli]	selbstverständlich
	to **promise** ['prɒmɪs]	versprechen
	to **justify** ['dʒʌstɪfaɪ]	rechtfertigen
	expense [ɪk'spens]	Kosten, Ausgabe
	perfectly ['pɜːfɪktli]	völlig
	period ['pɪəriəd]	Zeit(raum)
	to **interrupt** [ˌɪntə'rʌpt]	unterbrechen
	lifetime ['laɪftaɪm]	Lebenszeit, ein ganzes Leben
	to **save** [seɪv]	sparen
	to **replace** [rɪ'pleɪs]	ersetzen, austauschen
103	**ingredient** [ɪn'griːdiənt]	Bestandteil, Zutat
	durable ['djʊərəbl]	haltbar, langlebig
	beautifully ['bjuːtɪfli]	schön
	technically ['teknɪkli]	technisch
	instructions [ɪn'strʌkʃnz]	Bedienungsanleitung
	handle ['hændl]	(Hand-)Griff
	ergonomically [ˌɜːgə'nɒmɪkli]	ergonomisch
103t	**comfortable** ['kʌmftəbl]	bequem
	balanced ['bælənst]	ausgewogen
	accident ['æksɪdənt]	Unfall
	sharp [ʃɑːp]	scharf
	to **sharpen** ['ʃɑːpən]	schärfen
103	**bullet point** ['bʊlɪt pɔɪnt]	Stichpunkt
	fragile ['frædʒaɪl]	zerbrechlich
104	**comparison** [kəm'pærɪsn]	Vergleich
	competitor [kəm'petɪtə]	Konkurrent/in
	to **greet** [griːt]	(be)grüßen
104p	**hardback** ['hɑːdbæk]	gebundene Ausgabe
	via ['vaɪə]	über, per
	library ['laɪbrəri]	Bücherei, Bibliothek
	to **last** [lɑːst]	dauern, (durch)halten
	to **grind** [graɪnd]	mahlen
	voice [vɔɪs]	Stimme
	to **lease** [liːs]	leasen, mieten
	to **interpret** [ɪn'tɜːprɪt]	dolmetschen
	immediate [ɪ'miːdiət]	umgehend, sofortig
	quotation [kwəʊ'teɪʃn]	(Kosten-)Voranschlag
105	to **take care of** [teɪk 'keər əv]	sich kümmern um, sorgen für
105t	**comment** ['kɒment]	Bemerkung, Kommentar
	set [set]	Satz
106	to **peel** [piːl]	schälen
	to **pare** [peə]	schälen
	stockist [bi 'stɒkɪst]	Fachgeschäft
	replacement [rɪ'pleɪsmənt]	Ersatz
107	to **hesitate** ['hezɪteɪt]	zögern
	to **enquire about** [ɪn'kwaɪər əbaʊt]	sich erkundigen nach
	to **invest** [ɪn'vest]	investieren
	to **highlight** ['haɪlaɪt]	hervorheben
	huge [hjuːdʒ]	riesig
108	**exercise cycle** ['eksəsaɪz saɪkl]	Heimtrainer
	rating ['reɪtɪŋ]	Einschätzung, Beurteilung
	to **propose** [prə'pəʊz]	vorschlagen
	to **undertake** [ˌʌndə'teɪk]	vornehmen
	sales performance [ˌseɪlz pə'fɔːməns]	Verkaufszahlen
	recommendation [ˌrekəmen'deɪʃn]	Empfehlung
	in your opinion [ɪn jɔːr ə'pɪniən]	Ihrer Meinung nach
	to **continue** [kən'tɪnjuː]	fortfahren
	to **discontinue** [ˌdɪskən'tɪnjuː]	einstellen
109	**poor** [pʊə]	arm, schlecht, mangelhaft
	reliability [rɪˌlaɪə'bɪləti]	Zuverlässigkeit
	to **cover** ['kʌvə]	(ab)decken, behandeln

s **so** | t **tea** | v **van** | w **wet** | z **his** | ʃ **she** | ʒ **vision** | tʃ **chin** | dʒ **June** | θ **three** | ð **the** | ŋ **ring**

section ['sekʃn] Teil, Abschnitt
aim [eɪm] Ziel, Absicht
finding ['faɪndɪŋ] Ergebnis
conclusion [kən'klu:ʒn] (Schluss-)Folgerung
suggestion [sə'dʒestʃən] Vorschlag
to **examine** [ɪg'zæmɪn] untersuchen, prüfen
to **contrast** [kən'trɑ:st] gegenüberstellen
to **perform** (well/badly) [pə'fɔ:m] (gute/schlechte) Ergebnisse haben
particularly [pə'tɪkjələli] besonders
badly ['bædli] schlecht
to **recommend** [ˌrekə'mend] empfehlen
110 **confirmation** [ˌkɒnfə'meɪʃn] Bestätigung
to **reimburse** [ˌri:ɪm'bɜ:s] entschädigen, erstatten
reimbursement [ˌri:ɪm'bɜ:smənt] Entschädigung, Erstattung
receipt [rɪ'si:t] Empfang, Erhalt
to **insure** [ɪn'ʃʊə] versichern
111 to **rewrite** [ˌri:'raɪt] umschreiben
to **fit** [fɪt] passen (zu)
112 **damage** ['dæmɪdʒ] Schaden, Beschädigung
to **number** ['nʌmbə] nummerieren
113 **topic** ['tɒpɪk] Thema
in general [ɪn 'dʒenrəl] im Allgemeinen
entertainment [ˌentə'teɪnmənt] Unterhaltung
health [helθ] Gesundheit, Befinden
matter ['mætə] Ding, Angelegenheit
politics ['pɒlətɪks] (die) Politik
sarcasm ['sɑ:kæzəm] Sarkasmus
aggressive [ə'gresɪv] aggressiv

UNIT 10 MADE IN GERMANY

114 **sort** [sɔ:t] Art, Sorte
114t to **wash** [wɒʃ] waschen
along [ə'lɒŋ] entlang
corridor ['kɒrɪdɔ:] Gang, Korridor
115 **forged** [fɔ:dʒd] geschmiedet
proud of ['praʊd əv] stolz auf
current ['kʌrənt] gegenwärtig
traditional [trə'dɪʃənl] traditionell
craftsmanship ['krɑ:ftsmənʃɪp] Handwerkskunst, (handwerkliches) Können
step [step] Schritt, Stufe
skilled [skɪld] ausgebildet, Fach-
hi-tech [ˌhaɪ'tek] Hightech-, hochtechnisiert
computer-guided [kəm'pju:tə gaɪdɪd] computergesteuert
powerful ['paʊəfl] (leistungs)stark
to **take it in turns** [teɪk ɪt ɪn 'tɜ:nz] sich abwechseln
116 **customer support** [ˌkʌstəmə sə'pɔ:t] Kundendienst
raw material [ˌrɔ: mə'tɪəriəl] Rohstoff(e)
market research [ˌmɑ:kɪt rɪ'sɜ:tʃ] Marktforschung
advertising campaign [ˌædvətaɪzɪŋ kæm'peɪn] Werbekampagne
wholesaler ['həʊlseɪlə] Großhändler/in
to **oversee** [ˌəʊvə'si:] beaufsichtigen
annual report [ˌænjuəl rɪ'pɔ:t] Jahresabschluss, -bericht
finally ['faɪnəli] schließlich, zum Schluss
117 **scenery** ['si:nəri] Landschaft
lifestyle ['laɪfstaɪl] Lebensstil
partnership ['pɑ:tnəʃɪp] Zusammenarbeit
Cheers! [tʃɪəz] Prost!
pub [pʌb] Wirtshaus, Kneipe
to **imagine** [ɪ'mædʒɪn] sich vorstellen
way [weɪ] Hinsicht, Art (und Weise)
to **serve** [sɜ:v] servieren, anbieten
impression [ɪm'preʃn] Eindruck
open-minded [ˌəʊpən 'maɪndɪd] aufgeschlossen
conservative [kən'sɜ:vətɪv] konservativ
118 **dish** [dɪʃ] Gericht
starter ['stɑ:tə] Vorspeise
dessert [dɪ'zɜ:t] Nachspeise, Dessert
soup [su:p] Suppe
beef [bi:f] Rindfleisch
pork [pɔ:k] Schweinefleisch
veal [vi:l] Kalbfleisch
duck [dʌk] Ente
turkey ['tɜ:ki] Truthahn
liver ['lɪvə] Leber
sausage ['sɒsɪdʒ] (Brat-)Wurst
vegetable ['vedʒtəbl] Gemüse
sauce [sɔ:s] Soße
syrup ['sɪrəp] Sirup
fried [fraɪd] gebraten
roasted ['rəʊstɪd] gebraten, geröstet
boiled [bɔɪld] gekocht
pickled ['pɪkld] eingelegt
baked [beɪkt] gebacken
oven ['ʌvn] Herd
spicy ['spaɪsi] (stark) gewürzt, würzig
salty ['sɔ:lti] salzig
sweet [swi:t] süß
creamy ['kri:mi] sahnig
delicious [dɪ'lɪʃəs] köstlich, lecker
speciality [ˌspeʃi'æləti] Spezialität
house style ['haʊs staɪl] nach Art des Hauses
119 **relationship** [rɪ'leɪʃnʃɪp] Beziehung, Verhältnis
cold [kəʊld] Erkältung
120 **currently** ['kʌrəntli] momentan, zurzeit
power cable ['paʊə keɪbl] Stromkabel
to **finalize** ['faɪnəlaɪz] endgültig festlegen, zum Abschluss bringen
electricity [ɪˌlek'trɪsəti] Elektrizität, Strom
to **entertain** [ˌentə'teɪn] unterhalten
race [reɪs] (Pferde-)Rennen
120t **outside** [ˌaʊt'saɪd] draußen
bet [bet] Wette
to **realize** ['rɪəlaɪz] sich klar sein
optimism ['ɒptɪmɪzəm] Optimismus
specification [ˌspesɪfɪ'keɪʃn] Spezifikation, Vorgabe
insulation [ˌɪnsju'leɪʃn] Isolierung, Isolation
thick [θɪk] dick
loss [lɒs] Verlust
distance ['dɪstəns] Entfernung, Strecke
to **reflect** [rɪ'flekt] (sich) widerspiegeln
initially [ɪ'nɪʃəli] anfänglich, zuerst
long-term [ˌlɒŋ'tɜ:m] langfristig, Langzeit-
121 **delighted** [dɪ'laɪtɪd] (sehr) erfreut, entzückt
to **enclose** [ɪn'kləʊz] beilegen, beifügen
shortly ['ʃɔ:tli] in Kürze
to **appreciate** [ə'pri:ʃieɪt] dankbar sein
hospitality [ˌhɒspɪ'tæləti] Gastfreundschaft, -lichkeit
kindness ['kaɪndnəs] Güte, Freundlichkeit

æ hat | ɑ: arm | e pen | ɜ: her | ə ago | ɪ sit | i: see | i many | ɒ got | ɔ: saw | ʌ cup | ʊ put

	to **repay** [rɪ'peɪ]	sich revanchieren für
	to **brainstorm** ['breɪnstɔ:m]	(Ideen) sammeln
	socially ['səʊʃəli]	gesellschaftlich, sozial
	schedule ['ʃedju:l]	Zeitplan
125	to **wine and dine** [ˌwaɪn ən 'daɪn]	dinieren, essen gehen
	tip [tɪp]	Trinkgeld
	to **rely on** [rɪ'laɪ ɒn]	sich verlassen auf, abhängig sein von
	decent ['di:snt]	anständig
	wage [weɪdʒ]	Lohn, Gehalt

BUSINESS CORRESPONDENCE

141	**correspondence** [ˌkɒrɪ'spɒndəns]	Briefwechsel, Korrespondenz
142	to **update** [ˌʌp'deɪt]	aktualisieren, auf den neuesten Stand bringen
	sales literature ['seɪlz ˌlɪtrətʃə]	(Verkaufs-)Prospekt(e), Kataloge
	reference ['refərəns]	Zeichen, Bezug
	fee [fi:]	Gebühr, Honorar
	competitive [kəm'petətɪv]	konkurrenzfähig
	Yours sincerely [jɔ:z sɪn'sɪəli]	Mit freundlichen Grüßen
143	**Yours faithfully** [jɔ:z sɪn'sɪəli]	Mit freundlichen Grüßen
144	**trade journal** ['treɪd dʒɜ:nl]	Handelsblatt
	mutual ['mju:tʃuəl]	gemeinsam
	request [rɪ'kwest]	Anfrage, Anforderung
	recent ['ri:snt]	jüngst, kürzlich
	aerospace ['eərəʊspeɪs]	Raumfahrt-
145	**edition** [ɪ'dɪʃn]	Ausgabe, Auflage
	to **obtain** [əb'teɪn]	erhalten
	directory [də'rektəri]	(Inhalts-)Verzeichnis
	grateful ['greɪtfl]	dankbar
146	**storage** ['stɔ:rɪdʒ]	Lagerung
	warehouse ['weəhaʊs]	Lager(haus)
	adviser [əd'vaɪzə]	Berater/in
147	**extremely** [ɪk'stri:mli]	außerordentlich
	in due course [ɪn ˌdju: 'kɔ:s]	zu gegebener Zeit
148	**substantial** [səb'stænʃl]	ansehnlich, beträchtlich
149	**seller** ['selə]	Verkäufer/in
	satisfactory [ˌsætɪs'fæktəri]	zufrieden stellend, befriedigend
150	**grand total** [ˌgrænd 'təʊtl]	Endsumme
	introductory [ˌɪntrə'dʌktəri]	Einführungs-
	generous ['dʒenərəs]	großzügig
	cash discount ['kæʃ dɪskaʊnt]	Barzahlungsrabatt
	valid ['vælɪd]	gültig
	payment in full [ˌpeɪmənt ɪn 'fʊl]	vollständige Bezahlung
	certain ['sɜ:tn]	sicher, gewiss
	to **get in touch** [get ɪn 'tʌtʃ]	sich in Verbindung setzen
151	to **be willing** [bi 'wɪlɪŋ]	bereit/gewillt sein
	letter of credit [ˌletər əv 'kredɪt]	Akkreditiv, Kreditbrief
	to **dispatch** [dɪ'spætʃ]	(ab) schicken, aufgeben, (ver)senden
152	**translator** [træns'leɪtə]	Übersetzer/in
	subtitle ['sʌbtaɪtl]	Untertitel
	covering letter [ˌkʌvərɪŋ 'letə]	Begleitbrief
	to **apply for** [ə'plaɪ fə]	sich bewerben um
	daily newspaper [ˌdeɪli 'nju:zpeɪpə]	Tageszeitung
	to **involve** [ɪn'vɒlv]	umfassen, beinhalten
	field [fi:ld]	Bereich, Gebiet
	current affairs [ˌkʌrənt ə'feəz]	Tagesereignisse, -politik
	deep [di:p]	stark, tief
	opportunity [ˌɒpə'tju:nəti]	Gelegenheit, Chance, Möglichkeit
	valuable ['væljuəbl]	wertvoll
	contribution [ˌkɒntrɪ'bju:ʃn]	Beitrag
153	**response** [rɪ'spɒns]	Antwort
	resumé (AE) [rɪ'zju:m]	(tabellarischer) Lebenslauf
	present ['preznt]	gegenwärtig, jetzig
	duty ['dju:ti]	Aufgabe, Pflicht
	to **be an asset** ['æset]	von Wert sein, eine Stütze sein
	background ['bækgraʊnd]	Hintergrund, Herkunft
	to **require** [rɪ'kwaɪə]	benötigen
	communication [kəˌmju:nɪ'keɪʃn]	Kommunikations-
	knowledge ['nɒlɪdʒ]	Kenntnis(se)
154	**informal** [ɪn'fɔ:ml]	informell
	to **vary** ['veəri]	sich unterscheiden, variieren
	organizer ['ɔ:gənaɪzə]	Organisator/in
	association [əˌsəʊsi'eɪʃn]	Verband, Gesellschaft
	theme [θi:m]	Thema
	economy [ɪ'kɒnəmi]	Wirtschaft
	venue ['venju:]	(Tagungs-)Ort
	to **be payable** [bi 'peɪəbl]	fällig sein
	to **lead** [li:d]	leiten
155	**humble** ['hʌmbl]	bescheiden
156	**invitation** [ˌɪnvɪ'teɪʃn]	Einladung
	HR (human resources) [ˌhju:mən rɪ'sɔ:sɪz]	Personalabteilung
	recruitment [rɪ'kru:tmənt]	Einstellung (von Arbeitskräften)
	anniversary [ˌænɪ'vɜ:səri]	Jahrestag
	to **celebrate** ['selɪbreɪt]	feiern
	to mark the occasion [tə ˌmɑ:k ði ə'keɪʒn]	aus Anlass des Ereignisses
	celebration dinner [ˌselɪ'breɪʃn dɪnə]	Festmahl
	spouse [spaʊz]	Gemahl/in, Ehepartner/in
	Congratulations [kənˌgrætʃu'leɪʃnz]	Herzlichen Glückwunsch
157	**farewell** [ˌfeə'wel]	Abschieds-
	Christmas ['krɪsməs]	Weihnachten
	valued ['vælju:d]	geschätzt
	to **take place** [teɪk 'pleɪs]	stattfinden
	away on business [əˌweɪ ɒn 'bɪznəs]	geschäftlich unterwegs
	commitment [kə'mɪtmənt]	Verabredung
	to **regret** [rɪ'gret]	bedauern
	prior ['praɪə]	vorherig
	to **wish** [wɪʃ]	wünschen
	pleasant ['pleznt]	angenehm, nett
158	**reservation** [ˌrezə'veɪʃn]	Reservierung, Buchung
	VP (vice president) [ˌvaɪs 'prezɪdənt]	Vizepräsident/in
	publishing ['pʌblɪʃɪŋ]	Verlags-
	inclusive [ɪn'klu:sɪv]	einschließlich
159	to **ensure** [ɪn'ʃʊə]	sicherstellen
	to **settle** ['setl]	begleichen, bezahlen

u: **too** | u **actual** | aɪ **my** | aʊ **now** | eɪ **pay** | əʊ **home** | ɔɪ **oil** | ɪə **beer** | eə **hair** | ʊə **pure**

A–Z word list

Hier finden Sie die Wörter der *Unit word list* in alphabetischer Reihenfolge.
Die Zahl nach dem Stichwort bezieht sich auf die Seite, auf der das Wort zum ersten Mal erscheint.

p = das Wort befindet sich im Partner file
t = das Wort befindet sich im Transcript
AE = amerikanisches Englisch

A

absolutely *34* absolut
to **accept** *46* annehmen
acceptable *60t* annehmbar, akzeptabel
accident *103t* Unfall
according to *35* nach, entsprechend
account manager *7t* Kundenbetreuer/in
account *7t* (Stamm)Kunde
to **account for** (20%) *43t* (20%) ausmachen
accountant *81* Buchhalter/in
accounting *79* Rechnungswesen, (Bilanz-)Buchhaltung
across *28* waagerecht
activity *34* Aktivität, Beschäftigung
actual *42* konkret, wirklich
actually *30* eigentlich
to **adapt** *20t* anpassen
address book *13* Adressbuch
advance, in ~ *49* im Voraus
advanced *44* fortgeschritten
to **advertise** *59p* inserieren, werben (für)
advert(isement) *25t* Anzeige
advertising campaign *116* Werbekampagne
advice *58* Beratung
adviser *146* Berater/in
aerospace *144* Raumfahrt-
afterwards *72t* danach, hinterher
afraid, I'm ~ *24t* leider ...
again *9* wieder
age *35* Alter
agenda *69* Tagesordnung
aggressive *113* aggressiv
ago *13t* vor
to **agree** *35* zustimmen
aim *109* Ziel, Absicht
air freight *43* Luftfracht
airline *96t* Fluggesellschaft
A-levels *30* (*entspricht*) Abitur
all over *13t* überall (in)
allowed *52* erlaubt
almost *41* fast, beinahe
along *114t* entlang
also *20t* auch, außerdem
always *20* immer
amazing *66* erstaunlich
amount *85* Summe, Betrag
angrily *98* ärgerlich, wütend
angry *98* wütend, verärgert
anniversary *156* Jahrestag
annual report *116* Jahresabschluss, -bericht
another time *25* (später) noch einmal
anything else *49* noch etwas
anyway *72t* jedenfalls, sowieso
apartment (AE) *29* Wohnung
to **apologize** *49* sich entschuldigen
apology *94* Entschuldigung
to **applaud** *45* applaudieren
application *59* Bewerbung; *66* Anwendung, Verwendungszweck
to **apply for** *152* sich bewerben um
appointment *69* Termin, Verabredung
to **appreciate** *121* dankbar sein
approximately *8* ungefähr, zirka
area code (AE) *12* Vorwahl
arithmetic *81* Rechnen, Arithmetik
around *6* herum
to **arrange** *18* vereinbaren, verabreden
arrangement *70* Vereinbarung, Termin
arrival *97p* Ankunft
to **arrive** *32* ankommen
art gallery *23* Kunstgalerie
as a matter of fact *72t* eigentlich, tatsächlich
asap *56t* so schnell wie möglich
asset, to **be an ~** *153* von Wert sein, eine Stütze sein
association *154* Verband, Gesellschaft
to **assume** *103t* annehmen
at last *9* endlich
at the moment *18* im Augenblick
atmosphere *13t* Atmosphäre, Betriebsklima
to **attach** *49* beilegen, -fügen
attachment *49* Anlage
to **attend** *18* teilnehmen (an), besuchen
auctioneer *83* Auktionator
audience *45* Publikum, Zuhörer
authentic *60t* authentisch, echt
authority *47* Autorität
automatic(ally) *98* automatisch
automotive *60* Auto-
autumn *22* Herbst
availability *97* Verfügbarkeit
available *24* anwesend
average, on ~ *95* im Durchschnitt, durchschnittlich
away on business *157* geschäftlich unterwegs

B

Bachelor of Arts (BA) *41* 1. Staatsexamen in Geisteswissenschaften
Bachelor of Science (BSc/BS) *41* 1. Staatsexamen in Naturwissenschaften
background *153* Hintergrund, Herkunft
badly *109* schlecht
baked *118* gebacken
balanced *103t* ausgewogen
bank clerk *83* Bankangestellte/r
bank transfer *60* (Bank-)Überweisung
bankrupt *88* bankrott, pleite
bar, navigation ~ *59p* Navigationsleiste
barbecue *47* Grillparty
based in, to **be ~** *7t* den Firmensitz haben in
basically *60t* im Grunde
bathroom *29* Bad(ezimmer); auch AE: Toilette
beach *67* Strand
beautifully *103* schön
to **become** *30* werden
bedroom *97p* Schlafzimmer

bedtime *95* Schlafenszeit
beef *118* Rindfleisch
before *36t* vor
to **believe** *76* glauben
benefits *89* Vergünstigungen
Best wishes *48* Mit besten Grüßen
bet *120t* Wette
between *17* zwischen
bike, by ~ *20* mit dem Rad
bill *94p* Rechnung
biscuit *29* Keks
bit, a ~ *35t* ein bisschen, etwas
blade *90* Klinge
to **blame** *101* beschuldigen
board *35* (Wand-)Tafel
boiled *118* gekocht
book editor *83* Redakteur/in
to **book** *18* buchen, bestellen
booking *94p* Reservierung, Buchung
bookkeeper *83* Buchhalter/in
bookshop *61p* Buchhandlung
to **boom** *33* (auf)blühen, boomen
born, to **be ~** *30* geboren sein
both ... and *22* sowohl ... als auch
bottom line *66* Endergebnis
to **brainstorm** *121* (Ideen) sammeln
branch *37* Filiale, Niederlassung
briefcase *21* Aktentasche
to **bring forward** *72* vorverlegen
brochure *22* Broschüre, Prospekt
to **browse** *58t* surfen, stöbern, durchsehen
budget *37* Etat
to **build** *60* bauen
building *23* Gebäude
bulk discount *37* Mengenrabatt
bullet point *103* Stichpunkt
business activity *7* Geschäftstätigkeit
business agency *6* Geschäftsagentur
business diploma *30* Abschlusszeugnis als Diplomkaufmann/frau
business partner *6* Geschäftspartner/in
busy *20t* beschäftigt
button *59* Taste, Knopf
buyer *103* Einkäufer/in

C

to **call someone back** *24t* jdn. zurückrufen
called *6* namens
caller *24* Anrufer/in
to **cancel** *72* streichen, absagen
capital *10* groß
card *12* Visitenkarte
career *30* Karriere, Beruf
careful *58* sorgfältig
cargo *44* Fracht, Ladung
case *13t* Kiste; 84 Etui
case study *42* Fallstudie
cash discount *150* Barzahlungsrabatt
castle *22* Schloss
catastrophe *94p* Katastrophe
to **catch** *11* verstehen; 55 erreichen
cathedral *22* Dom
to **celebrate** *156* feiern
celebration dinner *156* Festmahl
cell phone (AE) *29* Mobiltelefon, Handy
centre *22* Zentrum
century *90* Jahrhundert
CEO (chief executive officer) *7t* (Haupt)Geschäftsführer/in
certain *150* sicher, gewiss
certainly *37* sicherlich, gewiss
chain *13* Kette
chair *21* Stuhl
challenging *82* herausfordernd
chamber of commerce *69* Handelskammer
charge *36* Kosten, Gebühr
to **check** *12* (über)prüfen
Cheers! *117* Prost!
chef *90* Chefkoch, Küchenchef
chemist *83* Chemiker/in
cheque *29* Scheck
child *20t* Kind
to **choose** *15* (aus)wählen
Christmas *157* Weihnachten
cinema *34* Kino
circle *53* Kreis
city centre *20t* (Stadt-)Zentrum
classroom *61* Klassenzimmer, -raum
clear *60t* klar, deutlich
client *7t* Kunde/Kundin
to **close** *31* schließen
closed corporation (AE) *77* GmbH
clothes *18* Kleidung
COD (cash on delivery) *60* Nachnahme, Barzahlung bei Lieferung
code *12* Vorwahl, Code
cold *119* Erkältung
to **collect** *13* sammeln; *55* abholen
college *31* (Fach-)Hochschule, Universität
colour *29* Farbe
column *47* Spalte
Come and join us *11* Kommen Sie zu uns
to **come in** *37* lieferbar sein
comfortable *103t* bequem
comment *105t* Bemerkung, Kommentar
commercial *22* Handels-, Geschäfts-
commitment *157* Verabredung
common *17* normal, üblich
communication *153* Kommunikations-
company *6* Unternehmen, Firma
company pension scheme *89* betriebliche Altersversorgung
to **compare** *8* vergleichen
comparison *104* Vergleich, Steigerung
competent(ly) *98* kompetent
competitive *142* konkurrenzfähig
competitor *104* Konkurrent/in
to **complain** *101* (sich) beschweren
complaining *94* Reklamieren, Beschweren
complaint *101* Beschwerde, Beanstandung
to **complete** *6* ergänzen, vervollständigen
complete *31* voll(ständig)
completely *89* völlig
complex *44* kompliziert, komplex
complicated *42* kompliziert
component *20t* Bauteil
composer *22* Komponist/in
computer-guided *115* computergesteuert

concern *90* Konzern
concert hall *22* Konzerthalle, -saal
conclusion *109* (Schluss-)Folgerung
condition *97* Bedingung
conference *11* Konferenz, Besprechung, Tagung
to **confirm** *49* bestätigen
confirmation *110* Bestätigung
Congratulations *156* Herzlichen Glückwunsch
to **connect** *58t* verbinden
conservative *117* konservativ
consignment *44* (Waren-)Sendung, Lieferung
construction *73* Bau
consultant *6* Berater/in
consumer *61p* Konsument/in
contact *6* Kontakt, Verbindung
to **contact** *58t* sich wenden an, Kontakt aufnehmen zu
to **contain** *59* enthalten
to **continue** *108* fortfahren
contract *56* Vertrag
to **contrast** *109* gegenüberstellen
contribution *152* Beitrag
convenient *97* bequem, angenehm
conventional *83p* konventionell
conversation *11* Gespräch, Unterhaltung
cookie (AE) *29* Keks
cooking *34* Kochen
copy *49p* Kopie
corporate *48* Firmen-
corporation *33* (Aktien-)Gesellschaft
to **correct** *8* korrigieren
correspondence *141* Briefwechsel, Korrespondenz
corridor *114t* Gang, Korridor
cost *60t* Kosten
counsellor *83* Berater/in
couple of times, a ~ *35t* ein paarmal
courier *43* Kurier
course *20* Kurs, Lehrgang
to **cover** *109* abdecken, behandeln
covering letter *152* Begleitbrief
craftsmanship *115* Handwerkskunst, (handwerkliches) Können
to **crash** *94p* abstürzen
creamy *118* sahnig
crime *33* Verbrechen, Kriminalität
crossword *28* Kreuzworträtsel
cultural *22* kulturell, Kultur-
cup *60t* Tasse
cupboard *21* Schrank
current affairs *152* Tagesereignisse, -politik
current *115* gegenwärtig
currently *120* momentan, zurzeit
curtain *21* Vorhang, Gardine
custom *45* Sitte, Brauch
customer *8* Kunde/Kundin
customer support *116* Kundendienst
CV (curriculum vitae) *31* Lebenslauf
cycling *34* Radfahren

D
daily newspaper *152* Tageszeitung
damage *112* Schaden, Beschädigung
dancing *35* Tanzen
data *35* Daten
daughter *25t* Tochter
day trip *34* Tagesausflug
deal *37* (günstiges) Angebot
dealer *59p* Händler/in
death *46* Tod
decent *125* anständig
to **decide** *60* (sich) entscheiden
decision *58t* Entscheidung
to **decrease** *91* abnehmen
deep *152* stark, tief
to **delay** *49* Verspätung, Verzögerung
delicious *118* köstlich, lecker
delighted *121* (sehr) erfreut, entzückt
to **deliver** *36* (aus)liefern
delivery *36* Zustellung, Auslieferung
dentist *38* Zahnarzt/-ärztin
to **depart** *96t* abreisen, abfahren, abfliegen
department *13t* Abteilung
department store *13* Kauf-, Warenhaus
departure *96* Abfahrt, Abreise, Abflug
to **describe** *19* beschreiben
description *85* Beschreibung
to **design** *49p* entwerfen, konstruieren
desk *21* (Schreib-)Tisch
dessert *118* Nachspeise, Dessert
details *13* Einzelheiten, Details
to **develop** *7t* entwickeln
dialogue *39* Dialog
diary *69* Terminkalender
dictionary *18* Wörterbuch
difference *17* Unterschied
different *35* unterschiedlich
difficult *41* schwierig
dinner *26* Abendessen
direct(ly) *47* direkt
directory *145* (Inhalts-)Verzeichnis
disabled *97p* (körper)behindert
disadvantage *94* Nachteil
disappointing *91* enttäuschend
to **discontinue** *108* einstellen
discount *36* Rabatt, Skonto, Nachlass
to **discuss** *19* besprechen, erörtern
dish *118* Gericht
to **dislike** *34* nicht mögen
to **dispatch** *151* (ab) schicken, aufgeben, (ver)senden
distance *120t* Entfernung, Strecke
to **distribute** *59p* vertreiben, (aus)liefern
distribution *31* Vertrieb, Auslieferung
to **disturb** *56t* stören
to **divide** *43t* (unter)teilen
division *42* (Betriebs-)Sparte
DIY *34* Heimwerken
to **do business** *45* Geschäfte machen
double *10* doppelt, Doppel-
doubt, without ~ *58t* ohne Zweifel
to **download** *59* herunterladen
to **downsize** *20* (Personal) abbauen
downtown (AE) *29* (im) Stadtzentrum
dramatic *92t* dramatisch
to **draw** *91* zeichnen
dream *75* Traum
dress down day *46* Tag mit legerer Kleidung
to **drink** *18* trinken
drive *37* Laufwerk

duck *118* Ente
due course, in ~ *147* zu gegebener Zeit
due *85* fällig
durable *103* haltbar, langlebig
during *88* während
duty *153* Aufgabe, Pflicht
dynamic *40* dynamisch

E

each *11* jede/r/s
early *28* früh
early bird *63* Frühaufsteher/in
to **earn** *43* verdienen
easily *99* leicht, einfach
east *23* Osten
eastern *23* östlich, Ost-
e-commerce *59p* elektronischer Handel
economy *154* Wirtschaft
edition *145* Ausgabe, Auflage
education *31* Ausbildung
effect *92t* (Aus-)Wirkung, Effekt
effective *31* effektiv, wirkungsvoll
eg (or e.g.) *43* z. B.
either *16* entweder
electrical technician *83* Elektriker, Elektrotechniker
electricity *120* Elektrizität, Strom
elevator (AE) *29* Fahrstuhl
emergency *48t* Notfall
to **employ** *13t* beschäftigen
employee *43t* Beschäftigte/r
employer *89* Arbeitgeber/in
to **enclose** *121* beilegen, beifügen
end *45* Ende, Schluss
energetic *31* energisch, tatkräftig
to **enjoy** *34* genießen, gern haben/tun
enough *48t* ausreichend
to **enquire about** *107* sich erkundigen nach
to **ensure** *159* sicherstellen
enterprising *83p* unternehmenslustig
to **entertain** *120* unterhalten
entertainment *113* Unterhaltung
enthusiastic *45* begeistert
environment *83p* Umwelt, Umfeld
equipment *33* Ausrüstung, Geräte
equivalent *77* Entsprechung
ergonomically *103* ergonomisch
estate agent *83* Immobilienmakler/in
etc *49* usw.
etiquette *47* Etikette
even *66* sogar (noch)
ever *67* je(mals), schon (ein)mal
exactly *6* exakt, genau
to **exaggerate** *46* übertreiben
to **examine** *109* untersuchen, prüfen
excellent *37p* ausgezeichnet
except *25p* außer
exceptionally *94t* außergewöhnlich
excerpt *66* Auszug
to **exchange** *12* (aus)tauschen
excited *79* (freudig) erregt
to **excuse** *9* entschuldigen
exercise *39* Übung
exercise cycle *108* Heimtrainer
exhibition *22* Ausstellung
to **expand** *19* sich ausdehnen, expandieren
to **expect** *85t* erwarten
expense *103t* Kosten, Ausgabe
expensive *13t* teuer
experience *31* (Berufs-)Erfahrung; *95* Erlebnis
expiry date *36t* Ablaufdatum
to **explain** *7t* erklären, erläutern
export sales manager *13p* Exportleiter/in
expression *8* Ausdruck
extension number *49* Durchwahlnummer
extensive *97p* ausgedehnt
extra *37p* zusätzlich
extract *40* Auszug
extreme(ly) *35* äußerst
extremely *147* außerordentlich
ex-works *60* ab Werk

F

face-to-face meeting *9* persönliche Begegnung
facility *90* Einrichtung
fact, in ~ *13t* tatsächlich
factory *7t* Fabrik
fair *31* angemessen
fairly *58t* ziemlich
to **fall asleep** *35* einschlafen
false *66* falsch
family name *17* Nach-, Familienname
famous *22* berühmt
fantastically *79* fantastisch
fare *97* Flugpreis
farewell *157* Abschieds-
fault *60t* Fehler, Schuld
favourite *34* liebst, Lieblings-
feature *37p* Merkmal, Eigenschaft
federal province *22* Bundesstaat
fee *142* Gebühr, Honorar
field *152* Bereich, Gebiet
figure *56* Zahl
file *21* (Akten-)Ordner
to **fill in** *15* eintragen, -setzen
to **finalize** *120* endgültig festlegen, zum Abschluss bringen
finally *116* schließlich, zum Schluss
finances *92* Finanzangelegenheiten
financial *58t* finanziell
to **find out** *33* herausfinden
finding *109* Ergebnis
fine, thanks; I'm ~ *9* Danke, gut
finished, to **be** ~ *24t* zu Ende sein
to **fire** *89* entlassen
first hand *30* aus erster Hand
first name *17* Vorname
to **fit** *111* passen (zu)
to **fix** *73* festlegen, -setzen
flag *53* Flagge, Fahne
flat *20t* Wohnung
flatscreen *37* Flachbildschirm
flight *9* Flug
flow chart *37* Flussdiagramm
fluent(ly) *31* fließend
to **fly** *55* fliegen
flyer *94* Flieger/in
focus *44* Schwerpunkt
following *49p* folgend
food *22* Essen, Nahrung(smittel)

foot *33* Fuß
for example *13t* zum Beispiel
foreign *6* ausländisch
forged *115* geschmiedet
to **forget** *101* vergessen
formal *46* formell, förmlich
to **found** *90* gründen
founder *90* Gründer/in
fragile *103* zerbrechlich
free, to **be** ~ *24t* frei sein
frequent(ly) *20* oft, häufig
fried *118* gebraten
friendly *13t* freundlich, informell
full name *31* voller Name
full, in ~ *60t* vollständig
fully *94p* vollständig
funny *35t* komisch, lustig
furniture *36* Möbel(stücke), Einrichtung
further *48* weiter

G **gallery** *28* Galerie
gap *15* Lücke
gas (AE) *29* Benzin
general, in ~ *113* im Allgemeinen
generally *47* im Allgemeinen, normalerweise
generous *150* großzügig
to **get back to someone** *24t* jdn. zurückrufen
to **get through** *24* durchkommen
to **get** *25t* jdn. (telefonisch) erreichen
glad *48* froh
go ahead *60t* schießen Sie los
to **go Dutch** *47* getrennt zahlen
Good afternoon *24t* Guten Tag! (nachmittags)
Good evening *25* Guten Abend
Good luck *69* Viel Glück
Good morning *24t* Guten Morgen
Good to see you *11* Freut mich, Sie zu sehen
goods *8* Ware(n), Güter
grand total *150* Endsumme
graphics *59p* Grafiken
grateful *145* dankbar
great *24t* groß(artig), gut
Great to see you *11* Ich freue mich sehr, Sie zu sehen
to **greet** *104* (be)grüßen
greeting card *13t* Glückwunschkarte
to **grind** *104p* mahlen
ground floor *29* Erdgeschoss
group *20* Gruppe
to **grow up** *95* aufwachsen
guarantee *37p* Garantie
to **guess** *68* erraten
guide *61p* (Reise-)Führer/in, Handbuch
guideline *52* Richtlinie
gym *34* Sportstudio

H **hair dryer** *94p* Fön
handle *103* (Hand-)Griff
handling *85* Bearbeitung, Beförderung
handmade *13t* handgemacht
handshake *47* Händedruck
to **happen** *24* passieren, geschehen
harbour *23* Hafen
hard *24t* schwer, schwierig
hardback *104p* gebundene Ausgabe
to **hate** *34* hassen, gar nicht mögen
Have a nice one *48t* Schönen Tag noch
head office *7t* Zentrale
heading *40* Überschrift
headline *66* Schlagzeile
headquarters *42* Hauptquartier, Zentrale
health *113* Gesundheit, Befinden
hectic *48* hektisch
to **hesitate** *107* zögern
hidden *16* verborgen
high quality *8* von hoher Qualität
high school diploma (AE) *30* Abschlusszeugnis der Oberschule
high *33* hoch
to **highlight** *107* hervorheben
hint *81* Hinweis
to **hire** *78* ein-, anstellen
historic *22* historisch
history *59* Geschichte
hi-tech *115* Hightech-, hochtechnisiert
to **hold a meeting** *91* eine Sitzung abhalten
Hold the line *25* Bleiben Sie dran
to **hold** *85t* warten
holiday *25* Ferien, Urlaub
homemade *92p* selbstgemacht
honest *46* ehrlich
honesty *47* Ehrlichkeit
to **hope** *48* hoffen
horizontal *16* horizontal, waagerecht
hospitality *121* Gastfreundschaft, -lichkeit
hour *33* Stunde
house style *118* nach Art des Hauses
How are you? *9* Wie geht es dir/Ihnen?
How do you do? *9* Es freut mich, Sie kennen zu lernen
huge *107* riesig
human resources (HR) *39* Personalabteilung
humble *155* bescheiden
hungry *94p* hungrig

I **idea** *23* Idee, Anregung
to **identify** *16* erkennen, identifizieren
ill *25* krank
illegal *50* verboten, illegal
illustrated *61p* illustriert
to **imagine** *117* sich vorstellen
immediate(ly) *46* sofort, umgehend
important *9* wichtig
impressed *35t* beeindruckt
impression *117* Eindruck
impressive *68* beeindruckend
in, to **be** ~ *24t* im Büro sein
inbound *97p* Ankunft
inbox *49* Posteingang
to **include** *43t* einbeziehen, umfassen
inclusive *158* einschließlich
income *43* Einkommen
incorporated *77* (als Kapitalgesellschaft) eingetragen
incorrect *51* falsch
to **increase** *80* steigern, erhöhen
indeed *72t* wirklich
indoors *35t* drinnen
industrial *22* Industrie-, industriell

infant *97* Kleinkind
informal *154* informell
ingredient *103* Bestandteil, Zutat
initially *120t* anfänglich, zuerst
inn *97p* (Land-)Gasthaus
inside *95* Innere/s
to **install** *20* installieren, einrichten, anschließen
instead *73* stattdessen
instructions *103* Bedienungsanleitung
instrument *34* (Musik-)Instrument
insulation *120t* Isolierung, Isolation
insurance company *8* Versicherungsgesellschaft
to **insure** *110* versichern
interesting *6* interessant
to **interpret** *104p* dolmetschen
to **interrupt** *103t* unterbrechen
to **introduce** *8* vorstellen
introduction *59* Einführung
introductory *150* Einführungs-
to **invent** *11* erfinden
to **invest** *107* investieren
investigative *83p* investigativ
investment market *48t* Anlagemarkt
invitation *156* Einladung
to **invite** *47* einladen
invoice *32* Rechnung
to **involve** *152* umfassen, beinhalten
It depends *34* Es hängt davon ab
item *36* Artikel, Gegenstand

J **job title** *13* Berufsbezeichnung
to **join** *30* gehen zu, anfangen bei
joint venture *6* Gemeinschaftsunternehmen
joke *35t* Witz, Scherz
journey *55* Reise, Fahrt
Just a minute *24t* Einen Moment, bitte
just *13t* nur, gerade
just over *13t* etwas über
to **justify** *103t* rechtfertigen

K **keeping fit** *31* Fitnesstraining
keyboard *37* Tastatur
keyword *58* Stichwort
Kind regards *48* viele Grüße
kindness *121* Güte, Freundlichkeit
kitchen *8* Küche
knife *8* Messer
to **know** *9* wissen, kennen
knowledge *153* Kenntnis(se)

L **ladies and gentlemen** *42* meine Damen und Herren
lake *23* (Binnen-)See
to **land** *55* landen
largest, third ~ *22* drittgrößte
to **last** *104p* dauern, (durch)halten
later *24t* später
to **laugh** *32* lachen
to **launch** *20* einführen, auf den Markt bringen
law firm *72* Anwaltskanzlei
lawyer *72* (Rechts-)Anwalt/Anwältin
to **lead** *154* leiten
leader *92p* Führer/in
leading *31* führend
leaflet *48t* Broschüre, Prospekt
to **lease** *104p* leasen, mieten
to **leave** (a message) *24* (eine Nachricht) hinterlassen
leisure *30* Freizeit
let's *29* lass uns
letter of credit *151* Akkreditiv, Kreditbrief
letter rack *21* Sortierbox
letterhead *85t* Briefkopf
to **level off** *91* sich einpendeln
librarian *83* Bibliothekar/in
library *104p* Bücherei, Bibliothek
licence *29* Lizenz
lifestyle *117* Lebensstil
lifetime *103t* Lebenszeit, ein ganzes Leben
limited company *77* Kapitalgesellschaft
line, on the other ~ *24t* auf der anderen Leitung
liver *118* Leber
lobby *93* Foyer, Eingangshalle
to **locate** *58* orten
located, to **be** ~ *23* sich befinden
location *97p* Lage
long-term *120t* langfristig, Langzeit-
to **look after** *33* betreuen
to **lose** *67* verlieren
loss *120t* Verlust
to **love** *33* lieben, sehr gern mögen
lunch *26* Mittagessen
lunchtime *69* Mittagszeit
luxury *61p* Luxus

M **magazine** *46* Zeitschrift
main point *13* Hauptpunkt
mainly *43t* hauptsächlich, vor allem
major *103t* groß, größer
maker *52* Hersteller
male *52* männlich
to **manage** *66* leiten
management trainee *30* Praktikant/in in der Geschäftsleitung
to **manufacture** *8* herstellen
manufacturing *44* Produktion, Fertigung
manufacturing company *8* Herstellerfirma
map *10* (Land-)Karte
market *13t* (Absatz-)Markt
market research *116* Marktforschung
market survey *35* Marktanalyse
Master of Arts (MA) *41* 2. Staatsexamen in Geisteswissenschaften
Master of Science (MSc/MS) *41* 2. Staatsexamen in Naturwissenschaften
to **match** *15* zuordnen
matter *113* Ding, Angelegenheit
maybe *8* vielleicht
meal *47* Essen, Mahlzeit
to **mean** *46* bedeuten, heißen
meaning *20* Bedeutung
mechanic *83* Mechaniker/in
medium *13t* mittlere
medium-sized *23* mittelgroß
member *73* Mitglied
memo *13* (Akten-)Notiz, Kurzmitteilung
memory *37p* Speicher
merger *56t* Fusion

message *24* Nachricht
method of payment *36* Zahlungsweise
middle-of-the-range *37p* aus dem mittleren Bereich
mid-morning *96t* vormittags
mile *33* Meile
mind, to **change one's** ~ *60t* seine Meinung ändern
missing *31* fehlend
mobile phone *9* Mobiltelefon, Handy
monthly *49* monatlich
morning *20* Morgen, Vormittag
mostly *34* hauptsächlich
mother tongue *31* Muttersprache
motorway *25t* Autobahn
mountain *33* Berg
mouse *37* Maus
to **move** *20t* umziehen
movie (AE) *29* (Spiel-)Film
must *45* müssen
mutual *144* gemeinsam

N to **name** *42* nennen
name badge *11* Namensschild
nationality *52* Staatsangehörigkeit
naturally *103t* selbstverständlich
near *26* nahe, in der Nähe von
nearby *97p* nahe gelegen, in der Nähe
nearly *35t* beinahe, fast
necessary *24* nötig, notwendig, erforderlich
necessary evil *47* notwendiges Übel
neighbour *34* Nachbar/in
never *20* nie(mals)
news *59* Nachricht(en)
next *25* nächste
Nice to meet you *9* Freut mich, Sie kennen zu lernen
Nice to see you again *9* Schön, Sie wieder zu sehen
nobody *94p* niemand
to **nod** *45* nicken
noisy *94p* laut
non-smoking *94* Nichtraucher-
noon *25* Mittag
normally *17* normalerweise
north *23* Norden
northern *22* nordlich, Nord-
not yet *22* noch nicht
note *8* Notiz
to **note** *25* notieren
notepaper *85t* Briefpapier
nothing *34* nichts
to **notice** *44* (be)merken
notice board *21* schwarzes Brett
to **number** *112* nummerieren
nurse *83* Krankenschwester, -pfleger/in

O **o'clock, at ...** *24t* um ... Uhr
objectively *101* objektiv
to **obtain** *145* erhalten
obviously *60t* offensichtlich, selbstverständlich
occasion, to mark the ~ *156* aus Anlass des Ereignisses
occasionally *20* gelegentlich
off, (£60) ~ *36t* Nachlass (von £60)
to **offer** *36t* anbieten
office manager *36* Büroleiter/in
office supplies *36* Büromaterial
often *18* oft, häufig
Oh dear *48* Ach du liebe Zeit
oil *95* Öl
old hand *81* alter Hase
once *55* einmal
one-way (AE) *97* nur Hinflug, einfach
open corporation (AE) *77* Aktiengesellschaft
to **open** *19* eröffnen
open-minded *117* aufgeschlossen
to **operate** *42* operieren
operations *42* Geschäfte, Aktivitäten
opinion, in your ~ *108* Ihrer Meinung nach
opportunity *152* Gelegenheit, Chance, Möglichkeit
opposite *35* Gegenteil
optimism *120t* Optimismus
or anything *35t* oder sowas
orchestra *35t* Orchester
order *36t* Bestellung
to **order** *70* bestellen
ordinary *103* gewöhnlich, normal
organizer *154* Organisator/in
originally *30* ursprünglich
other *92* andere/r/s
otherwise *96t* ansonsten
outbound *97p* Hin-, Abflug
outside *120t* draußen
outskirts *97p* Außengebiete, Stadtrand
oven *118* Herd
overland freight *43* Fracht über Land
overseas *69* ausländisch
to **oversee** *116* beaufsichtigen
own *37* eigen

P **PA** *57* persönliche/r Assistent/in
package *8* Paket, Bündel
packing *95* (Koffer-)Packen
paint *60* Farbe
paragraph *32* (kurzer) Artikel
to **pare** *106* schälen, schneiden
parent company *77* Muttergesellschaft
parking *97p* Parken, Parkmöglichkeit(en)
particularly *109* besonders
partnership *117* Zusammenarbeit
part-time *25t* Teilzeit-, Halbtags-
passport *95* Reisepass, Pass
pattern *20* Muster
to **pay** *36t* (be)zahlen
payable, to **be** ~ *154* fällig sein
payment in full *150* vollständige Bezahlung
to **peel** *106* schälen
pen *21* Kugelschreiber
pencil *21* Bleistift
percentage *43* Prozentsatz
perfectly *103t* völlig
to **perform** (well/badly) *109* (gute/schlechte) Ergebnisse haben
perfume *13t* Parfüm
perhaps *24t* vielleicht, eventuell
period *103t* Zeit(raum)
permanent *7t* ständig, Dauer-
permanently *95* permanent, ständig
personal *20* privat
personality *83* Charakter

personally *24t* persönlich
personnel *27* Personal
petrol *29* Benzin
pharmaceuticals *78* Pharmazeutika
pharmacist *83* Apotheker/in, Pharmazeut/in
phone, on the ~ *9* am Telefon
phone call *18* Anruf, Telefongespräch
photography *31* Fotografie
phrase *6* (Rede-)Wendung, Ausdruck
to **pick up** *63* abholen; *93* abheben
pickled *118* eingelegt
picture *18* Bild
pie chart *43t* Kreisdiagramm
piece *22* Stück
to **place an order** *36* eine Bestellung aufgeben
planner *56t* Terminplaner
plant *21* Pflanze
plastic *102* Kunststoff
to **play** *34* spielen
player *61p* Laufwerk
pleasant *157* angenehm, nett
Please, call me ... *11* Nennen Sie mich bitte ...
Pleased to meet you *6* Es freut mich, Sie kennen zu lernen
point (5.3) *43t* Komma (5,3)
police officer *83* Polizeibeamter/beamtin
policy *60t* (Firmen-)Politik
polite *46* höflich
politics *113* (die) Politik
poor *109* arm, schlecht, mangelhaft
popular *13t* beliebt, populär
population *22* Einwohner(zahl)
pork *118* Schweinefleisch
possible *15* möglich
possibly *99* möglicherweise
post code *12* Postleitzahl
postal address *12* Briefanschrift
to **postpone** *72* verschieben
potential *58t* möglich, potenziell
pottery *59p* Keramik, Töpferwaren
pound *37* Pfund (Sterling)
power cable *120* Stromkabel
powerful *115* (leistungs)stark
to **practise** *11* (ein)üben
to **prefer** *34* lieber mögen, bevorzugen
to **prepare** *44* vorbereiten
presence *58t* Anwesenheit, Präsenz
present *153* gegenwärtig, jetzig
presentation *35* Vorstellung, Präsentation
press release *80* Pressemitteilung
price list *49p* Preisliste
price range *13t* Preisgruppe, -segment
to **print** *46* drucken
printer *21* Drucker
prior *157* vorherig
private(ly) *77* privat
probably *44* wahrscheinlich
process *20t* Prozess, Ablauf
to **produce** *8* produzieren
professional *61p* Profi, Fachmann
profit *44* Profit, Gewinn
profitable *43t* gewinnbringend, rentabel
to **promise** *103t* versprechen
to **promote** *57* anpreisen, Werbung machen für
promotional *84* Werbe-
to **propose** *108* vorschlagen
proprietary limited company *77* GmbH
pros and cons *19* Für und Wider
proud of *115* stolz auf
to **provide** (a service) *8* (eine Leistung) anbieten, erbringen
provider *58* Anbieter, Versorger
provincial *22* Provinz-
pub *117* Wirtshaus, Kneipe
public limited company *77* Aktiengesellschaft
public relations *13p* Öffentlichkeitsarbeit
publishing *158* Verlags-
punctual *20* pünktlich
to **purchase** *80* (ein)kaufen
to **put someone through** *24t* jdn. verbinden, durchstellen

Q
qualification *30* Zeugnis
quantity (qty) *36* Menge, Quantität
quarter *91* Quartal
quarterly *91* vierteljährlich
query *85t* Frage
quotation *104p* (Kosten-)Voranschlag
to **quote** *61* ein Angebot abgeben

R
race *120* (Pferde-)Rennen
racquet *61p* (Tennis-)Schläger
rail *59* (Eisen-)Bahn
railway station *97p* Bahnhof
raincoat *95* Regenmantel
range *13t* Sortiment, Palette, Auswahl
rating *108* Einschätzung, Beurteilung
raw material *116* Rohstoff(e)
to **reach** (sb) *25* (jdn.) erreichen
to **realize** *120t* sich klar sein
really *33* wirklich, tatsächlich
to **rearrange** *15* umstellen
rebate *60* (Preis-)Nachlass, Rabatt
receipt *110* Empfang, Erhalt
to **receive** *75* erhalten, bekommen
recent *144* jüngst, kürzlich
reception area *33* Empfang(sbereich), Rezeption
reception desk *93* Rezeption, Empfang
receptionist *24t* Empfang(smitarbeiter/in)
to **recognize** *90* (an)erkennen
to **recommend** *109* empfehlen
recommendation *108* Empfehlung
recording *85t* Aufnahme, Aufzeichnung
recruitment *156* Einstellung (von Arbeitskräften)
to **refer to** *94* sich beziehen auf
reference *142* Zeichen, Bezug
to **reflect** *120t* (sich) widerspiegeln
to **refund** *60t* erstatten, zurückzahlen
region *42* Gebiet, Region
to **register** *90* eintragen (lassen), anmelden
registration form *93t* Anmeldeformular
to **regret** *157* bedauern
regularly *95* regelmäßig
to **reimburse** *110* entschädigen, erstatten
reimbursement *110* Entschädigung, Erstattung
relationship *119* Beziehung, Verhältnis
relatively *61p* relativ, verhältnismäßig

reliability *109* Zuverlässigkeit
to **rely on** *125* sich verlassen auf, abhängig sein von
to **remain** *91* bleiben
to **remember** *7* sich erinnern, daran denken
to **reorganize** *20* umorganisieren
to **repay** *121* sich revanchieren für
to **repeat** *36t* wiederholen
to **replace** *103t* ersetzen, austauschen
replacement *106* Ersatz
reply *16* Antwort
to **reply** *49* antworten
reply, in ~ *48* als Antwort
report *48t* Bericht
to **represent** *73p* vertreten, repräsentieren
representative *60* (Handels-)Vertreter/in
request *96* Bitte, Wunsch; *144* Anfrage, Anforderung
to **require** *153* benötigen
required, if ~ *85* falls erforderlich
research *57* Nachforschung(en)
research and development (R&D) *24t* Forschung und Entwicklung
reservation *158* Reservierung, Buchung
to **reserve** *70* reservieren (lassen)
response *153* Antwort
responsibility *31* Verantwortung
responsible *40* verantwortlich
result *35* Ergebnis
resumé (AE) *153* (tabellarischer) Lebenslauf
retail *79* Einzelhandel(sgeschäft)
retailer *8* Einzelhändler/in
to **return** *60* zurückgeben, -schicken
review *91* Rückblick
to **rewrite** *111* umschreiben
rhyme *10* Reim
to **ring** *9* klingeln, läuten
to **rise** *91* (an)steigen, anwachsen
river *22* Fluss
roasted *118* gebraten, geröstet
room *21* Zimmer, Raum
round *61* umher
round trip (AE) *97* Hin- und Rückflug
rule *94* Regel
to **run** *57* leiten, führen

S

safe *21* Tresor
sailing *31* Segeln
salary *82* Gehalt
sales *13t* Umsatz, Verkäufe
sales literature *142* (Verkaufs-)Prospekt(e), Kataloge
sales manager *7t* Verkaufsleiter/in
sales performance *108* Verkaufszahlen
sales representative *13t* (Handels-)Vertreter/in
salesperson *83* Verkäufer/in
salty *118* salzig
same *30* gleich
same-day *37p* am selben Tag
sarcasm *113* Sarkasmus
satisfactory *149* zufrieden stellend, befriedigend
satisfied *85t* zufrieden
sauce *118* Soße
sausage *118* (Brat-)Wurst
to **save** *103t* sparen
to **save face** *45* das Gesicht wahren
scale *60t* Skala
scene *95* Szene
scenery *117* Landschaft
schedule *121* Zeitplan
to **score** *83p* (Punkte) zählen
screen *97* Bildschirm
sea freight *43* Seefracht
search *58* Suche
secretary *38* Sekretär/in
section *109* Teil, Abschnitt
sector *92p* Sektor, Bereich
security *89* Sicherheit
to **seem** *94t* (er)scheinen
to **select** *58* auswählen
selection *93t* Auswahl, Angebot
to **sell** *7t* verkaufen
seller *149* Verkäufer/in
to **send** *36* senden, schicken
series *47* Serie, Reihe
to **serve** *117* servieren, anbieten
service company *8* Dienstleistungsunternehmen
set *105t* Satz
to **settle** *159* begleichen, bezahlen
to **shake** *52* schütteln
share *77* (Geschäfts-)Anteil, Aktie
share price *57* Aktienkurs
shareholder *77* Aktionär/in
sharp *103t* scharf, spitz, rasch, stark
to **sharpen** *103t* schärfen
sharply *91* rasch, schnell, stark
shipment *58* Sendung
shipping *58* Verfrachtung, Versand
shirt *18* Hemd
shopper *80* Käufer/in
shopping *34* Einkaufen
shortly *121* in Kürze
to **show** *45* zeigen
side *51* Seite
sight *22* Sehenswürdigkeit
signature *85* Unterschrift
similar *77* ähnlich
simple *13t* einfach
since *81* seit
single *93t* Einzel-
to **sit** *19* sitzen
site *19* (Stand-)Ort
situated, to be ~ *22* liegen
skiing *33* Skilaufen
skill *31* Fertigkeit, Fähigkeit
skilled *115* ausgebildet, Fach-
skirt *18* Rock
slightly *91* leicht, geringfügig
slip (of paper) *68* Zettel
small talk *33* (höfliche) Konversation
to **smile** *45* lächeln
to **smoke** *52* rauchen
snooker *34* Billard
so far *91* bis jetzt
soap *93* Seife
sociable *35* gesellig
social worker *83* Sozialarbeiter/in
socially *121* gesellschaftlich, sozial
to **soften** *101* abschwächen

solution *58* Lösung
to **solve** *58t* lösen
something *20* etwas
sometimes *20* manchmal
somewhere *56t* irgendwo
sort *114* Art, Sorte
sort of *96t* irgendwie
sound system *61p* Tonübertragungssystem
to **sound** *35t* sich anhören
soup *118* Suppe
south *13t* Süden
southern *23* südlich, Süd-
spare part *63* Ersatzteil
speaker *94* Sprecher/in
special offer *36* Sonderangebot
specialist *66* speziell
speciallty *118* Spezialität
specialized *58* spezialisiert
specification *120t* Spezifikation, Vorgabe
to **spell** *10* buchstabieren, schreiben
spelling *29* Rechtschreibung, Schreibweise
to **spend** (money) *78* ausgeben
spicy *118* (stark) gewürzt, würzig
sportswear *7t* Sportkleidung
sporty *35t* sportlich
spouse *156* Gemahl/in, Ehepartner/in
square *16* Quadrat
stable *91* stabil
staff *86* Personal, Mitarbeiter/innen
stairs *93t* Treppe(n)
starter *118* Vorspeise
start-up *6* Start-up(-Unternehmen)
to **state** *101* feststellen, angeben
to **stay** *35t* übernachten; *46* bleiben
steadily *98* stetig
steel *90* Stahl
step *115* Schritt, Stufe
still *30* (immer) noch
stock control *79* Inventur, Lagerhaltung
stockbroker *57* Börsenmakler/in
stockist *106* Fachgeschäft
to **stop** *43t* anhalten, aufhören
storage *146* Lagerung
storefront *80* Ladenfront
straight away *60* sofort, umgehend
to **study** *30* studieren
stupid *96t* dumm, blöde
style *97p* Stil
subject *25* Thema, Grund
subsidiary *69* Tochtergesellschaft
substantial *148* ansehnlich, beträchtlich
subtitle *152* Untertitel
subtotal *85* Zwischensumme
suburb *20t* Vorort, Außenbezirk
subway (AE) *29* U-Bahn
successful *40* erfolgreich
such as *28* wie zum Beispiel
to **suggest** *47* vorschlagen
suggestion *109* Vorschlag
suit *18* Anzug
suitable *54* geeignet, passend
suitcase *94p* Koffer
to **summarize** *58* zusammenfassen
summary *14* Zusammenfassung
summer *35t* Sommer
sunny *40* sonnig
superb *22* hervorragend
supplier *60* Lieferant/in, Zulieferer
to **supply** *36t* liefern
support *81* (technische) Hilfe
sure *42* sicher
surprised *47* überrascht, erstaunt
surprisingly *13t* überraschenderweise
surveyor *83* Gutachter/in, Landvermesser/in
sweet *118* süß
swimming *34* Schwimmen
symphony *35t* Sinfonie
syrup *118* Sirup

T

to **take a call** *24t* einen Anruf entgegennehmen
to **take care of** *105* sich kümmern um, sorgen für
to **take it in turns** *115* sich abwechseln
to **take notes** *20* (sich) Notizen machen
to **take place** *157* stattfinden
tale *95* Geschichte, Erzählung
task *69* Aufgabe
tax *61* Steuer
tea *26* Tee
teacher *34* Lehrer/in
technically *103* technisch
to **telephone** *24* anrufen, telefonieren (mit)
to **tell** *20* sagen, erzählen
term *60* Bedingung
terrible *25t* fürchterlich, furchtbar
terribly *72t* fürchterlich, furchtbar
theme *154* Thema
thick *120t* dick
thirsty *94p* durstig
though *72t* dennoch
thriving *22* aufstrebend
through, to **be** ~ *24t* sprechen mit
tie *18* Krawatte
tied up *73* beschäftigt
time *54* Zeit
timed, to **be** ~ *25t* mit der Zeitangabe versehen
timetable *98* Fahr-, Stundenplan
tip *125* Trinkgeld
tired *94p* müde
together *35* zusammen
tone *24t* (Signal-)Ton
tonight *29* heute Abend
toothbrush *94p* Zahnbürste
top *37p* Spitzen-, oberst
top three *35* die ersten drei
top to bottom, from ~ *16* von oben nach unten
topic *113* Thema
total, in ~ *13t* insgesamt
totally *56t* völlig, total
touch, to **get in** ~ *150* sich in Verbindung setzen
tour *35t* Tournee
towel *93t* Handtuch
town hall *22* Rathaus
to **trace** *58* zurückverfolgen, finden
to **track** *58* verfolgen, beobachten
trade discount *37* Händlerrabatt
trade fair *13* Handelsmesse

trade journal *144* Handelsblatt
trademark *90* Warenzeichen
trading terms *60* Handelsbedingungen
traditional *115* traditionell
traffic *25t* (Straßen-)Verkehr
trainers *7t* Turn-, Tennisschuhe
to **transfer** *25p* durchstellen
translation *28* Übersetzung
translator *152* Übersetzer/in
transportation *44* Transport, Beförderung
to **travel** *6* reisen
traveler (AE) *95* Reisende/r
trip *18* Reise
troubleshooter *95* Störungssucher/in
trousers *18* Hose(n)
true *20* richtig, zutreffend
truth *52* Wahrheit
to **try** *12* probieren, versuchen
turkey *118* Truthahn
turnover *13t* Umsatz
twin (room) *97p* Zimmer mit zwei (getrennten) Betten
type *59p* Art, Sorte, Typ
typical *17* typisch
typist *83* Schreibkraft

U
umbrella *84* (Regen-)Schirm
unclean *46* unsauber
underground *29* U-Bahn
to **understand** *36* verstehen
to **undertake** *108* vornehmen
unexpected *72t* unerwartet
unfortunately *69* unglücklicherweise, leider
unit price *36* Einzelpreis
unmarried *17* unverheiratet
to **unscramble** *10* entschlüsseln, in die richtige Reihenfolge bringen
unsure *83* unsicher, ungewiss
until *25p* bis
unusual *42* ungewöhnlich
up *33* oben
to **update** *142* aktualisieren, auf den neuesten Stand bringen
up-to-date *49* aktuell, modern
urgent *48t* dringend, eilig
to **use** *16* benutzen, verwenden
useful *23* nützlich
user *79* Anwender/in, Benutzer/in
usual *48* gewöhnlich, normal
usually *18* normalerweise, meistens

V
vacancy *59* offene Stelle
vacation (AE) *29* Urlaub, Ferien
valid *150* gültig
valuable *152* wertvoll
valued *157* geschätzt
to **vary** *154* sich unterscheiden, variieren
veal *118* Kalbfleisch
vegetable *118* Gemüse
venue *154* (Tagungs-)Ort
vertical *16* senkrecht, vertikal
vet *83* Tierarzt/-ärztin
via *104p* über, per
village *97p* Dorf
violin *35t* Geige
to **visit** *20* besuchen
visitor *23* Besucher/in, Gast
voice *104p* Stimme
voicemail *24* Mailbox
volume *61* Menge
VP (vice president) *158* Vizepräsident/in

W
wage *125* Lohn, Gehalt
warehouse *146* Lager(haus)
warehousing *58* Lagerung
to **wash** *114t* waschen
waste-bin *21* Papierkorb
watching TV *34* Fernsehen
way of life *47* Lebensweise
way *117* Hinsicht, Art (und Weise)
to **wear** *18* tragen, anhaben
weather *34* Wetter
web address *12* Internet-Adresse
weekend *35t* Wochenende
weight control *78* Gewichtskontrolle
to **welcome** *9* begrüßen
western *23* westlich, West-
whether *25* ob
while *75* während
whole of *97p* ganz
wholesaler *116* Großhändler/in
wide(ly) *66* weit
widescreen *61p* Breitwandbildschirm
wife *39* (Ehe-)Frau
willing, to **be** ~ *151* bereit/gewillt sein
window *21* Fenster
window shopping *34* Schaufensterbummel
to **wine and dine** *125* dinieren, essen gehen
winery *13t* Weinkellerei
to **wish** *157* wünschen
within *60t* innerhalb (von), in
without *22* ohne
to **wonder** *93t* sich fragen
wonderful *45* wunderbar, -voll
word order *20* Wort-, Satzstellung
to **work through** *49* durcharbeiten
workstation *37p* Arbeitsplatz
world-class *22* Weltklasse-
worldwide *8* weltweit
to **worry** *72t* sich Sorgen machen
to **write down** *12* aufschreiben

XYZ
years old *13t* ... Jahre alt
yesterday *32* gestern
young *34* jung
Yours faithfully *143* Mit freundlichen Grüßen
Yours sincerely *142* Mit freundlichen Grüßen

Important irregular verbs

Infinitiv	Vergangenheit	Partizip Perfekt	
be	was/were	been	*sein*
become	became	become	*werden*
begin	began	begun	*beginnen, anfangen*
break	broke	broken	*brechen, kaputtmachen*
bring	brought	brought	*bringen*
build	built	built	*bauen*
buy	bought	bought	*kaufen*
catch	caught	caught	*fangen*
choose	chose	chosen	*(aus)wählen, aussuchen*
come	came	come	*kommen*
cost	cost	cost	*kosten*
cut	cut	cut	*schneiden*
deal	dealt	dealt	*handeln, sich beschäftigen (mit)*
do	did	done	*tun, machen*
draw	drew	drawn	*zeichnen*
drink	drank	drunk	*trinken*
drive	drove	driven	*(Auto)fahren*
eat	ate	eaten	*essen*
fall	fell	fallen	*fallen*
feel	felt	felt	*(sich) fühlen*
find	found	found	*finden*
fly	flew	flown	*fliegen*
forget	forgot	forgotten	*vergessen*
get	got	got	*bekommen, gelangen*
give	gave	given	*geben, schenken*
go	went	gone	*gehen, fahren*
grow	grew	grown	*wachsen*
have	had	had	*haben*
hear	heard	heard	*hören*
hide	hid	hidden	*(sich) verstecken*
hit	hit	hit	*schlagen*
hold	held	held	*halten*
keep	kept	kept	*behalten*
know	knew	known	*wissen, kennen*
learn	learnt (learned)	learnt (learned)	*lernen*
leave	left	left	*(weg)gehen, (ver)lassen*
let	let	let	*(zu)lassen, erlauben*
lose	lost	lost	*verlieren*
make	made	made	*machen, tun*
mean	meant	meant	*bedeuten*
meet	met	met	*(sich) treffen*
pay	paid	paid	*(be)zahlen*
put	put	put	*legen, stellen, setzen*
read	read	read	*lesen*
rise	rose	risen	*steigen, sich erheben*
ring	rang	rung	*klingeln, anrufen*
run	ran	run	*laufen, verwalten*
say	said	said	*sagen*
see	saw	seen	*sehen*
sell	sold	sold	*verkaufen*
send	sent	sent	*senden, schicken*

set	set	set	*setzen, stellen, legen*
shake	shook	shaken	*schütteln*
show	showed	shown (showed)	*zeigen*
sing	sang	sung	*singen*
sit	sat	sat	*sitzen*
sleep	slept	slept	*schlafen*
speak	spoke	spoken	*sprechen*
spend	spent	spent	*ausgeben, verbringen*
stand	stood	stood	*stehen*
swim	swam	swum	*schwimmen*
take	took	taken	*nehmen*
teach	taught	taught	*unterrichten*
tell	told	told	*erzählen, sagen*
think	thought	thought	*denken, meinen*
understand	understood	understood	*verstehen*
wear	wore	worn	*tragen, anhaben*
win	won	won	*gewinnen*
write	wrote	written	*schreiben*

Quellenverzeichnis

Grafiken
Oxford Designers & Illustrators

Fotos
action press, Hamburg: S. 7/Krüger; **Argus**, Hamburg: S. 44/T. Raupach/P. Frischmuth; **The Bird Consultancy** for G-Mex Manchester: S. 102; **Jan Chipps Photography**, London: S. 7, 91, 93 (2), 103, 114; **COMSTOCK**, Luxemburg: S. 12, 13, 24, 36, 48, 56, 66, 69, 70, 79, 81, 104, 150; **Corbis GmbH**, Düsseldorf: S. 13/J. Andanson/RF, 24/M. Keller, 57/E. Bock/H. King/L. Williams/H. King/E. Ben-Shimon, 83/E. Wheeler, C. Savage, G. Disario, 60/J. Feingersh, 66/S.Terrill, 72/M. Keller, 73/J. Craigmyle, 78/ALAmo Tegta/R. Maass, 82/J. Palting/LWA-JDC, 85/P. Barton, 90/M. Keller, 93/C. Karnow, 96/L. Williams, 119/J. Henley, 142/J. L. Pelaez; **Corel:** S. 44, 54, 60, 67, 97, 114, 147, 158; **Das Fotoarchiv**, Essen: S. 61/B. Weller/J. Schumacher, 90/T. Mayer (2), 117/P. Hollenbach; **Getty Images**, München: Titelfotos, S. 6, 7 (3), 9, 12, 18, 19, 20/W. Hodges, 30, 32/J.T. Turner/T. McCormick, 33/J. Balog, 35/J. A. Rizzo, 36, 42/Chabruken, 44, 45/N. Clements, 54, 66, 67/K. Seaman/S. Murphy/D. Madison, 80/G. Buss, 91/J. Waterman, 92/J. Waterman, 94/P. Gridley, 95/D. Bosler, 105/C. Bissell, 109, 116/C. Thatcher, 118, 119/W. Hodges/S. Marks, 120/Real Life/G. Mortimore/R. Brimson, 121/R. Drury, 141; **IFA-Bilderteam**, Düsseldorf: S. 23/Lecom/EBI/P. Graf/Glück,67/G. Bumann, 146/Fufy; **Picture-Alliance**: S. 104/dpa-A. Petry/O. Berg, 144/dpa-F. P. Tschauner, 148/S. Mayr; **Stockfood**, München: S. 119; **Tourismusverband Linz**: S. 6, 22

Wir danken folgenden Firmen für die freundliche Unterstützung:

Adidas Deutschland, Herzogenaurach (S. 44)
Bettmer GmbH & Co. KG, Werbemittel, Anna-Birle-Str. 3, 55252 Mainz-Kastel, Tel: 0613472040; www.bettmer.de; mail@bettmer.de (S. 84)
Ed. Wüsthof Dreizackwerk, Solingen (S. 7, 103, 135)
Flughafen Linz GesmbH (S. 9 (3))
Fujitsu Siemens Computers, München (S. 37)
Heinz Kettler GmbH & Co. KG, Ense-Parsit (S. 108)
OTTO Marketing (S. 104)
Mit freundlicher Genehmigung der Sony Deutschland GmbH (S. 67)